KEYBOARDING AND BEYOND

KEYBOARDING AND BEYOND

Theodor Richardson

Charles Thies

MERCURY LEARNING AND INFORMATION
Dulles, Virginia
Boston, Massachusetts
New Delhi

Publisher: David Pallai

MERCURY LEARNING AND INFORMATION
22841 Quicksilver Drive
Dulles, VA 20166
info@merclearning.com
www.merclearning.com
1-800-758-3756

This book is printed on acid-free paper.

Theodor Richardson and Charles Thies. *KEYBOARDING AND BEYOND*
ISBN: 978-1-9364203-6-0

Library of Congress Control Number: 2012935717

121314321

I want to dedicate this book to my father, Dan Richardson; he taught me the value of education and has been a constant source of love and humor in my life. I hope I will always make you proud and always make you laugh.

— Theodor Richardson

To my mother, Lupe Thies, whose lifelong love for teaching and mentorship inspires my pedagogy and the profession I chose to follow.

— Charles Thies

Contents

Introduction

If you are new to typing or wish to learn proper hand positioning and form for using the keyboard effectively and efficiently, this textbook provides a complete solution to learning and practicing the use of the standard QWERTY keyboard. This text includes detailed instructions for each lesson and practice exercises to gain proficiency in using the keys added in each chapter. This text includes a total of 125 individual keyboarding lessons covering the entire keyboard as well as data entry, data organization, and the use of mobile typing and texting on non-standard keyboards and keypads.

Each chapter contains both keyboarding lessons and information for getting started in the use of productivity software such as word processing. The first six chapters cover the use of both the Windows and Macintosh versions of Microsoft Word as the predominant word processing software system in modern organizations. The coverage of this software includes everything from the basic layout and functionality of the software through advanced features for professional document creation.

The next section of the textbook focuses on managing and organizing data tables. This includes an introduction to the use of Microsoft Excel spreadsheet software for managing tables of data. The keyboarding lessons in this section are focused around table data entry, including spreadsheet data entry and tabbed tables of information.

The last section of the textbook addresses data entry in modern organizations. This provides an overview of how data is managed and used in modern organizations as well as an introduction to Microsoft Access for use in managing small data sets. The keyboarding lessons for this area focus on data entry in a form, whether it is on the Web or through a database management software system.

The Appendices of the textbook include information on mobile computing, typing, and texting as well as additional word processing software that can be used in place of Microsoft Word. This includes several keyboarding lessons that focus on texting and typing on mobile keypads.

Chapter Structure

Each chapter is structured to provide you with an overview of the concepts of one of the productivity software packages used for word processing, spreadsheet managements, and data entry. The majority of the chapters focus on the use of Microsoft Word for word processing; both the Windows and Macintosh versions of the software are addressed in the chapter content. Each chapter also contains keyboarding lessons for learning and practicing proper form in typing. These are reinforced with timed drills that can be completed on the software accompanying this text. A knowledge check is provided to allow you to test your comprehension of the chapter. Odd answers to the questions are provided at the back of the book. Additional exercises and discussion questions are presented to further explore the concepts of each chapter.

Student Resource DVD and Web site

The textbook provides a DVD contained in the back cover that includes chapter resources and the keyboarding software for completing the keyboarding exercises presented in the chapter. You will also find a repository of high resolution images from the chapters. Additional video tutorials and resources are available on the companion Web site for the book at *www.keyboardingandbeyond.com*; you can register for a free account to access the student materials.

Instructor Resource DVD and Web site

The instructor DVD contains all of the solutions for the exercises and knowledge checks and PowerPoint presentations for each chapter. Instructors can register for the instructor materials online at *www.keyboardingandbeyond.com*.

Acknowledgments

I am very proud of the book you now hold in your hands and I want to thank you for choosing it over others. It has been my goal to shape this into a self-sufficient guide to getting started in word processing and typing no matter what background you may have in the subject. It is the result of the combined creative forces of everyone who has worked to make it possible, and I want to offer my sincere thanks to them all. I want to thank Katie Kennedy for her continued support, patience, and understanding as well as her seemingly superhuman ability to deal with me under stress. She has once again proven herself as the master of Excel and her experience and expertise has allowed the spreadsheet content to be accessible. I also want to thank my grandparents, Leonard and Sylvia Ullom, and my parents, Dan and Deborah Richardson, for giving me such a wonderful upbringing, perpetual support, and helping me to capitalize on the opportunities that have led to my lifelong dream of seeing a book of my own creation in print. I would like to thank my publisher, David Pallai, and my co-author and friend, Charles Thies, for seeing another project through to completion. Last and certainly not least, I want to thank you, dear reader, for your support.

— Theodor Richardson

I would like to say a special thank you to several people. To my wonderful wife, Lea, who would accompany me with a cup of coffee every night as I typed another page. My sons, Matt and Will, whose constant smiles energized me every day, bringing me closer to the finish line towards the completion of this book. To my parents, David and Lupe, who influenced who I have become. To Ted, my friend and co-author, whose encouragement and mentorship has led to another successful book project. To David Pallai whose leadership has guided us to the completion of yet another successful project. A special thank you to the professors and students who chose this book for their courses. We realize this book would not be possible without your support. Finally, thank you to all of those involved in this project that we never met, but know worked tirelessly into the night to meet the tight deadlines to move this book from an idea to reality.

— Charles Thies

Word Processing and the QWERTY Keyboard

IN THIS CHAPTER

This chapter presents an introduction and background to word processing, which is part of a larger classification of applications called productivity software, and an overview of the common QWERTY keyboard found on most computer systems today. This chapter will also introduce you to Microsoft® Word® (on both the Windows® and Macintosh® platforms), the preferred business software for word processing and document creation. You will learn the application interface and document management. Once you complete the chapter, you will be able to:

- Locate and use the File menu to create and manage documents

- Access the help files for an application

- Construct a new word processing document

- Navigate the application interface for Microsoft Word

- Use the home row keys, the spacebar, and the Enter key on the QWERTY keyboard

1.1   KEYBOARDING LESSON

Each chapter presents a keyboarding lesson for shaping and enhancing your typing ability as you learn about the use of word processing software. In this chapter, you will learn the layout of the QWERTY keyboard, practice with the spacebar and Enter key, and learn proper hand positioning for the home row keys.

1.2   INTRODUCTION TO WORD PROCESSING

Word processing is the digital process of document creation and it is the most common task in any modern business environment. The history of word processing is a story of the gradual automation of producing formerly hand-written documents. The technology of word processing as we know it today originated with the printing press. The first printing presses utilized moveable type (sets of letters and punctuation that could be rearranged to form words and sentences and fitted to a machine) to create an automatic ink duplicate of a hand-written work. This was the advent of mechanically created type (a process called typesetting) but it would take time for industrialization to allow for the creation of mechanically created type on an individual basis, which was still a long way from using the digital format that is ubiquitous today.

As mechanization improved through the mid-1800s, it became possible to create a machine for use by an individual as a substitute for hand writing text, called the typewriter, which used metal prongs to strike an ink ribbon to create each letter on the page. Businesses were the first to adopt the technology because it increased their productivity and by the early 1900s the technology was available for household use. The typewriter continued to evolve and accommodate greater flexibility of use and even limited reuse of typed text. It is not surprising then that this would be one of the first business areas to make use of computing technology, beginning with magnetic data storage to preprocess sentences before they were typed on the page and continuing through to automated electronic spelling checks.

The typewriter (whether mechanical or electrical) is now a historical artifact. Today, typing is almost universally performed on computers, but the terminology and standard keyboard configuration of laptop and desktop computers are retained from the pioneering days of the typewriter. The term "word processing" was coined by IBM in the 1960s for its electronic typewriters that were capable of storing the keys typed, editing the content, and printing the result through the use of electronic memory; this entire process was performed on a "word processor." The terms word processor and word processing have remained from these early days and now apply to a class of software applications used to produce electronic documents for business and personal use.

The history of the typewriter and its gradual adoption as well as the gradual inclusion of computing elements began in the mid-1800s with individually produced mechanized machines. A lot of the terminology for the key names (such as the shift and enter keys) retain their naming from the mechanical function they performed as well as the keyboard as the most common interface device. It also intertwines with the cultural revolution of the spread of computing and the rapid increase in computing power. The 1980s, when the personal computer saw widespread adoption and use, was one of the last eras where partially computerized typewriters, called word processors, were physical devices instead of a software class on a computer. You can find complete histories of the typewriter and its impact by using a search engine such as Google® (*www.google.com*) or Bing® (*www.bing.com*) and searching for the "history of word processing" or "typewriter history."

Word processing is one component of the larger class of *productivity software* that drives most businesses and helps individuals organize and manage tasks. This chapter will introduce you to the Microsoft Word application, the most common word processing application in use in the business environment, for both Windows and Macintosh computers. You will also learn the layout of the standard QWERTY keyboard and learn the first set of keys for proper and proficient typing.

As you progress through this text, each chapter will introduce new material for enhancing your understanding of word processing and the features it offers, complete with application projects using the software. Each chapter also contains a keyboarding lesson to teach proper typing technique and guide you to proficiency; the keyboarding lessons are complete with exercises you can perform on your own or using the software included with the book (you can get more information on the keyboarding software included with the text in Chapter 1.3.4). The final two chapters of this book introduce spreadsheet software (Chapter 7) and database software (Chapter 8) which are common applications for data entry, another area in which typing skills are essential; these chapters also include keyboarding lessons and exercises for practice. The appendices of the book provide additional applications of typing skills (such as texting on mobile devices and smart phones) and additional practice exercises for discipline-specific documents such as movie scripts and legal letters.

WORD PROCESSING *in modern terms is the use of a computer system to create, manipulate, and share text. The traditional means of word processing is through the use of the keyboard and mouse, though modern speech recognition programs allow you to create text from audio input.*

PRODUCTIVITY SOFTWARE *is a program that assists you in performing tasks that are necessary for you to accomplish at home or in the workplace. Productivity is a measurement of how much you can accomplish in a given period of time, a concept that will be revisited in the discussion on evaluating typing speed.*

MICROSOFT WORD

Microsoft Word is the word processing application within the Microsoft Office® software suite. Microsoft Office is an example of a software suite that is used for productivity. A *software suite* is a collection of individual programs that are used to perform related tasks; in the case of Office, this is the management of documents for word processing, presentations, spreadsheets, and e-mail. Microsoft Word will be the primary software application used for the study of word processing; you will get to see examples of spreadsheet and database software from the Microsoft Office suite toward the end of the book.

NOTE

If you do not already have Microsoft Office installed on your machine, you can get a trial version of the 2010 software for Windows from the Office home page at *www.office.com* (select the *Products* link at the top of the page to get to the Office download). To get a trial of the 2011 version of the Office software for Macintosh, go to *www.microsoft.com/mac*. You can purchase the software directly from Microsoft for unlimited use as well.

Companies like JourneyEd™ (*www.journeyed.com*) offer discounted professional software to students. If you are using another site to get a discount on your software, remember that whenever you purchase software from a source other than the official vendor, you should make sure the site is legitimate before you attempt to make a purchase or enter any personal information. This is part of being a responsible Web user and protecting yourself from identity theft.

Microsoft Word 2010 uses a ribbon interface; this is a type of interface that uses larger icons than a standard toolbar to organize productivity. Each ribbon contains multiple panels of grouped commands; the different ribbons are accessed by the name of the ribbon across the top of the ribbon interface. Each ribbon name is called a tab on the ribbon interface. Microsoft Word 2011 uses a combination of the ribbon interface and traditional menus. For the most part, there is little difference in functionality between the Office 2010 and Office 2011 versions of Microsoft Word. The differences are mainly in the placement of commands between the two versions, and these will be pointed out in the text. You access the programs that are part of Office on a Windows machine by selecting the *Start* menu, choosing *All Programs*, and then choosing *Microsoft Office*; you will then see a listing of programs from which to choose. For word processing, you will choose *Microsoft Word*.

To access Office 2011 on the Macintosh, you may be able to click the icons installed on the Dock (when you installed the software, you probably had the option to place the shortcut icons there). If you do not have the icons on your Dock, you can access the programs in the Office 2011 suite by selecting *Macintosh HD* (or whatever name you have given your machine) from the desktop, opening the *Applications* folder, and then opening the *Microsoft Office 2011* folder. Select *Microsoft Word* from the available programs.

The functionality between the two versions of Microsoft Word is very similar, but they do have decidedly different layouts. The next two sections provide an overview of the application interface, which is an example of a graphic user interface (GUI). You may jump to whichever section applies for the computer you are using. You should open your Word application to follow along with the interface and descriptions so you are familiar with where to find the commands you need.

NOTE

If you are new to typing or word processing documents, the blinking vertical line in the document display is the cursor. This denotes the current location at which text will be added to the document when you strike (or type) keys on the keyboard. You can adjust this position using the directional arrows on the keyboard or by moving the mouse to where you want the cursor and left-clicking on that spot.

1.3.1 Anatomy of Microsoft Word 2010

When you open Microsoft Word 2010 on a Windows machine, it will create a new blank document by default, called *Document1*. If you have used Word in the past, the number of the document will increase (to *Document2*, *Document3*, etc.). Figure 1.1 shows an example of the standard application interface for Word 2010. Across the top of the window for each open document is the Quick Access toolbar, which contains shortcuts to commonly used commands. By default, Save, Undo, and Redo are included as direct links. The arrow beside the Undo

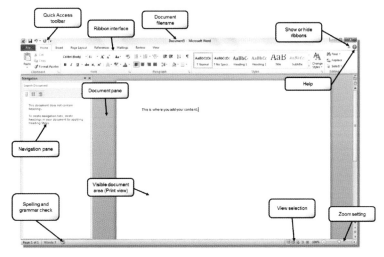

▼ **FIGURE 1.1** Anatomy of Word 2010

command contains a buffer list of prior actions that can be undone; all of the actions after the one selected will be undone if this list is used. The Microsoft Word icon in the far-left corner contains commands for moving and resizing the window. The far right of the interface contains icons to minimize the window (which removes the document from the screen while keeping it open), maximize the window (to take up the full available space of the computer screen), or close the document and the window.

The ribbon interface for Word 2010 is beneath the toolbar. The File menu can be found to the left of the ribbons that are available. The Home ribbon is the first ribbon you will see. This ribbon, shown in Figure 1.2, contains common formatting commands for your document. You can also manage styles from this ribbon, which you will learn about in Chapter 2. The other commands here to note are represented by the Find, Replace, Copy, Cut, and Paste icons. You will use these extensively in creating documents in Chapter 3.

▼ **FIGURE 1.2** Home ribbon in Word 2010

The Insert ribbon, shown in Figure 1.3, is used to add special content to your document; this includes tables, images, drawing objects, and clip art. There are special document elements available in this ribbon as well, particularly the Header, Footer, Cover Page, Blank Page, and Page Break (which immediately pushes subsequent content to the next page regardless of whether there is room left on the current page). Other formatting options include Drop Cap, Symbols, and Hyperlinks. You can add a hyperlink to an external document or Web page, or link to a section within the current document (defined as a bookmark). The contents of this ribbon will be covered in Chapter 4.

▼ **FIGURE 1.3** Insert ribbon in Word 2010

The Page Layout ribbon is the next one in line, as shown in Figure 1.4. This ribbon allows you to control the size of the document, document orientation for printing, indents, spacing, and alignment. These aspects of the ribbon are discussed in Chapter 3.

▼ **FIGURE 1.4** Page Layout ribbon in Word 2010

The References ribbon is used for documents that require citations, endnotes, and footnotes. This ribbon is covered in Chapter 6. This is also where you can create a table of contents; you can see an example of the References ribbon in Figure 1.5.

▼ **FIGURE 1.5** References ribbon in Word 2010

The Mailings ribbon is used to construct documents such as envelopes and labels and individualize mailing documents for letters to multiple recipients. This is one of the more advanced features of Microsoft Word. You can see the Mailings ribbon in Figure 1.6; the functionality of this ribbon is covered in Chapter 3.

▼ **FIGURE 1.6** Mailings ribbon in Word 2010

The next ribbon is the Review ribbon, shown in Figure 1.7. This ribbon contains the icon for Spelling and Grammar, which should be used to review any document prior to submitting it; clicking this icon will start parsing your document for known spelling and grammar errors and prompt you to correct them. Additional research tools like the Thesaurus and Word Count are also located here, as well as the ability to turn on Track Changes and add and remove comments, which are useful when working on a collaborative document. The Review ribbon is covered in Chapter 5.

▼ **FIGURE 1.7** Review ribbon in Word 2010

The View Ribbon is the last standard ribbon and is shown in Figure 1.8. You can change the view of the document in this ribbon. Unlike some of the other programs in the Office suite, there is not usually a reason to deviate from the Print Layout for most word processing documents; this view shows the text broken up into pages where the editable regions are bright white and anything not on the printed page is shown as a gray background. The main functionality of the View ribbon is discussed later in this chapter.

▼ **FIGURE 1.8** View ribbon in Word 2010

The bottom of the standard interface contains page information, word count, a proofing error indicator, and View and Zoom settings. You can see the current page in which you are working and the total number of pages in the document. The word count defaults to the total number of words in the document; if you have some text selected, the words in that selection are displayed as a fraction of the total word count. The View settings are shortcuts to the different views available. To change the zoom percentage, you can use the slider or the + and – buttons. The zoom percentage is how much the document is magnified from standard print/ screen size. A zoom of 100% is the actual size of the document.

1.3.2 Anatomy of Microsoft Word 2011

The main difference you may notice between Word 2010 and Word 2011 is the inclusion of the menu bar in Word 2011. The menu bar is standard with any Macintosh software application, and it contains a lot of the functionality of the ribbon interface plus some convenient shortcuts that are not easily accessible from the ribbon. The menu bar is located beside the Apple® menu at the top of the computer screen; the menu choices begin with the Word menu and include the File menu and Help menu. In the document window itself (shown in Figure 1.9) are the icons to close the document, minimize it, or maximize it on the screen. Beneath those are the Quick Access toolbar icons. By default, there are more of these icons in Word 2011 than there are in Word 2010; these include shortcuts to the standard File menu commands (such as New, Open, Save, and Print), along with Cut, Copy, Paste, Undo, Redo, and Format Painter.

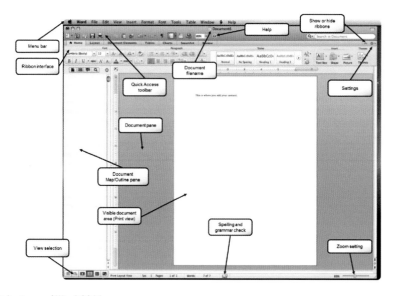

▼ **FIGURE 1.9** Anatomy of Word 2011

The Quick Access toolbar also contains an icon to open the Help interface; this appears as a circle with a question mark inside of it. Beside the Quick Access toolbar is a text box for searching the document; you simply type a keyword into the box and press *Enter* or click on the magnifying glass icon to perform the search. The ribbon interface is beneath this toolbar.

The Home ribbon for Word 2011, shown in Figure 1.10, contains the tools you will need to format your text. This includes the Font and Paragraph panels for altering various settings that affect how your text will display. You also have access to the available styles in this ribbon, which are covered in the next chapter. In Word 2011, you can also insert pictures and shapes from the Home ribbon. The functionality of the Home ribbon for Word 2011 is covered in Chapters 2 and 4.

▼ **FIGURE 1.10** Home ribbon in Word 2011

The Layout ribbon, shown in Figure 1.11, contains all of the tools for setting up the pages of your document. These include setting whether you want your document layout to be *Portrait* (the standard printed page with the longer side having the vertical measurement) or *Landscape* (where the shorter side is the vertical measurement). You can also set your margins from this ribbon. The margin is the amount of white space between the edge of the printed page and the beginning of your content; these typically default to 1″ on each side. This ribbon allows you to add page breaks, set the number of columns in your document, and use advanced functionality, such as adding a watermark to the document or changing the background color of the page. The main functionality of the Layout ribbon is covered in Chapter 3.

▼ **FIGURE 1.11** Layout ribbon in Word 2011

The Document Elements ribbon, shown in Figure 1.12, allows you to add common items to your page. These include a cover page, a blank page, and various types of page breaks. You can add a Table of Contents, Header, and Footer to your document from this ribbon using the predefined formats; this functionality is addressed in Chapter 4. This ribbon also includes tools for using references and citations; this functionality is covered in Chapter 6.

▼ **FIGURE 1.12** Document Elements ribbon in Word 2011

The Tables, Charts, and SmartArt ribbons are used to add advanced features to your document. These ribbons are shown in Figure 1.13. The functionality for each of these is covered in Chapter 4.

▼ **FIGURE 1.13** Tables, Charts, and SmartArt ribbons in Word 2011

The Review ribbon is used primarily for editing collaborative documents for which you want to track changes. This also contains commands for sharing documents with others. Some of the features in this ribbon are discussed in Chapter 6. You can see an example of the Review ribbon in Figure 1.14.

▼ **FIGURE 1.14** Review ribbon in Word 2011

The bottom of the interface includes shortcuts for changing the view of the document. The views included here are Draft, Outline, Publishing, Print, Notebook, and Full Screen. In addition to the view selection, the bottom of the interface has several other convenient data points. You will see the page number you are currently on out of the total page count. You will also see your current word count; if some of the document text is selected, you will see the word count of the selected text out of the total word count. There is also an indicator for spelling and grammar errors; a green check mark means there are currently no mistakes in the document and a red *X* indicates that there are errors according to the spelling and grammar rules of Word 2011. Finally, at the far right of the bottom interface is the current zoom percentage (this is a percentage of actual document size, which is 100%); you can adjust the slider setting to change the zoom.

1.3.3 The File Menu

Whenever you open Word from either a desktop icon or the Start menu of a Windows machine, it will open with a new blank document. You can save this document with a name of your choosing using the *Save As* command in the *File* menu (the File menu is shown in Figure 1.15). The File menu and the help files should be the first items you locate in any new software system. The File menu exists in almost all software applications written today and enables you to perform the essential tasks of creating a new file, opening an existing file, saving a file, printing a file, and exiting the program. The File menu is typically located at the left side of the software interface. Figure 1.15 shows the File menu for Word. In Word 2010, the File menu (which is also called the Backstage view in the Office 2010 suite) is found to the far left on the ribbon interface. In Word 2011, it is located beside the Apple menu at the top of the computer screen.

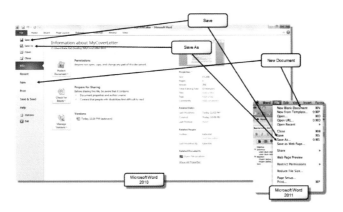

▼ **FIGURE 1.15** File menu in Word

When you select the *Save As* command, it will open a Save As dialog box, as shown in Figure 1.16. This allows you to select the location where you want to store your file. You can select the folder you want to use from the right-hand Navigation pane of the dialog box. The contents of the active folder are shown at the left side of the Navigation pane. Select the *New Folder* icon to create a new folder for use inside the current folder. Finally, you can type a name for your file and select the file type you want for your document. The default file type for Microsoft Word is *Word Document (.docx)*. Save your document in a new folder called *Keyboarding* on either your hard drive or on a removable storage device with the filename *MyNewDocument*.

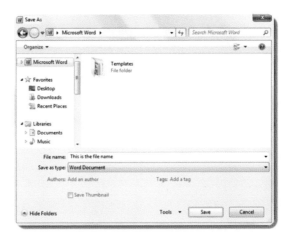

▼ **FIGURE 1.16** Save As dialog box in Word

Whenever you are working on a document, you should make sure to save it often. Your software could quit because of a machine error or a glitch and any unsaved progress on your work could be lost. You could also accidentally delete a portion of your work or make a change that the Undo command cannot correct; if you have saved your document before these changes, you can close the current document and open the saved version to get back to where you were.

Activity 1 – Saving and Opening Files

You should practice saving and opening documents to see how the word processing software interacts with the file system of the operating system. If you have not done so, you should create a folder called *Keyboarding* somewhere on your computer (this should be located somewhere in your document libraries or inside your *My Documents* folder where you can locate it easily). You should already have your initial file (that opened by default when you started the program) which was saved as *MyNewDocument*. Create a new document and save it (using the default file extension selected in the dialog box) as *Activity1*. Close these two files and follow the instructions below to open them again. If your software application closes when you close these files, as in the case of the Windows version which closes when there are no open documents, you should start it again from the operating system. By the end of this section, you should have both *MyNewDocument* and *Activity1* open again.

To open an existing document in Word, select the *File* menu and then choose *Open*. This will display an Open dialog box, as shown in Figure 1.17. The left-side Navigation pane is similar to the Save As dialog box where you can navigate to the folder you want to open. The right side of the dialog box lists the contents of the current folder. You can select any of the files with file types that can be opened in Word; the name of the file will display in the *File name* field and you can click the *Open* button (or simply double-click the name of the file).

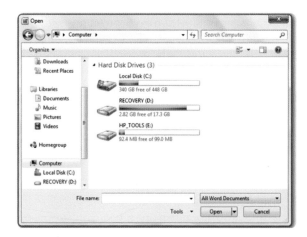

▼ **FIGURE 1.17** Open dialog box in Word

You can also start typing the name of the file you want to open in the File name field of the Open dialog box. A drop-down menu will appear from the File name field, displaying all of the filenames within the active folder that match the partial string of characters you have typed. You can then select an item from the list instead of typing the entire filename or manually sorting through all of the contents of the active folder.

If you are relatively new to computing, there are several essential commands found within the File menu with which you should become familiar:

- *New*—The New command is used to create a new file of the type associated with the program. In the case of Word, this file is a word processing document. The New command may present you with several alternatives if the program supports different document types or document creation options. By default, you will want to select *Blank Document* as your choice for creating an empty document.

- *Save As*—This command opens a dialog box to allow you to select the name, file type, and location to which you would like your file stored; this operates on the file that is currently active in the program. If you have already saved your document and want to save a copy or save it with a different name, you can do so with this option. For Word, the default file type is *Word Document* (*.docx*), but there are several alternative file types available when saving a document including *Portable Document Format* (*.pdf*). It is important to use Save As to save a new file you have created so your work will not be lost if there is a problem with the software system or you close it by accident.

- *Save*—The Save command allows you to save the file that you currently have open within the software application; this is useful for making sure your recent changes are retained in the document. The first time you save the document after it is created, this command will typically function like the Save As command.

- *Open*—The Open command is used to reopen existing documents. Selecting this command opens a dialog box that is similar to the one used to save documents and allows you to select a document from the current folder on the right-hand side of the dialog box. You can also type the name of the file you want to open in the File name field, and any files that are a match to the partial string you have typed will appear in a box as options to select.

- *Print*—This command allows you to send the current file to an installed printer. Printing requires additional hardware and a driver installation for that hardware to work. In Office 2010, you are given a software-based print option of *Send to OneNote 2010* as a possible printer regardless of what other printers you have installed. If you have installed Adobe Acrobat® Professional, you will also get the software-based option of printing to a *Portable Document Format* (*.pdf*) file.

- *Exit*—Selecting this command will close the program. Make sure you have saved all of the work you wish to keep before selecting this option.

OFFICE 2011 On a Macintosh, closing the windows of the program will not exit the program entirely. To close Word 2011 on the Macintosh, you must select the Word menu and choose Quit Word to fully close the program.

Document Types

There are several options for saving your files from Word. The default file type for the Word application is Word Document which has a file extension of *.docx*. This is selected by default when you save the document. You can also use the compatibility format for Word documents so that the documents you create can be viewed in older versions of Word without issues; this document format is called Word 97–03 and has the document extension *.doc*. Using the *.doc* file format disables the new features of Word but preserves backward compatibility with prior versions; the need for this is becoming less common since the 2007 and 2008 versions of Word use the new *.docx* format and features. In addition to these options, you can also save your document from the Word application in other file formats:

- A Portable Document Format (PDF) file (which uses a *.pdf* extension) is constructed from printing commands and it produces a static document that cannot be edited or reformatted without specialized software. Unlike the native Word file format, which can change depending on the software version and installed fonts, there is no variance in the display of a PDF file (a format that was invented by the Adobe company). This means it will display for the viewer exactly as you intend it to be seen. You can create a PDF file of your Word document by selecting *PDF* as the file type in the Save As dialog box in both Word 2010 and Word 2011. The most common application for viewing PDF files is the Adobe Reader®, which is available in a free version from *www.adobe.com* (by typing "Adobe Reader" in the search box).

- The XML Paper Specification (XPS) format is the Microsoft version of a PDF; this type of file requires a special viewer for the application type but it has the same fixed display property of the PDF document. The document extension for this type of file is *.xps*.

- The Web Page format saves the document in HyperText Markup Language (HTML) for use in Web browsers and storage on Web servers for remote access. HTML is an interpreted display, so it will look different in different Web browsers. Word does not create clean code for the Web, so you should not use it as a primary Web development tool. The file extension for this is *.htm* or *.html*.

- Rich Text Format (RTF) was invented by Microsoft in 1987; it is a common format for word processing that can be used by multiple, cross-platform word processing applications for document exchange. This is a safe alternative file format if the destination of the file is not another Word product but it will disable the advanced display features and text modifications available in Word and retain only basic formatting such as bold and italic text. The file extension for RTF is *.rtf*.

- Plain text will save the contents of the document without any formatting effects or modifiers. This type of document format can be read by basic text applications like Notepad and Notepad++ which do not allow formatting alterations for text content. The document extension for this type of file is *.txt*.

- OpenDocument Format is an open standard for word processing that is compatible with the OpenOffice.org application suite. Not all of the features available in Word have an equivalent in this format, so the document may not display accurately in this file format. You can find more information on the use of OpenOffice.org as an alternate word processing software solution in the appendices of this book.

Activity 2 – File Types

Now that you have an understanding of the different types of file formats that are available for saving a document from Word, you should create a new document and save it using the default file format as *Activity2*. You should add a line of text to the document such as "This is my new application document." Now, save the document in the folder for this chapter with each of the following file formats: PDF, XPS, RTF, Web Page, and Plain Text. Depending on the type of file format you select, you may need to re-open the original document to save it in a new format. What are the application icons for each of these formats that appear as the default program to open them (such as the system's default Web browser for the Web page version of the file)?

1.3.5 Document Management

Whenever you are working on a project, it is important to manage the files associated with that project. Throughout the rest of this text, you will be creating projects in every chapter. You should be sure to keep your work organized—not just for the purposes of learning but also for the general management of productivity. You should already have a folder for this text called *Keyboarding*. To further manage your projects, you should create a new folder within it for each chapter and title each one following the naming format of *Chapter1* for this chapter. It is a good idea to create folders to manage your different responsibilities so you can find items when you need them; the same rules that apply to filing and sorting paper documents also apply to organizing electronic documents.

1.3.6 Locating Help Files

Help files are almost always included in a software system. These files allow you to get definitions of elements in the software system and obtain help in performing common tasks and troubleshooting. On a Windows machine, pressing the *F1* key will activate the Help interface for whatever program you currently have selected (if you are using the operating system when you press *F1*, you will open the help interface for the operating system). On a Macintosh, the Help interface is available by selecting the *Help* menu at the top of the screen; this will be context-sensitive for the program you have active. The Word Help interface is shown in Figure 1.18. Most help files, including those in Office, allow you to search for entries using a keyword search.

▲ **FIGURE 1.18** Word Help interface in Word

Document Views

There are a variety of display modes available in Word for looking at your documents; these are called views. You can select the view in Word 2010 from the bottom of the interface or by using choosing it on the View ribbon. The default view is called the Print Layout view and it shows what the document will look like when it is printed out on paper. The other available options are Full Screen Reading, Web Layout, Outline, and Draft.

The Full Screen Reading view shows the document with the maximum amount of screen space devoted to the content. Web Layout shows the contents of the page as they would look if the page were converted to an HTML document. Outline view shows the levels of the document and is similar to an outline of content; you can promote or demote content using this view and select how many levels of headings you want to see. Draft view works like Print Layout view but without showing the text as it would appear on the printed page.

> **OFFICE 2011** Word 2011 also allows you to select the view of your document. The default view is called the Print view. Views can be changed using the icons at the bottom of the Word 2011 interface. The options available here are similar to those found in Word 2010; the options include Draft, Outline, Full Screen, Publishing, and Notebook views. Draft view shows your document without the page formatting. Outline view shows the contents of your document arranged as an outline where you can see higher level headings for text farther to the left. Full Screen view is a special mode that shows your document on the full screen without any desktop interface, as shown in Figure 1.19; when you are in this view, you have access to just a subset of the normal formatting commands. Select *Exit* to return to the standard Print view. Publishing view and Notebook view are special formats for text documents that require your document to be created in or converted to the format for use; Notebook Layout view is similar to Office OneNote 2010 for Windows.

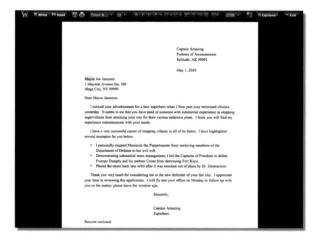

▼ **FIGURE 1.19** Full Screen view in Word 2011

One item to note here is the *Navigation Pane* checkbox on the View ribbon; this will show or hide the Navigation pane, which provides you with an outline or preview of your document in a separate, mobile pop-up window. By default, you should make sure this checkbox is selected to provide you with an easy means of navigating your document and identifying search results.

The Navigation pane within the Word 2010 interface has three tabs. The first tab (which looks like a small document with outline format) is a display of the document outline by heading; you can adjust the number of levels of the document outline to display by right-clicking on a heading and choosing *Show Heading Levels* and the level you want to show. The Browse tab displays a thumbnail view of the pages of your document so you can jump quickly to a page by clicking its thumbnail. Finally, the Browse Results tab shows the results of a keyword search of the document using any keywords entered in the text box above the tabs.

OFFICE 2011 The Document Map in Word 2011 is the equivalent of the Navigation pane in Word 2010 and allows you to see an outline of your document. To open the Document Map, select the *View* menu, choose *Sidebar*, and then choose *Document Pane*. The four tabs across the top of the Document pane correspond to Thumbnails, Document Map, Reviewing, and Find and Replace. The Thumbnail pane shows a miniature version of the pages of your document as they appear when printed. The Document Map pane shows the outline of the document arranged according to the document headers. The Reviewing pane identifies comments and tracked document changes. The Find and Replace pane will locate instances of the text you enter in the Find text box and allow you to select options for replacing that text with what you enter in the Replace text box. The Document pane is useful for jumping quickly through your document and seeing an outline of the text you are constructing.

1.3.8 Customizing the Quick Access Toolbar

By default, the Quick Access Toolbar in Word 2010 gives you the commands to Save, Undo, and Redo, but you can change this to include any of the commands that you use frequently. You can use the Customize Quick Access Toolbar icon beside these choices; this allows you to select from the most common commands or choose *More Commands* to select from the list of available commands for the software. You can see the Customize Quick Access Toolbar icon in use in Figure 1.20.

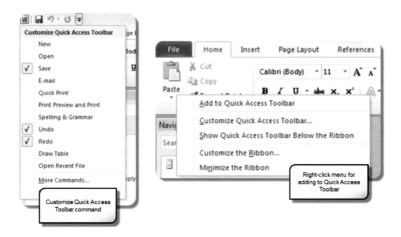

▼ FIGURE 1.20 Customizing the Quick Access Toolbar

You can also add commonly used commands to your Quick Access Toolbar by right-clicking on the command icon in the ribbon interface and selecting the *Add to Quick Access Toolbar* choice that appears in the menu, which is also shown in Figure 1.20. This will create a shortcut icon without text in the Quick Access Toolbar. You can remove any of the items added to the Quick Access Toolbar by right-clicking the icon and selecting the *Remove from Quick Access Toolbar* selection in the menu that appears. You should use the Quick Access Toolbar to save time in navigating the ribbon interface for the commands that you use most often.

> **OFFICE 2011** To modify the Quick Access Toolbar in Word 2011, you must redefine it as a menu. You can do this by selecting the View menu, choosing Toolbars, and selecting Customize Menus and Toolbars. When the new dialog box opens, choose the Commands tab to add any additional commands you want on your toolbar interface.

1.4 KEYBOARDING I

Your goal for using the keyboard should be what is called *touch typing*. Touch typing is when you can use the keyboard without looking at the letters you are typing and without pressing too hard on the keys (you should just press hard enough for the key press to register). This first lesson will guide you through the placement of your hands on the keyboard and will introduce you to the home row keys. The home row keys are the ones where your fingers will naturally reside as you type; all of the other keys will be learned as an offset to the home row key position for each finger. The method used for these keyboarding lessons is the *add-a-key* method, meaning you will focus on mastering one key at a time and adding a new key with each numbered lesson at the end of the chapter. You should familiarize yourself with the elements of the keyboard presented in the chapter content and pace yourself through the individual lessons at the end of the chapter. It is ideal if you master one lesson before moving on to the next. It is important to train your hand positioning and movement correctly to maximize your typing speed and minimize the number of errors that you make.

TOUCH TYPING *is the process by which you position your hands on the keyboard and type using your sense of touch without looking at the keys you are pressing. This is the goal of learning to type because it increases your productivity when you can focus your sight on the source material and output instead of where your hands are moving.*

The **HOME ROW KEYS** *are the keys on which you place your fingers at rest when typing. The standard placement for the left hand is the keys A through F and the standard placement for the right hand is the keys J through L and the semicolon (;) key. After any displacement to strike a key on the keyboard, your fingers should return to the home row keys at the default placement.*

ADD-A-KEY *is a method of learning to type where you start with a single key and, when that is mastered, add a new key to increase proficiency. This method involves repetition typing with a focus on error-free results and speed of typing. When you have reached proficiency with the key, you should be able to strike it without looking at the key.*

1.4.1 The QWERTY Keyboard

The QWERTY keyboard has been the standard typing interface since at least the patent containing it in 1878 but probably closer to its invention by C. L. Sholes for his "Type-Writer" in the 1860s. This keyboard, also called the "Universal" keyboard, is named for the arrangement of the first six letters on the top row of letter keys. You can see an example of the modern QWERTY keyboard in Figure 1.21. The rows of keys were placed diagonally to accommodate the mechanical levers between the keys.

▼ **FIGURE 1.21** Example of the QWERTY keyboard

While the QWERTY is standard in its arrangement of numbers and letters, some of the peripheral keys such as the arrow keys and function keys, are located in different places on different computers, so you should take the time to examine your own machine to find the keys you need. The first introduction to keyboarding (or typing) will come with the home row keys and how to place your hands over the keyboard for the most effective way to type. You should consider comfort and dexterity with your hand placement to make sure you can reach the keys with the necessary fingers to minimize motion over the keys for maximum effectiveness.

1.4.2 The Home Row Keys

The home row keys are where your fingers will be placed on the keyboard when you are about to type and where your fingers will return when you are done pressing keys. You can see an illustration of how your fingers should be placed on the home row keys in Figure 1.22. Your left hand should be placed such that from your little finger (or pinky finger) on your left hand to your index finger rest over the A through F keys respectively. Your right hand should be placed such that your index finger to your little finger rest over the J through L and semicolon keys respectively. The G and H keys are also part of the home row, but these will be reached by moving your left and right index finger to the key from the rest position and are introduced later in the lessons.

▼ **FIGURE 1.22** Home row keys and finger positioning

Proper Hand Placement

You should place your hand on the keyboard such that your fingers rest gently on the assigned home row keys as shown in Figure 1.23. You can place your wrists against your desk or the bottom of the laptop or you can suspend them in the air; this decision is a matter of comfort. You should try to find a comfortable resting position with your hands in the proper location over the keyboard (with both thumbs easily able to strike the spacebar) that is natural for you; this will help you avoid fatigue. Your arms will generally be slightly curved to the side and should not be rigid in position. Once you have your fingers over the correct keys in the home row, try extending your fingers one by one to make sure they have mobility over the rest of the keyboard without pain or difficulty and adjust your overall posture and position so you can make these motions easily. The F and J keys typically have some tactile modification so they are easily recognizable by touch, such as a raised groove at the bottom of the key; this will help you find the proper hand position without visually referencing the keyboard.

▼ **FIGURE 1.23** Hand placement on home row keys

If you have trouble getting settled in a natural position over the keyboard, you can consider ergonomic solutions which are tailored to the natural angles and positioning of the body. However, the keyboards designed for this tend to be expensive and non-standard. You should also be mindful of your posture when you are seated at your computer to type. Arching your back to type may cause cramping and discomfort; you should try to keep a good straight posture as much as possible when you type. You also want to make sure any reference (or source) material, the material that you are copying, is easily visible; this tends to be a distance of 24 to 36 inches on average, though this will vary with lighting and eyesight considerations.

Activity 3 – Home Row Key Practice

Now that you have a comfortable position in which to type, you should open a new Word document and name it *Activity3*. You should then type using only the home row keys on which your fingers naturally rest to get a feel for how to press the keys lightly and how gently your fingers should rest over the keyboard. As an added challenge, you should try to type words using only these keys without moving your fingers from their default positions.

Spacebar and Enter Keys

Two other keys with which you will need to be familiar quickly are the enter key and the spacebar. The enter key is located in the home row keys on the right-hand side of the keyboard. You will strike this key with your right pinky by moving your pinky finger only from the semicolon key past the apostrophe key to the enter key. The movement should be smooth without moving your entire hand. It may take some time to get accustomed to the motion so that it feels natural. You can see an illustration of this in Figure 1.24.

▼ **FIGURE 1.24** Pinky movement to enter key

The other key you will use often is the spacebar. This is the long key that has no marking on it two rows down from the home row keys. You will strike this key with either of your thumbs. You should practice this motion as well without moving your fingers from the default keys over which they should rest.

Activity 4 – Space and Enter Key Practice

Create a new Word document called *Activity4*. Start by placing your hands in the default position over the home row keys. Press the spacebar and enter keys alternately until you get a cadence for typing on the two keys. Now try to strike keys using your other fingers without moving them from their default position (other than the right pinky which moves to strike the enter key). You should practice moving from the semicolon to the enter key several times until the movement becomes natural.

1.4.5 The Keyboarding Software

The keyboarding software that accompanies this text can be used to perform all of the lessons in this text. It uses a timer system that will either count down for timed activities or count up until the exercise is complete to give you an estimation of your time as well as calculate the errors present in what you have typed. It is designed to run on a Web browser and it can be opened locally from the accompanying DVD or online from the companion Web site for the book at *www.keyboardingandbeyond.com*. To use the companion Web site, you must register for a free account by clicking the *Register* link on either the side navigation or the top banner. You can see an example of the software interface in Figure 1.25.

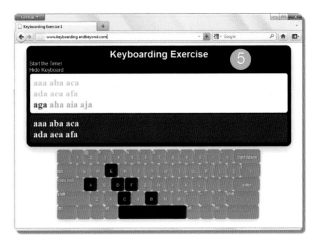

▼ **FIGURE 1.25** Included keyboarding software interface

You can access the software from the DVD by opening the chapter for which you are doing exercises, choosing the Software folder, and then clicking on the file name of the keyboarding lesson you want to complete (such as *Lesson1_1.htm* for Lesson 1.1). This will open the exercise in a Web browser window. You must click the *Start the Lesson* link to start the timer and allow you to start typing the solution; your typed text will automatically populate the correct field, so you do not need to use your mouse after clicking the *Start the Lesson* link. If you are completing the exercises from the Web site *www.keyboardingandbeyond.com*, when you have logged in with your free registered account, you can click the Lessons link on the main navigation panel on the left and then select your lesson or drill from the list that appears on the right.

While the timer is running, all of your keystrokes will be recorded on the page and used to calculate your speed, errors, and overall timing. You can restart the lessons at any time by clicking the *Restart Lesson* link that appears when the timer is active. You can only restart a keyboarding drill after the timer has expired or you have obtained your results; lessons are for practice, but the drills at the end of the chapter are a test of your proficiency so you should complete them without restarting.

The software is optimized to run in Firefox version 4.0 and higher (available for free download on Mac, PC, and select mobile devices from *www.firefox.com*), though you should not experience display issues in any updated version of modern browsers such as Internet Explorer or Safari. From the menu, you will simply select the lesson that you want to complete and choose the "Start" button to begin the timer and start recording your keystrokes. When you start the lesson, all of the prior text entered will be removed. This software disables the default behavior of certain keys that are used for navigating the Web, such as the backspace key, but this is necessary to process the keystrokes properly; this is inherent to the page and these keys will resume functionality on any other page or Web site you use.

1.4.6 Keyboarding Lessons 1–15

By the time you have completed the following lessons, you will have practiced all of the keys highlighted in dark blue in Figure 1.26. You should concentrate in these lessons on learning the hand motion necessary to reach the keys without looking at them. The more you practice, the better your form will become and the more your speed will increase.

▼ **FIGURE 1.26** Keyboarding I keys and hand motion

The software included with the text and available online at *www.keyboardingandbeyond* *.com* will time the lessons and alert you to any mistakes made while entering the text for these exercises. Because this is practice, you should feel free to redo these lessons and activities as much as you need to improve your performance and form.

Lesson 1.1 J Key

In this lesson, you will use your right index finger to press the J key as well as using the spacebar with your thumbs and the enter key with your right pinky. The software will count up the amount of time it takes for you to complete the task, so you can take as long as you need and retry the exercise to improve your time.

Type the following:

```
j jj jjj jj j j jj jjj jj j
j jj jjj jj j j jj jjj jj j
j jj jjj jj j j jj jjj jj j
jj jjj j jj jjj j jj j jj j jjj j jj
jj jjj j jj jjj j jj j jj j jjj j jj
```

Lesson 1.2 K Key

You will now add the K key to your hand motion using your right middle finger. You will begin by practicing with the K key and then include the J key which you have already learned. The software will count up the amount of time it takes for you to complete the task, so you can take as long as you need and retry the exercise to improve your time.

Type the following:

```
k kk kkkk kk k kk kkkk kk k kk
k kk kkkk kk k kk kkkk kk k kk
j jk jkj jj kk jk kj jkj jj k
j jk jkj jj kk jk kj jkj jj k
jkjkjkjkjkjj kkjkjkjkjkjk jj kk jk kj kk jj
```

Lesson 1.3 L Key

This time you will include the L key in your typing using your right ring finger. You should once again concentrate on form over speed. The software will count up the amount of time it takes for you to complete the task, so you can take as long as you need and retry the exercise to improve your time.

Type the following:

```
l lll l lll l lll l ll l ll ll ll lll l
l lll l lll l lll l ll l ll lk lk lkl l
l ljl l ljl l lkl l lj l lj lk lk lkl j
l lkl l lkl l ljl l lk l lk lj lj ljl j kk ll j
l ljl l ljl l lkl l lj l lj lk lk lkl j ll kk j
```

Lesson 1.4 Semicolon Key

In this lesson, you will use your right pinky finger to type the semicolon (;) key. In proper use, the semicolon key receives only a single space after use. This means your right pinky will be pressing both the semicolon key and the enter key using swift motion back and forth. The software will count up the amount of time it takes for you to complete the task, so you can take as long as you need and retry the exercise to improve your time.

Type the following:

```
;; ;; ;; ;; ;;; ; ;;; ; ;;
j; k; l; ;l ;k ;j ;; l;l k;k j;j ;;
;j; ;k; ;l; ;;k ;;j ;jkl; ;lkj; ;jkl ;lkj ;
;
;
;kk ;ll; ;jj; ;jj ;ll ;lj ;jk ;jl ;kl jl k; jl k; ;j lk
;kk ;ll; ;jj; ;jj ;ll ;lj ;jk ;jl ;kl jl k; jl k; ;j lk
```

Lesson 1.5 Right Hand Practice

For this lesson, you will use the home keys for your right hand along with the spacebar and enter keys to enter the text. You should try to focus on tapping the keys lightly so that you strike them just hard enough to type the character and then release pressure on the key. The software will count up the amount of time it takes for you to complete the task, so you can take as long as you need and retry the exercise to improve your time.

Type the following:

```
jjj kkk lll ;;; lll kkk jjj kkk lll ;;;
;;;jjj lllkkk jljljl k;k;k; ;j;j; ;k;k; ;l;l;
jkjk klkl jljl k;k; jk jl j; k; kj kl ;j ;k ;l
jkl;jkl;jkl;;lkj;lkj;lkj jkl jkl jk jk j j;
l; l; l; k; k; j; j; kl; kl; ;lk ;lk ;j;j
j;j;k; k;l;l; ljljl kjkjk kllk kjjk k;;k
```

Lesson 1.6 F Key

In this lesson, you will begin using the keys for your left hand. You will learn each key for your left hand first before using the keys from your right hand other than the enter key which is assigned to the right pinky finger. The software will count up the amount of time it takes for you to complete the task, so you can take as long as you need and retry the exercise to improve your time.

Type the following:

```
f ff ffff fff ffff fff ff f
f ff ffff fff ffff fff ff f
fff ff ff ff fff ff ff fff f ff fff
fff ff ff ff fff ff ff fff f ff fff
f fff ffff ff ff fff f ffff f ffff ff ff
```

Lesson 1.7 D Key

In this lesson, you will add the D key used by your left middle finger. The software will count up the amount of time it takes for you to complete the task, so you can take as long as you need and retry the exercise to improve your time.

Type the following:

```
ddd dd d dddd dd dd dd ddd d d
ddd dd d dddd dd dd dd ddd d d
ddd df d dffd df dd df dfd d f
fdf ff dd f d f d f d ddd fff dfd fdf
fdfdfd dd ff ddfdd ffdff dfdfd ff f d dd ddd d
```

Lesson 1.8 S Key

For this lesson, you will use your left ring finger to type the S key in addition to the keys you have already learned for your left hand. The software will count up the amount of time it takes for you to complete the task, so you can take as long as you need and retry the exercise to improve your time.

Type the following:

```
s ssss sss sss sss ssss ss s ss s ss
sds sfs sss ss sd sf fs sf sd ds sds sss sss
sfs sds fds fds ffs dds ssd ssf ffs dds ffd ddf
sfs sds fds fds ffs dds ssd ssf ffs dds ffd ddf
sfsd sdsf fdfd sfsf sdsd dsds dfdf sfsf fsfs dsds
```

Lesson 1.9 A Key

In this lesson, you will use the A key in addition to the keys for your left hand which you have already learned. The software will count up the amount of time it takes for you to complete the task, so you can take as long as you need and retry the exercise to improve your time.

Type the following:

```
a aa aaa aa aaa aa aa aa a aaa
ad da af fa as sa asa ada afa fada dafa
sasa adaf fada dasa fasa sad das fas saf
sads dass sass fass fad fada sasa fads dafs
safda afdsa sadfa fada sada dasa dfsa sadf
```

Lesson 1.10 Left Hand Practice

In this lesson, you will practice using each of the home row keys at rest assigned to your left hand. The only other keys you should use are the enter key and spacebar. The software will count up the amount of time it takes for you to complete the task, so you can take as long as you need and retry the exercise to improve your time.

Type the following:

```
sad sad dad fads safsa dasa ds
fasf fads sads dasa sa sa as as add add
dad dad add sad fad fads sa sa da fa fa
da sa dasa sada fasa safa asaf adaf asa dsd
fsd dsf dfa ad sf as df fd sa da fs fa ds das
sa fa da fd fs fa ds da df fd fa sa dsd dad fsf dad
```

Lesson 1.11 Both Hand Practice

In this lesson, you will use all of the home row keys that are assigned to your fingers at rest. The only finger which should move from the assigned keys in this lesson is the right pinky finger which is used to strike the enter key. The software will count up the amount of time it takes for you to complete the task, so you can take as long as you need and retry the exercise to improve your time.

Type the following:

```
jkl; asdf ;lkj fdsa asdf jkl; ;lkj fdsa asdf jkl;
;als kdjf jf kd ls ;a a; sl dk fj jl fs k; da ;s al
jd fk ks sl ;a a; a;sldkfj jfkdls;a jas kas lass;
lad lass sall; saj; jas; kas sak; jasa dafa kasa lasa
ja;f;a ks la ;a jf kd ls ;a ;sldkfja fjdksla; jlsf k;da
lak jak kas kaj lak laj as add dad fad lass lad ;; aa jj ff
kk dd l;
```

Lesson 1.12 H Key

To type the H key, you need to move your right index finger one key to the left on the home row. You will practice this motion in the following exercise. Your right index finger and your right pinky are the only fingers which should move from the assigned home row keys at rest. The software will count up the amount of time it takes for you to complete the task, so you can take as long as you need and retry the exercise to improve your time.

Type the following:

```
hhh jj hh hjjh hh jj jjj hhh jj hhh jj hhh jj hh
has sah lass lash hash sha jha kha lha jha dha sha fha
had dad add lass lad lash jas jah has had fad
add has had jad jas has had jas jad jaad haas saah hasa
dasa has das dad kad kash lash jash dash
```

Lesson 1.13 G Key

To type the G key, you will move your left index finger one key to the right of its rest position on the F key. The rest of your left hand should remain over the respective at rest keys on the home row when you move your index finger to type the G key. The software will count up the amount of time it takes for you to complete the task, so you can take as long as you need and retry the exercise to improve your time.

Type the following:

```
g gg ggg gfg ff ff gg fgf gfg ggg ff g
gas sag hash gash dad add shag gag jag gak lag gall
gh hf gj fg jh hj gf fgf hjh jhj gfg ;; j; g; h;
as dad had lash; lash had lad lass lag gash; fash shaf
jads kads gads hads fads lads ;ads das; dasl ;a ls kd jf hg gh
fj dk sl a;
```

Lesson 1.14 Both Hand Practice

In this lesson, you will use the entire set of home row keys you have learned so far along with the spacebar and enter key. You should concentrate on your form in this lesson and repeat it as necessary to improve your time and your proficiency with the finger motion. You should concentrate on striking the keys just hard enough to type the letter before releasing pressure. The software will count up the amount of time it takes for you to complete the task, so you can take as long as you need and retry the exercise to improve your time.

Type the following:

```
jfj fjf kdk dkd lsl sls ;a; a;a aja ;f; ljl lfl aja afa
jlsffslj a;ls kdjf jfkd ls;a j jj kk f ff dd jfj kdk lsl
has has has sash sash dad add as has had fad ad lass lad lad
lass lass; gas gas gash has hash sh sh sha sha sha ash ash
kaja ajak lajak jakal dakal lal lad kad klad glad klad;; ;
ghgh jfjf kdkd lsls ;a;a jgfh dksl a;fj a;gh gha; ;ahg ;ajf
```

Lesson 1.15 Practice and Review

In this lesson, you will practice typing all of the keys you have learned so far. The timer for this exercise counts down, so you should try to gain enough proficiency and speed to complete the exercise in its entirety before the timer runs out. Because you are still learning, you should repeat this exercise as necessary until you are able to complete it with time left on the timer!

Type the following:

```
sasha has a glad dad; lass sad das add; lad kass sad glass;
has a sasha dad add; lass a glad fad dad; sad lass sad dad sad lad;
```

had has sad had; jag hag kag lag; saf; had sad lad lass dad add;
jhag ghaj jak kaj lak kaj lal gag hah faf daf dafa
sash has had add dad das ad add fad glad sad glass fad dad ad
add lass lad fash lash
gash glass dad das has sash had sash gash lash jas;
add dad glad sad fad gad lad kad;
lass has das fas gas hash jash kash lash;

CHAPTER SUMMARY

This chapter introduced you to the fundamental concepts and operations for creating, saving, and opening simple word processing documents. Word processing is the most common productivity application in businesses and organizations. In addition, this chapter covered the use of common File menu commands for most software applications, keyboard productivity shortcuts, and file and file type management. The next chapter expands on the use of word processing software to create more advanced documents and give you exposure to the more complex formatting available in document creation. The menus and tasks introduced will help you navigate the word processing software as you continue to explore document creation and typing. You should now be familiar with the layout of the standard QWERTY keyboard and how to position your hands for keyboarding. Once you have completed the keyboarding lessons for this chapter, you should be proficient with the use of the home row keys, the spacebar, and the enter key; the next step is to master the top row keys, which will be your first significant finger movement to another row of keys.

CHAPTER KNOWLEDGE CHECK

1 Word processing is the _____ of document creation and it is the most common task in any modern business environment.

- ○ **A.** Digital evolution
- ○ **B.** Digital process
- ○ **C.** Electronic process
- ○ **D.** All of the above
- ○ **E.** None of the above

2 _____ in modern terms is the use of a computer system to create, manipulate, and share text.

- ○ **A.** Electronic processing
- ○ **B.** Digital processing
- ○ **C.** Word processing
- ○ **D.** AutoCorrect

3 This command opens a dialog box to allow you to select the name, file type, and location to which you would like your file stored; this operates on the file that is currently active in the program.

○ **A.** Save As Command

○ **B.** Print Command

○ **C.** Command Line Environment

○ **D.** All of the above

4 The Home ribbon in Word 2010 is where you find _____ commands such as Bold, Italics, style settings, and list settings.

○ **A.** Mailing

○ **B.** Reference

○ **C.** Formatting

○ **D.** None of the above

5 The File menu exists in almost all software applications written today and enables you to perform the essential tasks of creating a _____.

○ **A.** New file, opening an existing photo, saving a file, printing a file, and exiting the program

○ **B.** New file, opening an existing file, saving a file, printing a file, and exiting the program

○ **C.** New file, opening an existing file, inserting a graph, printing a file, and exiting the program

○ **D.** New file, opening an existing file, saving a file, changing fonts, and adjusting font size

6 Touch typing is when you can use the keyboard _____ at the letters you are typing and without pressing too hard on the keys (you should just press hard enough for the key press to register).

○ **A.** Without looking

○ **B.** While looking

○ **C.** Tapping

○ **D.** None of the above

7 If you are new to typing or word processing documents, the blinking vertical line in the document display is the _____.

○ **A.** System type

○ **B.** Pointer

○ **C.** Cursor

○ **D.** None of the above

8 You can place your wrists against your desk or the bottom of the laptop or you can suspend them in the air; this decision is a _____.

○ **A.** System standard
○ **B.** National Standardized Typing Standard
○ **C.** Matter of comfort
○ **D.** All of the above
○ **E.** None of the above

9 The References ribbon is used for documents that require _____.

○ **A.** Citations, endnotes, or footnotes
○ **B.** Headers, body, or conclusion
○ **C.** Citations, paragraphs, and references
○ **D.** None of the above

10 The _____ keyboard has been the standard typing interface since at least the patent containing it in 1878 but probably closer to its invention by C. L. Sholes for his "Type-Writer" in the 1860s.

○ **A.** ALPHA
○ **B.** STANDARD
○ **C.** QWERTY
○ **D.** None of the above

CHAPTER EXERCISES

1. For your first exercise, open the Word application by selecting it from the Start menu. Use the New command to start a new document. Once you have opened the new document, return to the file menu and select the Save as command. Use the Save as command to save the new file to the My Documents folder and selecting a name that will accurately describe the contents of the file.

2. Open a new document from the Word application file menu. For this exercise you will learn to work with file types. The Word application allows you to save your document in a variety of file types. These file types can easily be recognized by looking at the three or four characters after the period contained in the file name you have chosen. A Word 2010 file extension is .docx. Save your new file with an easily identifiable name as you did in Exercise 1, except this time when the Save as dialogue window appears select a name and then select the Save as Type drop down menu box and select a PDF type. Saving your file in this fashion will create a protected document that other users can open using a PDF reader such as Adobe Acrobat Reader.

3. For this exercise you will learn how to apply templates stored within the Word application. Select the file menu and then select the New command. From Available Templates near the top of the window select Sample Templates. A new list of available business letter templates appears with several designs. Open the desired template and save to your favorite location, such as to the My Documents locations on your computer.

4. Developing professional documents can be a time intensive process. This requires that you be sure you do everything possible to preserve your original documents. The Word application has several features that will help you safely recover your files from accidental deletions and even power outages. One of these features is the automatic save which is set to automatically save your documents every 10 minutes. For this exercise select the Options command from the file menu which results in the window displayed in Figure 1.27. Next you should be sure the *AutoRecover information every* selection has a checkmark in the check box and finally adjust the minutes to five so that your work is automatically saved every five minutes. To show your instructor you have completed this exercise simply press the Ctrl key + Alt key + Print Screen key to copy your screen and then left click in a Word document at the position where you would like to paste your screen shot and your image will appear.

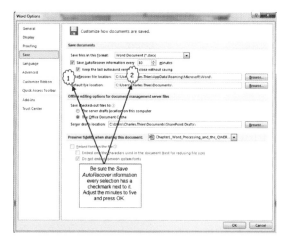

▼ FIGURE 1.27 Save as options

If you're using a Macintosh computer and you're using Microsoft Word 2011 then you can complete the same exercise with the exception of a couple of different steps as shown in Figure 1.28 below. On the Mac you will need to open the file menu and select Save As. When the Save as dialogue window opens you will notice that on the bottom left side of the window there is an options button. Select the Options button and the Save options window opens. Be sure to select the Save AutoRecover information every check box if it is already not checked and change your minutes to 5. To show your instructor you have completed this exercise, simply press the Command + Shift + 3 keys to copy your screen, which will be saved as a PNG file on your desktop. You can paste this image into a Word document that will show your instructor you completed the exercise.

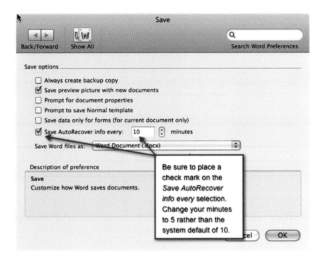

▼ **FIGURE 1.28** Save as options on a Macintosh

5. Organizations today constantly struggle to protect their intellectual capital. Intellectual capital is an organization's "know how" skills they develop over time. For this assignment let's suppose you are working on an important memorandum that contains confidential information relating to a new fuel formula that helps vehicles burn cleaner significantly protecting the environment. As you previously learned, please create a new Word file and name it *NewFuelforAmerica.docx* and save it to your favorite location. With the document open we are going to learn to encrypt and password protect the document (Note: The encryption option is not available for Word 2011). Open the file menu and press the Info command and select the Protect Document as shown in Figure 1.29. For this assignment select the Encrypt with Password option and select a password with no more that fifteen characters using a combination of numbers, letters, and characters.

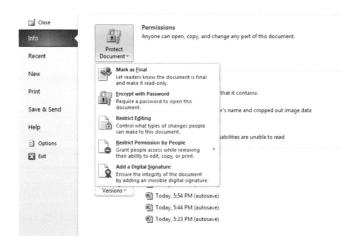

▼ **FIGURE 1.29** Encrypt with Password options

If you're using a Macintosh computer and you're using Microsoft Word 2011 then you can complete the same exercise with the exception of a couple of different steps. Microsoft Word 2011 allows you to protect your document but does not use encryption, so this means you must also rely on keeping your files safe in a secure location. It is also important that you do not exceed fifteen characters or you will not be able to open the document on a Microsoft version of Word 2010. To password protect the document simply open Word 2011 and select Preferences, Personal Settings and Security. Performing these steps produce a window as shown in Figure 1.30. There are three options to protect your document that include:

- Require a password to open
- Require a password to edit
- Suggest read-only mode

Make the changes, press OK and re-enter your password in the confirm dialogue. To show your instructor you have completed this exercise, simply press the Command + Shift + 3 keys to copy your screen, which will be saved as a PNG file on your desktop. You can paste this image into a Word document that will show your instructor you completed the exercise.

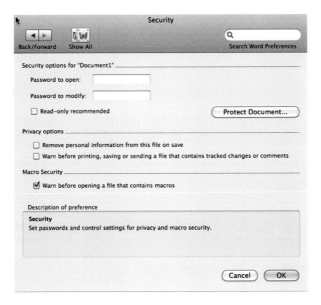

▼ **FIGURE 1.30** Word 2011 Document Password Options

CHAPTER REVIEW QUESTIONS

The following five questions apply to the Windows version of Microsoft Word 2010:

1. Please define and contrast the differences between Word Processing and Productivity Software. How does Word processing affect productivity in the business environment?

2. Locate the help file for Microsoft Word. Using the help file and using the search window research the backstage view within the Word application. Write a short paragraph identifying the major features and options available in this view.

3. Most software applications you use will require routine maintenance that includes downloading updates available from the software developer. Microsoft is very good about providing routine updates for your software. For this exercise you will need to check for any updates available for your installed copy of Microsoft Word. Proceed to the backstage and press the help command, once you have performed these steps, investigate what is needed to search and install current system updates for your version of the software application. Please list the steps required as proof to your instructor that you have completed the exercise.

4. For the following exercise you will explore and identify the View ribbon within the Microsoft Word environment. Please identify all of the groups available within the View ribbon, particularly change your document views and Show view in different configurations. Once you have explored these areas describe what happened when you changed the configurations and explain when you might use each of these views.

5. For this next exercise, the focus is Microsoft 2011 for the Macintosh operating system. Please locate and identify the help menu. Type the word "template" in the search window and identify an easy way to create business cards using the Word application.

The following five questions apply to the Macintosh version of Microsoft Word 2011:

6. Using Word 2011, please load one of the sample documents available in the student CD and find the menu option that gives you the ability to save a document. Please rename your document and select save as and a name for your new file. Please save the file as a .pdf file type. To show your instructor you have completed this exercise, simply press the Command + Shift + 3 keys to copy your screen, which will be saved as a PNG file on your desktop. You can paste this image into a Word document that will show your instructor you completed the exercise.

7. For the following exercise you will explore and identify the tabbed ribbon environment within the Microsoft Word 2011 environment. Please identify all of the groups available within the View ribbon, particularly change your document views and Show view in different configurations. Once you have explored these areas describe what happened when you changed the configurations and explain when you might use each of these views.

8. In this exercise you will become familiar with the different views available within Word 2011. Please open a new document and select the View from the menu tool bar. Please compare and contrast the different views available for your document.

9. In this exercise you will check for updates to assure your copy of Word 2011 is current. Please select the help menu and identify the option for an application update. Please explain the steps that you took and list the results.

10. For this exercise you will explore and identify Ribbon Preferences. Locate the gear on the top right hand side of your Word window and select Ribbon Preferences. Please explore the settings available and identify the results. Which option do you prefer in relation to your Ribbon settings?

KEYBOARDING DRILLS

1. Type as much of the following as you can in thirty seconds; try to complete the exercise before the timer runs out if possible. You can use the included software to track your time, speed, and errors:

```
sad sad dad fads safsa dasa ds
fasf fads sads dasa sa sa as as add add
dad dad add sad fad fads sa sa da fa fa
;;;jjj lllkkk jljljl k;k;k; ;j;j; ;k;k; ;l;l;
jkjk klkl jljl k;k; jk jl j; k; kj kl ;j ;k ;l
```

2. Type as much of the following as you can in thirty seconds; try to complete the exercise before the timer runs out if possible. You can use the included software to track your time, speed, and errors:

```
jkl; asdf ;lkj fdsa asdf jkl; ;lkj fdsa asdf jkl;
;als kdjf jf kd ls ;a a; sl dk fj jl fs k; da ;s al
jd fk ks sl ;a a; a;sldkfj jfkdls;a jas kas lass;
lad lass sall; saj; jas; kas sak; jasa dafa kasa lasa
ja;f;a ks la ;a jf kd ls ;a ;sldkfja fjdksla; jlsf k;da
```

3. Track your time and focus on your form to type the following with as few errors as possible. You can use the included software to track your time, speed, and errors:

```
jfj fjf kdk dkd lsl sls ;a; a;a aja ;f; ljl lfl aja afa
jlsffslj a;ls kdjf jfkd ls;a j jj kk f ff dd jfj kdk lsl
has has has sash sash dad add as has had fad ad lass lad lad
lass lass; gas gas gash has hash sh sh sha sha sha ash ash
```

```
kaja ajak lajak jakal dakal lal lad kad klad glad klad;; ;
ghgh jfjf kdkd lsls ;a;a jgfh dksl a;fj a;gh gha; ;ahg ;ajf
```

4. Track your time and focus on your form to type the following with as few
   errors as possible. You can use the included software to track your time,
   speed, and errors:

```
sasha has a glad dad; lass sad das add; lad kass sad glass;
has a sasha dad add; lass a glad fad dad; sad dad sad lad;
had has sad had; jag hag kag lag; saf; had sad lass dad add;
jhag ghaj jak kaj lak kaj lal gag hah faf daf dafa
sash has had add dad das ad add fad glad sad glass fad dad ad
add lass lad fash lash
gash glass dad das has sash had sash gash lash jas;
```

5. Type as much of the following as you can in one minute. You can use the
   included software to track your time, speed, and errors:

```
jfj fjf kdk dkd lsl sls ;a; a;a aja ;f; ljl lfl aja afa
jlsffslj a;ls kdjf jfkd ls;a j jj kk f ff dd jfj kdk lsl
has has has sash sash dad add as has had fad ad lass lad lad
lass lass; gas gas gash has hash sh sh sha sha sha ash ash
kaja ajak lajak jakal dakal lal lad kad klad glad klad;; ;
ghgh jfjf kdkd lsls ;a;a jgfh dksl a;fj a;gh gha; ;ahg ;ajf
jkl; asdf ;lkj fdsa asdf jkl; ;lkj fdsa asdf jkl;
;als kdjf jf kd ls ;a a; sl dk fj jl fs k; da ;s al
jd fk ks sl ;a a; a;sldkfj jfkdls;a jas kas lass;
lad lass sall; saj; jas; kas sak; jasa dafa kasa lasa
ja;f;a ks la ;a jf kd ls ;a ;sldkfja fjdksla; jlsf k;da
lak jak kas kaj lak laj as add dad fad lass lad ;; aa jj ff
```

Typography and Top Row Keys

This chapter presents an overview of typography and font choice in constructing documents. You will learn to modify the display of fonts in your document according to size, spacing, and other text modifications for emphasis. You will also explore common formatting shortcuts and how to manage and apply styles in a document. In addition, you will continue to learn to type using the keyboard by adding the top row keys to the lessons. Once you complete the chapter, you will be able to:

- Understand the characteristics of a font

- Modify the display of text in your document by font, size, and spacing

- Change the justification of your text

- Use formatting shortcuts and styles

- Type on the home row keys and top row keys without looking at the keyboard

TYPOGRAPHY

Typography is the process of arranging letters in a specific arrangement to make language readable from the outcome. This was once a specialized occupation, but with the advent of personal computing, typography is something in which everyone who types a document participates. The typeface, size, and spacing of the letters are all contributing factors to typography; these are all choices that are made in composing any document you write.

A typeface is a collection of symbols that form an alphabet; each typeface has its own unique style of display, such as the typefaces Times New Roman and Arial, two common typefaces installed on most machines. It is very likely that you will see the typeface confused with the term *font* (as in the case of Word) since they are almost synonymous. A font is actually a combination of a typeface and a size, so 10-point Arial would be a font. With the advent of digital typography, such as that used in Microsoft Word, the font selection is typically separate from the sizing, making the choice of typeface and font virtually indistinguishable. Now, you would simply select Arial as your font and set the size of the type separately.

> **TYPOGRAPHY** *is the process of arranging letters and punctuation to create a readable outcome in any document. Most typography is done for artistic reasons, but readability and clarity should be primary concerns in any typography effort.*
>
> *A* **TYPEFACE** *is a complete set of keyboard characters in one particular style (the style is the name of the typeface). Most typefaces support standard sizes as well as bold and italic variants.*
>
> *A* **FONT** *is a typeface combined with a set size, such as 10 pt Arial. In most modern computing systems, fonts support use with size modifications, so the terms typeface and font are becoming synonymous.*
>
> *A* **SERIF** *is a decoration on a letter of text. This is a non-essential element that graphically enhances a character without adding any new information; these are mostly used to enhance readability by distinguishing the letters from each other and for artistic effect.*
>
> **MONOSPACING** *in terms of typing is the characteristics of all letters typed occupying the same horizontal space regardless of the inherent letter size.*

There are two major classifications of fonts: serif and sans-serif. A *serif* is a text decoration added to letters of the font, such as you would find in Times New Roman. Sans-serif means a font without these text decorations present. You can see examples of both types of fonts in Figure 2.1.

Times New Roman – serif

Batang – serif

Jokerman – serif

Arial – sans-serif

Dotum– sans–serif

Verdana – sans-serif

◀ **FIGURE 2.1** Examples of serif and sans-serif fonts

The font is also determined by the size of the text. Most modern fonts accommodate multiple sizes with the same display. A pixel is the smallest unit of display on your computer monitor; the standard resolution for a computer is 72 pixels per inch. In the world of typesetting, there are 72 points per inch, meaning that a point is roughly equivalent to a pixel on the screen. Therefore, a 12 point (abbreviated *12 pt*) font would occupy roughly 12 pixels of space on a digital display. A less common measurement you may see is a pica; a pica is equivalent to 12 points. Pica rulers are most common in desktop publishing applications.

There are two types of spacing available in the design of fonts: monospacing and proportional spacing. *Monospacing* is when all of the characters in the font occupy the same horizontal width when typed; this was the common case for most fonts in mechanical typewriters because the motion of the typing carriage was fixed. Proportional spacing on the other hand allows letters to occupy only the space each one needs to display. The spacing between adjacent letters in a font is also established by default, but you can adjust this manually; this process of adjustment is called *kerning*. Adjusting the spacing between words is called *tracking*. The spacing between lines (which is typically part of paragraph formatting) is called *leading*.

Activity 5 – Typing Practice with Fonts

In this activity, you should create a new document called *Activity5* and save it in a folder for your Chapter 2 projects. Next, you will select ten different fonts installed on your computer from the dropdown list in the Font panel of the Home ribbon and type one sentence in each font. Identify each font as either serif or sans-serif and then identify whether it is a monospaced font or a proportional font.

The choice of font for a project varies greatly. When you are creating printed material, serif fonts are generally accepted as the standard. In digital display such as PowerPoint® slides, sans-serif is considered the better option. With the variety of fonts available from which to choose, it is a matter of creative choice. However, as a general rule of design, you should have no more than two fonts occupying the same document. More than this makes the arrangement look haphazard and poorly planned.

There are a variety of typefaces or fonts that come installed on any modern computer system, but it is possible to add new typefaces or fonts and install your own. The most common type of font that works on almost all systems is a TrueType® font; this is a font that contains additional display information so it accommodates multiple size settings beyond the standard set common to most fonts. These are also noted for nearly identical display across different operating systems. A TrueType font file will have the extension *.ttf*; when you find a font file like this (whether you download it from the Web or get it from someone else) on a Windows 7 machine you can double-click the file for a preview window like the one shown in

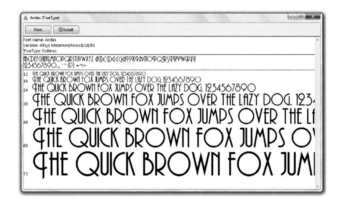

▲ **FIGURE 2.2** Windows 7 font preview

Figure 2.2. This shows the font display for all of the available characters in the available common sizes.

The button that says Install can be used to automatically add the font to the computer so it becomes available for use in any program that supports the use of fonts, like Word. You can also manually move the font file to the Font Directory for Windows located at *C:/Windows/ Fonts* on your machine. When you move the font to this folder, it will be ready to use. You may need to restart the program in which you want to use the font after it is installed.

OFFICE 2011 To install a typeface or font on a Mac OS X® Lion® machine, you should start by double clicking the file. This will open a preview window showing examples of the text in specific sizes. At the bottom of the window is a button that says *Install Font*. If you click this, the typeface will be added to your machine as a choice in any program that supports the use of fonts.

2.2 FORMATTING TEXT

Text entry can be done in simpler programs like Notepad®, but the real benefit of word processing software is the ability to format and change the appearance of text. The ability to design the appearance of your text, add additional media to your documents, and share your documents in multiple formats is where word processing stands out against simple text editors. Word has all of these features available to turn the plain text you added to your document into a professional-looking project. The Home ribbon contains most of the functionality you will need for formatting text. In particular, the Font panel and Paragraph panel will manage most of the display settings for your text.

2.2.1 The Font Panel

The Font panel is common to most of the Office programs and not just Word. This panel, located on the Home ribbon, contains the formatting commands for changing the typeface (or font), size, style, and color of your text as well as adding text effects and text decorations. The default font for a new document is Calibri (Body) on Windows and Cambria (Body) on the Macintosh. Enter some text in your document (you can do this by practicing the keys you have learned on the keyboard), select all of the text in your document by using the *Select All* keyboard shortcut (*Ctrl-A* on Windows and *Command-A* on the Macintosh), and select *Times New Roman* from the dropdown *Font* list.

> A keyboard shortcut is a productivity tool that allows you to perform a repeated task by pressing a modifier key (such as the Control or Command key) along with a standard keyboard key to initiate an action. There are several common keyboard shortcuts that will be covered throughout the book.

NOTE

The Font panel is shown in Figure 2.3. Remember that changes to the Font panel settings apply only to text that is selected when the changes are made. If no text is selected, the settings will be changed for text that is added at the current cursor location until another section of formatted text is encountered. By default, the format of new text that you enter will be consistent with the text immediately before it (to the left) in the document.

▼ **FIGURE 2.3** Word Font panel in the Home ribbon

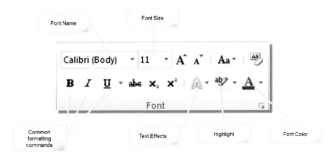

You can change the size of your text (called the font size) in a number of ways: by selecting a preset value from the drop-down Font Size field, typing a number manually in the Font Size field, or using the Grow Font and Shrink Font icons to increment or decrement the size of the font. Select all of your text and change the font size to *12*. Font sizes are set in point values; a point is roughly equivalent to a pixel on the screen.

<table>
<tr>
<td>NOTE</td>
<td>There are several keyboard shortcuts for the common formatting enhancements. To bold text, use *Ctrl-B* (or *Command-B* on the Mac); to italicize text, use *Ctrl-I* (or *Command-I*); and to underline text, use *Ctrl-U* (or *Command-U*). These act as a toggle, so repeating the command will turn off the effect.</td>
</tr>
</table>

You should not add text effects to a business or formal letter. Readability and clarity are essential for these document types. However, you should take note of the styles that you can apply to your text in the Font panel. Bold, Italic, and Underline are all means of adding emphasis to your text. Bold will make the text thicker and darker, Italic will slant the text, and Underline will add a line under the text. You should note that underlining text is considered outdated and the better way to add emphasis is with bold and italic text. Strikethrough retains the text but crosses it out; this is used to show completed tasks in a list of tasks or to retain editing marks in a legal or fixed document. The strikethrough used to be an indicator of an error correction in typewritten documents, but there is no need for this use in modern word processing software except in situations that require its use such as the preceding examples.

Activity 6 – Modifying Text

For this activity, you should create a new *Activity6* document and enter several lines of text. This is a good opportunity to challenge yourself by creating as many words as possible from the keys you have learned. When you have finished adding text, modify the font of several words and add bold and italic highlights. Save your work.

You can use the Text Highlight Coloroption to highlight your text; this is similar to using a highlighter marker on paper. The text will remain visible, but it will be emphasized so it can be quickly found later. The color of the highlighter can be changed, allowing you to color-code text. To get rid of an existing highlight, select the highlighted text, click the drop-down arrow under the *Text Highlight Color* icon, and choose *No Color*.

To change the color of the text itself, you use the Font Color icon. Clicking on the drop-down arrow opens a menu from which you can select any of the colors of the current theme setting and standard colors. You can also utilize custom colors or a gradient by selecting these options from the menu. Finally, using the Clear Formatting icon (which looks like an eraser) will remove any changes you have made to the formatting of the selected text and reset it to the default font settings for the document.

In Word 2010, the expansion icon in the lower-right corner of the Font panel opens the Font dialog box. The Font dialog box is shown in Figure 2.4.

◀ **FIGURE 2.4** Font dialog box in Word

This dialog box allows you to configure the font, size, effects, and enhancements for your text in a single interface. Of particular note is the ability to change the underline style of your text from the default thin solid line to a preset number of selections included a dotted line, broken line, wavy line, and double line. The Advanced tab also allows you to alter the default kerning for the font.

> **OFFICE 2011** In Word 2011, you open the Font dialog box by selecting the *Format* menu and choosing *Font*.

2.2.2 Text Effects

You can also use the Text Effects icon on the Font panel to modify your text even further. You should note that these effects are specific to Microsoft Office, so you may want to avoid their use if the document is destined for another program or format such as OpenDocument Format. Not all of the text effects are backwards compatible, either; earlier versions of Word will ignore the text effects it cannot display. You can see an example of the pop-up menu that activates when you click the Text Effects icon in Figure 2.5.

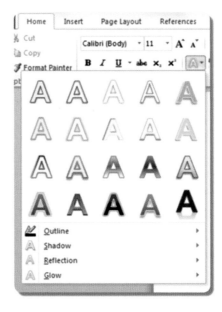

◀ **FIGURE 2.5** Text Effects menu in Word 2010

In addition to the preset selection of styles, you can also modify individual elements of the text in the areas of Outline, Shadow, Reflection, and Glow. You can see several examples of these in Figure 2.6. There are a variety of settings to adjust in each category.

Times New Roman 18pt

Arial 22pt

Broadway 22pt

Courier New 20pt

◀ **FIGURE 2.6** Text effect examples

- Outline sets the effects for the outer line around the characters; you can set the color, weight (width of the line), and the line style from this menu.

- For Shadow, you can select the shadow display for the characters. The options for shadowing are presented visually so you can choose the effect you want to portray. If you understand the settings, you can also select Shadow Options to define your own effect, but the standard shadowing effects like Outer shadow will likely suffice for most cases.

- Reflection will create a transparent, faded copy of the text as though it were placed on a reflective surface. This can be a nice effect to create emphasis but it should be used sparingly. Like Shadow, there is also an option to configure your own reflection setting with Reflection Options.

- Glow adds a colored glowing effect to your text. You can select how far you want the glow to extend from the characters and choose the color of the glow effect. You can also configure your own glow effect by selecting Glow Options.

Activity 7 – Text Effects

Create a new document called *Activity7*. Try to determine the fonts and effects used on the text in Figure 2.6 and recreate them in your own document.

2.2.3 The Paragraph Panel

The Paragraph panel is located beside the Font panel on the Home ribbon and is shown in Figure 2.7. This panel provides options for bullets and numbering, outline formatting, text indent (to increase or decrease paragraph indentation), text alignment, and spacing between lines (called leading). Text alignment will be a bigger concern when you start adding complex visual elements to your word processing documents. For now, though, you should use the Align Text Right icon to align

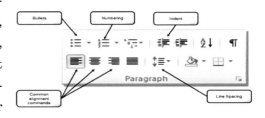

▼ FIGURE 2.7 Word Paragraph panel in the Home ribbon

your text to the right margin of your document (the margins should be set at the default letter size for now, meaning your text will be 1" from the right edge of the paper when printed). The default setting is for text to be aligned to the left. The other two options for aligning text are Center and Justify. Selecting Center will line up the midpoint of the line of text with the midpoint of the page so it takes up equal space on both sides. Selecting Justify will force the text to occupy the entire space between the left and right margins of the page, adding additional space between words to force the content to fit.

The Line Spacing icon allows you to select the number of lines of space given for each line of text (by default, this is set at 1.15 lines of space per line in the menu); this spacing is based on the font size of the text, so double spacing (two lines of space per line of text) for a 12 pt font will be equal to 24 points of space, but for an 18 pt font will be 36 points of space. There are also a few options for paragraph spacing. The Paragraph dialog box offers a more detailed selection of options for line spacing.

In Word 2010, click the expansion icon in the lower-right corner of the Paragraph panel to open the Paragraph dialog box. When you open the dialog box, it should default to the *Indents and Spacing* tab, which is where you change the settings for the line spacing. In the *Spacing* area, select *At Least* under the *Line Spacing* entry, and in the *At* field, enter *16 pt*.

This will add some additional space to each line and make your text more readable without wasting too much space. The preset *Single* and *Double* values are also commonly used for formatting, using either one or two times the font size of the line as the vertical space between lines of text.

OFFICE 2011 In Word 2011, you activate the Paragraph dialog box by selecting the *Format* menu and choosing *Paragraph*.

2.2.4 Using and Managing Styles

Another element of the Home ribbon is the Styles panel. A *style* is a predefined set of formatting enhancements and adjustments. There is a default set of styles from which to choose, including six different heading styles (Heading 1 through Heading 6) that are treated differently from ordinary text in assisting you with your document outline (as shown in the Navigation pane).

*A **STYLE** is a collection of formatting effects and enhancements used to modify text in a consistent manner. Applying a style to a selection of text will add all of the defined formatting effects and enhancements of that style without the need to individually recreate them.*

Select your first line of text and apply the style *Heading 1* from the Styles Panel of the Home ribbon. You should notice that there are six heading styles already defined for you to use; these each have a representation in the outline of your document with Heading 1 being the highest level and Heading 6 being the lowest above plain text. You can add additional heading levels to create a more complex outline of your document.

NOTE The default style used in any Microsoft Word document is *Normal*. This is a predefined style that defaults to whatever setting is established at installation. You can edit the Normal style just as you can with any other style and all of the text that has Normal as a style will update to reflect the changes. The functionality of updating all of the text formatted with a style at once is one of the benefits of using styles in a document.

In Microsoft Word 2010, you can select the Change Styles icon and select a predefined document style from the list that you would like to use. To see the effect of this, you should select the *Distinctive* choice under the *Style Set* menu within the *Change Styles* icon. You can also click the expansion icon of the Styles Panel to open the Styles Pane.

OFFICE 2011 In Microsoft Word 2011, the equivalent to change the style settings for the document is the *Change Quick Styles settings* icon from which you can also choose the *Distinctive* option. You can open the Styles panel in Word 2011 by selecting the *Manage styles* icon.

You can select the text you want to modify and click any of the styles in the menu to apply it to your selected text. You can use the dropdown arrow for the style and select *Modify* to adjust individual elements of the style just as you would using the Font Dialog Box from the previous section. You can create a new style using the *New Style* icon. You can see an example of the Styles pane in Figure 2.8.

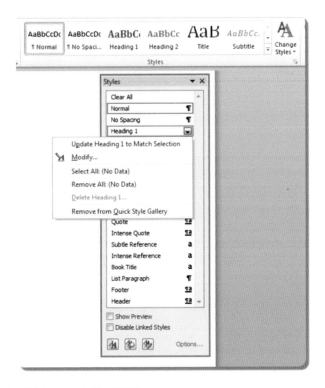

◀ **FIGURE 2.8** Styles panel and Styles pane in Word 2010

To duplicate styles from another document in Microsoft Word 2010, you can click on the *Manage Styles* icon of the Styles pane. This will open the Manage Styles Dialog Box; click on the *Import/Export* button at the bottom of this dialog.

> **OFFICE 2011** To access the Manage Styles Dialog Box in Microsoft Word 2011, select the *Format* menu and choose *Style*. When the dialog box opens, click the *Organize* button.

You will now see style listings for two files. The file you are developing is on the left and by default the global template *Normal.dotm* is on the right. You can close the Normal.dotm file (using the *Close File* button) and select the file whose styles you want to duplicate using the *Open File* button. Once you have the document open, you can use the mouse to select the styles you want to add to your current document and then use the *Copy* button (which will have a directional arrow showing you where the copies will be placed) to move them over to the current file. This is mostly used when you are composing a joined series of documents where you want the formatting to be uniform across multiple separate documents.

2.2.5 Format Painter

It is important to give any document you create a consistent look and feel. You have already learned about managing styles, but another way to provide consistency is to use format painting. This process takes the formatting modifications from the currently selected text and applies them to any text that is highlighted after you click the Format Painter icon. This icon, which looks like a paintbrush, is located in the Home ribbon in Word 2010.

> **OFFICE 2011** The Format Painter in Word 2011 is located by default in the Quick Access toolbar across the top of the interface.

2.2.6 Bullets and Numbering

Bulleted and numbered lists are a great way to quickly organize data. Numbered lists imply an order, such as you would find in a standard document outline for a research paper. Bulleted lists have no inherent order, so this is useful when the items either all have equal importance or the sequencing is irrelevant. Make sure you have multiple lines of text in your document beneath the header; you can continue your typing practice if you need to add more text.

Select four lines of text and then click the *Bullets* icon in the *Paragraph panel* of the *Home* ribbon. This will automatically convert your items to an unordered list of elements. You can change the style of the bullet point by selecting from among the available options in the drop-down arrow menu for the Bullets icon, shown in Figure 2.9. You can also define a custom bullet style by selecting *Define New Bullet*. This will open a dialog box allowing you to select a symbol, image, or letter from a particular font (like *Wingdings* or *Webdings*) for your bullet point.

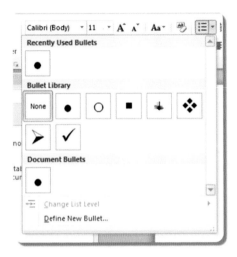

There are similar options available from the Numbering icon's drop-down arrow menu. You can see an example of this in Figure 2.10. The significant difference between numbering and bullets is the inclusion of ordering in a numbered list.

The numbering options available include letters, numerals, and Roman numerals (a system that uses specific letters to represent numeric values such as *I* for one and *V* for five); you can choose from the predefined set or you can choose *Define New Number Format* to create custom styles.

Activity 8 – Numbered Lists

Create a new document called *Activity8* and enter at least eight lines of text. Group the first four lines of text into a numbered list and group the next four lines into an alphabetized list. You will create both of these by selecting the Numbering icon and choosing an option from the menu.

2.2.7   The System Clipboard

The system clipboard is temporary storage for anything you copy from a document or folder which allows you to use it again elsewhere. When you copy an object or a grouping of text to the clipboard, the formatting and content are all retained. The copied material can then be pasted in another location in any of the productivity software programs. For instance, you can copy formatted text from Word and paste it into PowerPoint and it will retain any formatting that was applied to it. Similarly, you can copy a chart from Excel® and paste it into a Word document. This interoperability and the ease of use of the clipboard make it a valuable tool for productivity.

The three commands that apply to the clipboard are:

- *Copy*—The Copy command is used to make a duplicate of selected text or objects in a document. Copy will leave the original source of the material intact in the document and make a duplicate on the clipboard. The Copy icon looks like two sheets of paper overlapping each other. The shortcut for the Copy command is *Ctrl-C* on a Windows machine and *Command-C* on a Macintosh machine.

- *Cut*—The Cut command functions like Copy except it removes the original source material from the document (whether it is text or an object) and places it on the clipboard. The Cut icon is traditionally a pair of scissors; the shortcut for the Cut command is *Ctrl-X* on a Windows machine and *Command-X* on a Macintosh machine.

- *Paste*—The Paste command is used to place the contents of the clipboard at the active cursor location within a selected document. Whether the contents are then removed from the clipboard depends on the specific program; in Word, they are not removed and can be pasted multiple times. The Paste icon looks like either a clipboard or a bottle of rubber cement (which was traditionally used to place clippings of documents in other documents). The shortcut for Paste is *Ctrl-V* on Windows and *Command-V* on Macintosh.

If you copy formatted text from one document and paste it into a document location that does not allow formatting, such as Notepad on a Windows machine, the text will be pasted and the formatting will be removed. The spacing of the letters (such as blank space characters created using the spacebar or tab indents from the Tab key) will be retained to match the way the keys and spacing are defined in the target document. This can actually be helpful for removing unwanted formatting from Web documents or PDF files.

In Word, you are given a choice of options when you paste something from the clipboard. This appears as a clipboard icon, which opens to a menu when you place an object from the clipboard, as shown in Figure 2.11. Typically, these options are whether you want to keep the formatting from the source, whether

▼ **FIGURE 2.11** Paste Options menu in Word

you want to match the formatting to that of the document where you are placing the text (called *Merge Formatting* in Word 2010), or whether you want to retain the text without the formatting. These options vary from program to program. Try this functionality yourself by typing a simple line of text in your open document, selecting it, cutting it from the document, and pasting it back into the document. If you open the clipboard icon, you will see the available paste options.

2.3 KEYBOARDING II

By now, you should have a lot of practice with the use of the home row keys. In this set of lessons, you will learn how to type using the top row keys. These are the line of keys directly above the home row; you can see the location of the top row keys in Figure 2.12. Each of your fingers will extend above and to the left to reach the assigned top row key with your index finger and pinky finger being assigned additional keys to cover the entire row.

▼ **FIGURE 2.12** Primary top row keys

2.3.1 Top Row Keys

The top row keys include the Q key through the P key. There are three additional punctuation keys in this row on the right hand side that you will learn later. This row also includes the tab key, which is used to align spacing in a document or indent text; this key is reached with the left pinky finger. Whenever you are using the top row keys, you should keep your

▲ **FIGURE 2.13** Finger motion for primary top row keys

fingers in place on the home row keys and only extend the assigned finger to reach out to the top row key to strike it. This should be a concise movement and it may take practice to be able to do it with all of your fingers without moving the rest of your hand. You can see an illustration of the necessary finger movements to reach the top row keys in Figure 2.13.

2.3.2 The Tab Key

The tab key was originally used to format data in a tabular form (hence the name, which is an abbreviation of "tabulate") without having to repeatedly use the spacebar. This would advance the position on the page to the next horizontal tab stop. In mechanical typewriters, a tab stop was a predetermined location where a mechanical carriage would halt; tab stops in software are predefined positions that can be manually altered. In Word, the tab key is used to

▲ **FIGURE 2.14** Tab stops indicated beneath the ruler in Word

indent the first sentence in a paragraph and it can be used to increase the overall indentation of a paragraph of text. If you view the rulers in Word (which you can activate by selecting the checkbox for Ruler on the View ribbon), you can see the tab stops indicated as dots beneath the rule line, as shown in Figure 2.14.

The tab key on the keyboard is reached by moving the left pinky to the far left end of the top row keys. This is a useful key to learn as it will help you properly align text in a document and move from element to element in such items as HTML forms on the Web, spreadsheets, and databases. In general, a tab is roughly equivalent to 5 presses of the spacebar.

NOTE In applications, the tab is counted as a single character where pressing the spacebar five times would create five characters in the document despite the nearly equivalent distance of white space.

Keyboarding Lessons 16–30

By the time you have completed the following lessons, you will have practiced all of the top row keys highlighted in dark blue in Figure 2.15. You should concentrate in these lessons on learning the hand motion necessary to reach the keys without looking at them and keeping your hands in place while one finger reaches to the desired key to strike it. The more you have practice with this, the better your form will become and the more your speed will increase.

▼ **FIGURE 2.15** Keyboarding II keys and hand motion mapping

The software included with the text and available online at *www.keyboardingandbeyond.com* will time the lessons and alert you to any mistakes made while entering the text for these exercises. Because this is practice, you should feel free to redo these lessons and activities as much as you need to improve your performance and form.

Lesson 2.1 The U Key

In this lesson, you will use your right index finger to press the U key as well as using the keys you have already learned. You should focus on your form and keep your hands positioned over the home row keys while you move only the necessary finger to strike the keys you wish to type. The software will count up the amount of time it takes for you to complete the task, so you can take as long as you need and retry the exercise to improve your time.

Type the following:

```
uuuu jjjj uuuu uujj ujuj juju huju hjuh
uuuu jjjj uuuu uujj ujuj juju huju hjuh
hug ugh jus huff dull sulk gulf fluff
ju ku lu ;u au su du fu gu hu uj uk ul
uk ul lll asdfukl; ku lu ;u ;j juh huj
hug ugh jus huff dull sulk gulf fluff
```

Lesson 2.2 The I Key

In this lesson, you will use your right middle finger to press the I key as well as using the keys you have already learned. You should focus on your form and keep your hands positioned over the home row keys while you move only the necessary finger to strike the keys you wish to type. The software will count up the amount of time it takes for you to complete the task, so you can take as long as you need and retry the exercise to improve your time.

Type the following:

```
iiii kkkk iiii iikk ikik kiki kiik ikki
iiii kkkk iiii iikk ikik kiki kiik ikki
if gill dill fill kid sigh sail fail high
ik il ij i; ai si di fi il ik ij ih ;i
jui kui lui l;i ais sid dif fig hij lik
if gill dill fill kid sigh sail fail high
```

Lesson 2.3 The O Key

In this lesson, you will use your right ring finger to press the O key as well as using the keys you have already learned. You should focus on your form and keep your hands positioned over the home row keys while you move only the necessary finger to strike the keys you wish to type. The software will count up the amount of time it takes for you to complete the task, so you can take as long as you need and retry the exercise to improve your time.

Type the following:

```
oooo llll oooo ooll olol lolo lool ollo
oooo llll oooo ooll olol lolo lool ollo
hook look good hood hoof foul hola soul
oj ok ol o; oa so do fo go ho lo; ;ol
lok kol lol aos sod fog hoj jok kol
hook look good hood hoof foul hola soul
```

Lesson 2.4 The P Key

In this lesson, you will use your right pinky finger to press the P key as well as using the keys you have already learned. You should focus on your form and keep your hands positioned over the home row keys while you move only the necessary finger to strike the keys you wish to type. The software will count up the amount of time it takes for you to complete the task, so you can take as long as you need and retry the exercise to improve your time.

Type the following:

```
pppp ;;;; pppp pp;; p;p; ;p;p ;pp; p;;p
pppp ;;;; pppp pp;; p;p; ;p;p ;pp; p;;p
pod; gap; pass; soup; plaid; plough;
;p p; pl pk pj ph pa ps pd pf pg po pi pu
aps spd dpf fpg hph jpj kpk lpl
pod; gap; pass; soup; plaid; plough;
```

Lesson 2.5 The Y Key

In this lesson, you will use your right index finger to press the Y key as well as using the keys you have already learned. You should focus on your form and keep your hands positioned over the home row keys while you move only the necessary finger to strike the keys you wish to type. The software will count up the amount of time it takes for you to complete the task, so you can take as long as you need and retry the exercise to improve your time.

Type the following:

```
yyyy jjjj yyyy yyjj yjyj jyjy hyjy hjyh
yyyy jjjj yyyy yyjj yjyj jyjy hyjy hjyh
guy yay yak you ugly sassy lassy flashy
yj yk yl y; yay s yd yf yg yj yu yh
yhju ujhy yjhu uhyj ays syd dyf gyh hyj jyk kyl
guy yay yak you ugly sassy lassy flashy
```

Lesson 2.6 Right Hand Practice

For this lesson, you will use the home keys and top row keys for your right hand along with the spacebar and enter keys to enter the text. You should try to focus on tapping the keys lightly so that you strike them just hard enough to type the character and then release pressure on the key. The software will count up the amount of time it takes for you to complete the task, so you can take as long as you need and retry the exercise to improve your time. You should focus on your form and typing cadence (or rhythm) in completing this exercise.

Type the following:

```
ujuj yhyh ikik olol p;p; yuiop yuiop
ypuoi iopuy ulojp hpoiu yolkp yoiul;
lip look pull pill yolk loop look kooky
jhj jyj juj jyuhj killjoy pool loop hull lull
pill joy poll; lollipop; pool yol loy uio oiuy oih oig
pill joy poll; lollipop; pool yol loy uio oiuy oih oig
lip look pull pill yolk loop look kooky
```

Lesson 2.7 The R Key

In this lesson, you will use your left index finger to press the R key as well as using the keys you have already learned. You should focus on your form and keep your hands positioned over the home row keys while you move only the necessary finger to strike the keys you wish to type. The software will count up the amount of time it takes for you to complete the task, so you can take as long as you need and retry the exercise to improve your time.

Type the following:

```
rrrr ffff rrrr rrff rfrf frfr grfr gfrg
rrrr ffff rrrr rrff rfrf frfr grfr gfrg
or rad rill ruff ross hard rally rough
rf rg rd rs ra ar jr kr lr yr hr
```

```
raf rsf rdr rdf fdr ras sar dar raf
or rad rill ruff ross hard rally rough
```

Lesson 2.8 The E Key

In this lesson, you will use your left middle finger to press the E key as well as using the keys you have already learned. You should focus on efficient finger motion and keeping your hands over the home row keys. The software will count up the amount of time it takes for you to complete the task, so you can take as long as you need and retry the exercise to improve your time.

Type the following:

```
eeee dddd eeee eedd eded dede deed edde
eeee dddd eeee eedd eded dede deed edde
see are free seed deed grease lease please
ea es ed ef er eg ej ek el eh ey
aes aed sed ser sef stf seg stg srg efr
see are free seed deed grease lease please
```

Lesson 2.9 The W Key

In this lesson, you will use your left ring finger to press the W key as well as using the keys you have already learned. You should focus on keeping your hand over the home row keys and moving only the necessary finger to strike the keys you wish to type. The software will count up the amount of time it takes for you to complete the task, so you can take as long as you need and retry the exercise to improve your time.

Type the following:

```
wwww ssss wwww wwss wsws swsw swws wssw
wwww ssss wwww wwss wsws swsw swws wssw
awe well wish wash swell wake walk jowl jewel
aw sw dw fw jw kw lw ew rw yw uw iw ow pw
sew wer rew weg wet jef kel lep pel yeh heg
awe well wish wash swell wake walk jowl jewel
```

Lesson 2.10 The Q Key

In this lesson, you will use your left pinky finger to press the Q key as well as using the keys you have learned so far. The software will count up the amount of time it takes for you to complete the task, so you can take as long as you need and retry the exercise to improve your time. You should focus on the form of your finger moving to the upper row while keeping your hand and the remaining fingers positioned over the home row keys.

Type the following:

```
qqqq aaaa qqqq qqaa qaqa aqaq aqqa qaaq
qqqq aaaa qqqq qqaa qaqa aqaq aqqa qaaq
aqua quad quell liquid quail squid opaque
aq sq dq fq gq hq jq kq lq qw qe qr qy
aqs aqd aqf aqg aqh aqj aqk aql sql qws qwe qwd qrf qef
aqua quad quell liquid quail squid opaque
```

Lesson 2.11 The T Key

In this lesson, you will use your left index finger to press the T key in addition to the keys you have already learned. The software will count up the amount of time it takes for you to complete the task, so you can take as long as you need and retry the exercise to improve your time. You should focus on the precision of the finger motion and keeping your hand in place over the home row while only your finger moves.

Type the following:

```
tttt ffff tttt ttff tftf ftft gtft gftg
tttt ffff tttt ttff tftf ftft gtft gftg
tell teeth total quest plate stress lateral
ta ts td tf tg th tj tk tl tq tw te tr
tas tsd tdf tfg thj tkl tq tw te trt tyt tut tot tpt
tell teeth total quest plate stress lateral
```

Lesson 2.12 Left Hand Practice

In this lesson, you will practice using each of the home row keys and top row keys assigned to your left hand. The only other keys you should use are the enter key and spacebar. The software will count up the amount of time it takes for you to complete the task, so you can take as long as you need and retry the exercise to improve your time.

Type the following:

```
rfrf tftf eded wsws qaqa trewq trewq
tqrwe ewqrt rswfq gqwer twsdq twers
wet feet dread sweat treat start street
aws sed drf ftg gaq fsw fde rtf frgtf grft tfrg fgrt
qwerty asdfg ta qg wf rs de ya qh wg st ef dr
wet feet dread sweat treat start street
```

Lesson 2.13 Both Hand Practice

In this lesson, you will use all of the home row keys and the top row keys that you have learned. The software will count up the amount of time it takes for you to complete the task, so you can take as long as you need and retry the exercise to improve your time. You should focus on your form and minimizing the errors in your typing.

Type the following:

```
qp wo ei rut y qlp paq qao wsi edi rfu
qq pp w woo ee ii rr uu tt yy yu tr tg yh
squirt dart grasp poise loop lip wasp pass quilt quip post grasp
poise swear tear glass lass dad add plaster respire require
attire try tire wire prairie tripe tart trade dirt squirt pert
terse jersey the that hat tap part harp group pour wet two pout
squirt dart grasp poise loop lip wasp pass quilt quip post grasp
poise swear tear glass lass dad add plaster respire require
```

Lesson 2.14 Practice and Review

In this lesson, you will practice typing all of the keys you have learned so far. The timer for this exercise counts up, so while your speed should still be a consideration, you should focus on the form of your finger reaching between the keys and moving across the rows. You should repeat this exercise as necessary until you are able to complete it without errors.

Type the following:

```
taq plo plt ply plu qwk qwe qej tyr gyt fru his sai oas osl
aqo pos wep per ioe urt yue pqo ioq wio peo per pas dfe ghr jku
aqua west trust tressle pass trespass sip pill glass list tryst
poise post port troll lost first third fourth fifth eighth
taq plo plt ply plu qwk qwe qej tyr gyt fru his sai oas osl
aqo pos wep per ioe urt yue pqo ioq wio peo per pas dfe ghr jku
```

Lesson 2.15 Typing Speed Test

In this lesson, you will practice typing all of the keys you have learned so far including the home row keys and the top row keys. The timer for this exercise counts down, so you should try to gain enough proficiency and speed to complete the exercise in its entirety before the timer runs out. Because you are still learning, you should repeat this exercise as necessary until you are able to complete it with time left on the timer!

Type the following:

```
op wo ei ri tut y yt ur ie ow pq
aqw lop loi polite grip pri post ost os the he she it is as
qp wo ei rut y al sk dj fh gy ht she he it is as is was will
the there ere ear ea oi ois oise serif sa as was qw pru pri pra
per se serif stre strut stra sti ir ai ei ur or re ra ri ru
shore rest est ist ust ast past last trust rest lest pest
were retire ire yr pyre pour pout post quarry quest quality
```

CHAPTER SUMMARY

This chapter introduced you to the main concepts of typography and the settings you can use in Microsoft Word to adjust the display of text in your document. This includes the choice of typeface (or font) and font size. Additional text decorations such as bold, italics, and underline and even color choice are also available for use in Word to modify the text display. Advanced features such as text effects for shadows, outlines, glow, and reflection are also useful in creating text that stands out in a document. By the time you have completed the keyboarding lessons for this chapter, you should be proficient in using both the home row and top row keys. When you are using the software application for timing your exercises, you should try to get to at least 25 words per minute at this stage of your typing development.

CHAPTER KNOWLEDGE CHECK

1 _____is the process of arranging letters in a specific arrangement to make language readable from the outcome.

- ○ **A.** Typing
- ○ **B.** Typography
- ○ **C.** Autocorrect
- ○ **D.** None of the above

2 A *typeface* is a complete set of keyboard characters in one particular style (the style is the name of the typeface).

- ○ **A.** True
- ○ **B.** False

3 This is a non-essential element that graphically enhances a character without adding any new information:

- ○ **A.** Serif
- ○ **B.** Font
- ○ **C.** Color
- ○ **D.** All of the above

4

Text entry can be done in simpler programs like Notepad, but the real benefit of word processing software is the ability to format and change the appearance of text.

- ○ **A. True**
- ○ **B. False**

5

To install a typeface or font on a Mac OS X Lion machine, you should start by double clicking the _____.

- ○ **A. Window border**
- ○ **B. Toolbar**
- ○ **C. File**
- ○ **D. All of the above**

6

The Font panel is common to most of the _____ and not just Word.

- ○ **A. Office programs**
- ○ **B. Software programs**
- ○ **C. Client applications**
- ○ **D. None of the above**

7

In Word 2011, you open the Font dialog box by selecting the _____ menu and choosing _____.

- ○ **A. Save, Font**
- ○ **B. Format, Print**
- ○ **C. Format, Font**
- ○ **D. None of the above**

8

To access the Manage Styles Dialog Box in Microsoft Word 2011, select the _____ and choose _____.

- ○ **A. Format menu, Style**
- ○ **B. Toolbar menu, Format menu**
- ○ **C. Print menu, Save as**
- ○ **D. None of the above**

9

The Format Painter in Word 2011 is located by default in the _____ across the top of the interface.

- ○ **A. Word toolbar**
- ○ **B. Quick Access toolbar**
- ○ **C. Print menu**
- ○ **D. None of the above**

10 To bold text in Word, use *Control* (or *Command*) + _; to italicize text, use *Control* (or *Command*) + _; and to underline text, use *Control* (or *Command*) + _.

- ○ **A.** B, T, U
- ○ **B.** A, I, U
- ○ **C.** B, I, U
- ○ **D.** None of the above

CHAPTER EXERCISES

The following five questions apply to the Windows version of Microsoft Word 2010:

1. For this first exercise using Word 2010, create a new document and save it as *lastname_chp2exercises.docx* in your designated location. Use this document as your answer sheet for all of the exercises. From the Home ribbon tab, explore the font group and write a short paragraph using the Verdana font type and using the 12 pt font size. Give the paragraph an interesting title and change the font type of the title to Arial and apply bold and italic formatting.

2. Using Figure 2.16 match the letters to the correct parts of the image.

___Font Type

___Font Size

___Bold

___Italic

___Underline

___Text Effects

___Text Highlight Color

___Font Color

___Font Dialogue Box

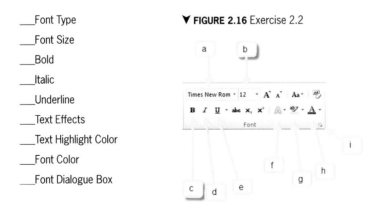

▼ **FIGURE 2.16** Exercise 2.2

3. Type the following words in a new paragraph: "This is my first experience using the paragraph panel in Microsoft Word 2010." Now highlight the sentence holding down the left button on your mouse and dragging to the end of the sentence. Proceed to the paragraph panel and center the sentence on your page using the center option. Once you have completed this task, press enter and select either a bullet format or number format of your choice from the paragraph panel and write a list of six features you have learned about in this lesson.

4. Using Figure 2.17 match the letters to the correct parts of the image.

___Numbering

___Bullets

___Indent

___Alignment

___Line and Paragraph Spacing

___Bottom Border

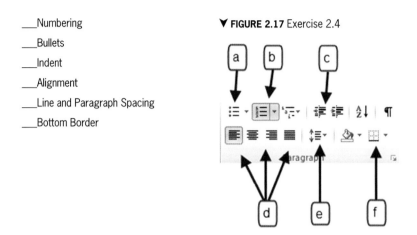

▼ **FIGURE 2.17** Exercise 2.4

5. In this exercise, you will practice managing style in your document. Copy and paste the paragraph you wrote for the first exercise along with the list. Now using the Styles group from the Home tab change the style on just the paragraph and list. Remember to save all of the work you have done to this point.

The following five questions apply to the Macintosh version of Microsoft Word 2011:

6. For this exercise using Word 2011, create a new document and save it as *lastname_chp2exercises.docx* in your designated location. Use this document as your answer sheet for all of the exercises. From the Home ribbon tab, explore the font group and write a short paragraph using the Verdana font type and using the 12 pt font size. Give the paragraph an interesting title and change the title font type to Arial and apply bold and italic formatting to the title.

7. Using Figure 2.18 match the letters to the correct parts of the image.

___Font Type

___Font Size

___Formatting Commands

___Text Effects

___Text Highlight Color

___Font Color

___Font Dialogue Box

▼ **FIGURE 2.18** Exercise 2.7

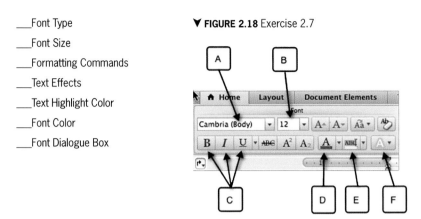

8. In Word 2011, type the following sentence: "This is my first experience using the paragraph panel in Microsoft Word 2010." Now highlight the sentence holding down the left button on your mouse and dragging to the end of the sentence. Proceed to the paragraph panel and center the sentence on your page using the center option. Once you have completed this task, press enter and select either a bullet format or number format of your choice from the paragraph panel and write a list of six features you have learned about in this lesson.

9. In this exercise, you will practice managing style in your document. Copy and paste the paragraph you wrote for the first exercise along with the list. Now using the Styles group from the Home tab change the style on just the paragraph and list. Remember to save all of the work you have done to this point.

10. Using Figure 2.19 match the letters to the correct parts of the image.

___Numbering

___Bullets

___Indent

___Alignment

___Line and Paragraph Spacing

___Bottom Border

▼ **FIGURE 2.19** Exercise 2.10

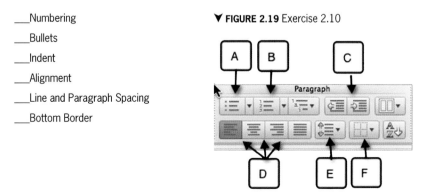

CHAPTER REVIEW QUESTIONS

1. Define and contrast a typeface and a font.

2. Using the skills that you have learned in this chapter, write a short business memo notifying employees of a new medical benefit that will be implemented shortly, providing a date and time for an informational meeting to discuss the new plan. Use the Font panel and Paragraph panel to align the text and add appropriate formatting.

3. Please discuss and list the important elements that you should use when writing a formal business letter. Specifically, from your readings, what were the two most important elements to include?

4. Please explain the difference between text effects and styles. How can these be used to create a professional document?

5. How do you add a new style to Microsoft Word? Please explain the steps used to perform the action.

6. How do you access the system clipboard and how does it work? Please explain the steps used for either the Word 2010 or 2011 version depending on which one you are using.

7. Please explain how the tab key works and how tab stops relate to its use.

8. What are the common shortcut keys on the Windows or Macintosh computer, specifically used to add formatting to text?

9. Define and explain the term typography in your own words. How is typography used to change the appearance of a document? (Please be sure to use the terminology used throughout the chapter.)

10. What is a keyboard shortcut and where are these commonly used? Please explain if a secondary process exists to perform the same action without the keyboard shortcut.

KEYBOARDING DRILLS

1. Type as much of the following as you can in thirty seconds; try to complete the exercise before the timer runs out if possible. You can use the included software to track your time, speed, and errors:

```
tqrwe ewqrt rswfq gqwer twsdq twers
wet feet dread sweat treat start street
aws sed drf ftg gaq fsw fde rtf frgtf grft tfrg fgrt
qwerty asdfg ta qg wf rs de ya qh wg st ef dr
lip look pull pill yolk loop look kooky
jhj jyj juj jyuhj killjoy pool loop hull lull
pill joy poll; lollipop; pool yol loy uio oiuy oih oig
pill joy poll; lollipop; pool yol loy uio oiuy oih oig
lip look pull pill yolk loop look kooky
```

2. Type as much of the following as you can in thirty seconds; try to complete the exercise before the timer runs out if possible. You can use the included software to track your time, speed, and errors:

```
squirt dart grasp poise loop lip wasp pass quilt quip post
grasp poise swear glass lass dad add plaster respire require
attire try tire wire prairie tripe tart trade dirt squirt pert
terse jersey the hat tap part harp group pour wet two pout
yhju ujhy yjhu tfrg grtf gfrt rthg lop pol aqws defr kilo
yhju ujhy yjhu tfrg grtf gfrt rthg lop pol aqws defr kilo
```

3. Track your time and focus on your form to type the following with as few errors as possible. You can use the included software to track your time, speed, and errors:

```
aqo pos wep per ioe urt yue pqo ioq wio peo per pas dfe ghr
aqua west trust tressle pass trespass sip pill glass list
poise post port troll lost first third fourth fifth eighth
taq plo plt ply plu qwk qwe qej tyr gyt fru his sai oas osl
growl lower rest squirt list post polyp swallow sparrow
growl lower rest squirt list post polyp swallow sparrow
```

4. Track your time and focus on your form to type the following with as few errors as possible. You can use the included software to track your time, speed, and errors:

```
op wo ei ri tut y yt ur ie ow pq
aqw lop loi polite grip pri post ost os the he she it is as
qp wo ei rut y al sk dj fh gy ht she he it is as is was will
the there ere ear ea oi ois oise serif sa as was qw pru pri
per se serif stre strut stra sti ir ai ei ur or re ra ri ru
shore rest est ist ust ast past last trust rest lest pest
were retire ire yr pyre pour pout post quarry quest quality
or rad rill ruff ross hard rally rough
aqua quad quell liquid quail squid opaque
```

5. Type as much of the following as you can in one minute. You can use the included software to track your time, speed, and errors:

```
hug ugh jus huff dull sulk gulf fluff
if gill dill fill kid sigh sail fail high
hook look good hood hoof foul hola soul
pod; gap; pass; soup; plaid; plough;
guy yay yak you ugly sassy lassy flashy
or rad rill ruff ross hard rally rough
see are free seed deed grease lease please
awe well wish wash swell wake walk jowl jewel
tell teeth total quest plate stress literal
```

Document Creation and Bottom Row Keys

This chapter focuses on the creation of new documents as either blank documents or through the use of templates. In this chapter, you will learn how to format the document margins and columns and how to add elements like headers and footers. You will also learn to add elements like a cover page and table of contents to your document. You will learn to add the bottom row keys to your typing skills; this means you will have the ability to type the entire alphabet when you have completed the practice lessons. Once you complete the chapter, you will be able to:

- Create a new document from a template

- Format the layout of the document and add document elements

- Construct a formal business letter with all of the necessary components

- Utilize shortcuts for managing and creating files

- Utilize the bottom row keys with proper typing form

3.1 CREATING DOCUMENTS IN WORD

You already have practice creating new documents in Word, but there are a wide variety of options available with the document creation process. The standard method for creating a blank document is using the *File* menu, selecting *New*, and then choosing *Blank Document*. However, as you can see in Figure 3.1, there are a large variety of templates that you can use to construct specific documents such as resumes, cover letters, and other common business documents.

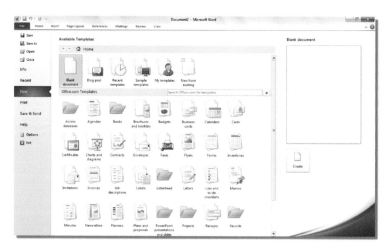

◀ **FIGURE 3.1** Word options for creating a new document

3.1.1 Using Document Templates

A *template* is a preformatted placeholder document for your content; you can build your own instance of the document using the predefined areas where you can add objects and text, knowing what it will look like when you are finished. It is possible to modify templates just like any other document (you can even create custom templates by saving your document as a Word Template), but templates save you work in formatting the document yourself or formatting the same document repeatedly. Document templates are a great way to get started with formatting if you are unsure of what your document should look like and you are creating a common type of document.

In Word 2010, you can create a new document from a template by selecting the *File* menu and choosing *New*. Beneath the blank document types that you can select are the available template selections. As an example, you can select *Resumes and CVs* and *Basic resumes* and then choose one of the options from the window shown in Figure 3.2.

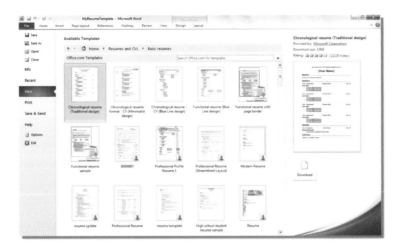

◀ **FIGURE 3.2** Template selection in Word 2010

In Word 2011, you can create a new document from a template either by selecting the *File* menu and choosing *New from Template* or by clicking the *New from Template* icon in the Quick Access toolbar. This will open the Word Document Gallery shown in Figure 3.3; this is the same gallery that appears when you first open Word 2011 without another document open. From this interface, select *Resumes* and choose one of the templates. You can select whichever one you want, but the Blocks Resume is a versatile option.

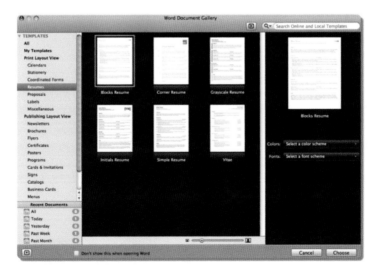

◀ **FIGURE 3.3** Template selection in Word 2011

Your new document based on the template will open in a new window of Word. You will save this document just like any other blank document you have created. Note that all of the stylistic elements and categories of information that are necessary for a resume are included in the template; this is true of all of the available templates as they tend to be created to include as many elements as possible necessary for the document type. It is important to remember, though, that not all of these elements may apply to every document you are creating.

Activity 9 – Template Usage

Create a new document from a template of your choice; you should select a different category from what you know and try something new. Save this document first as a regular document called *Activity9*. Now alter the document however you want and save it as a Word Template file. What is the document extension for this file and what happens when you attempt to open it by double clicking on the file?

3.1.2 Setting a Page Layout

At this point you should create a new blank document and add text using the home row keys and top row keys; you are then going to format the page layout. You have the flexibility in word processing documents to choose the size of your pages. While most home and office printers only accommodate 8 ½" by 11" paper size, you can customize the document to whatever dimensions you need up to 22" by 22". There are predefined sizes you can use for envelopes and legal documents as well. You can select your page size in Word 2010 by activating the Page Layout ribbon and choosing the *Size* icon; this opens a menu for you to select an existing size or customize your own.

> OFFICE 2011 In Word 2011, the *Size* icon is located in the Layout ribbon. The function performed is the same as it is in the Word 2010 counterpart.

You can change other properties of your document as well. One such change is the orientation of the page; by default, blank documents have a Portrait layout, meaning the longer side of the page is the vertical side. The other option is a Landscape layout, where the shorter side of the page is the vertical side. You can change your document from Portrait to Landscape layout using the *Orientation* icon in the Page Layout ribbon (or the Layout ribbon in Word 2011). The *Margins* icon is another useful tool to locate and it can be found on the same panel with the Orientation and Size icons; the *Normal* margin setting of 1" on all sides is what should be used for constructing most documents as this provides a comfortable margin for printers which need to utilize some of the edge space of the page to grip and feed it through the mechanical print wheel.

Activity 10 – Modifying Page Layout

Start this exercise with a new document called *Activity10*. Type some text in the document to practice your typing skills. Now modify the margins of the page to be 2" on each side (using Custom Margins) and change the page layout to landscape. Now try changing the document size to the different size options available. Save your document in Tabloid size.

You can see the exact size of your document and position of elements in your text using the rulers and gridlines built into Word. The Ruler gives you the spacing of the text compared to real inches and centimeters on the printed document; as mentioned in the previous chapter, the tab stops are also noted below the ruler itself. This is helpful if you need to place elements within a certain range or confined area for printing (such as printing labels or envelopes). Gridlines give you a cross section of the ruler lines so you can position elements more exactly within the document; this is similar to using graph paper for a visual layout. The default gridlines are 1/8" apart. You can enable Gridlines from the View ribbon where you activate the Ruler and Navigation pane.

OFFICE 2011 The ruler in Word 2011 can be activated or deactivated by selecting the *View* menu and choosing *Ruler*. The gridlines options in Word 2011 are located in the Layout ribbon; you can select the checkbox next to *Gridlines*. These will appear when you select an object that can be repositioned on the document.

Like the Navigation pane, the rulers and gridlines can be distracting when you are creating a document and focusing on the visual layout and elements. You can activate these settings for planning your document and then deactivate them later as needed. When planning your document, you may also want to change the zoom setting using the slider bar at the bottom of the Word interface.

3.1.3 Formatting Columns

While the format of the documents you create will vary by their purpose, you may sometimes need multiple columns to format your document correctly. To change the number of columns for your document, you can simply select the text you want to change and choose the *Columns* icon. This is located on the Page Layout ribbon in Word 2010 (and the Layout ribbon in Word 2011). You can select from any of the predefined column divisions for the selected text or you can select the *More Columns* option from the dropdown list to get access to more advanced options (this is labeled simply *Columns* in Word 2011). You can see an example of the advanced menu and a sample two column result in Figure 3.4.

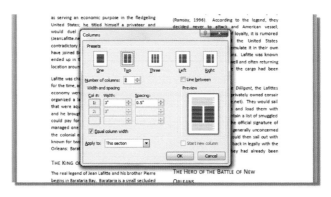

◀ **FIGURE 3.4** Advanced column configuration and two column formatting of text

You can choose any of the predefined options from this dialog box or you can create your own columns with customized widths. You can also choose whether you want to apply the column formatting to the entire document or just from that point forward. You can convert the text back and forth into different column settings as needed by highlighting what you want to change and selecting the number of columns from the Columns icon. If you add additional media elements to your page that do not line up within the text, this may alter the display of the columns, so you may want to wait and format your column settings last if it is not consistent throughout the entire document.

Activity 11 – Column Formats and Text Flow

Text flow is how text continues past one part of a page into another; in ordinary documents, text flows into new pages when it overflows, but this behavior changes when you have multiple columns in your document. Create a new document called *Activity11* and change it to two-column format. Enter text in the document until you see how text moves from one column to the next. How does it flow into the next column and how does it flow into the next page?

3.1.4 Page Setup

The expansion icon on the Page Setup panel of the Page Layout ribbon opens the Page Setup dialog box. From here, there are three tabs of options from which to choose: Margins, Paper, and Layout as shown in Figure 3.5. Though it is rare to use different paper settings for different parts of your document, this is not the case with margins.

From the Page Layout dialog box, you can set the margins for one section of your document at a time. This is useful for academic or business reports which require a larger top margin on the first page than on the rest of the subsequent pages. You can create this effect by setting the margin for the first page and then placing the cursor at the top of the second page and using this dialog box to change the margin settings for the selected text and choose *This point forward* in the *Apply to* selection box. If you have any text selected, the only options you will have will be *Selected text* and *Whole document*, which you would not want in this case.

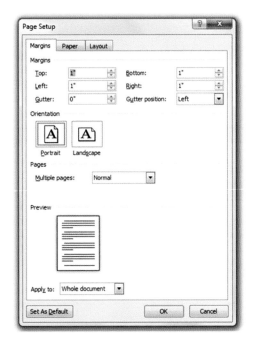

▲ **FIGURE 3.5** Page Setup dialog box in Word 2010

OFFICE 2011 In Word 2011, the Document dialog box is where you will find similar settings to the Page Layout dialog box. This contains the Margins and Layout tabs for customizing document settings. You can access this dialog box by selecting the *Format* menu and choosing *Document*.

3.2 COMMON DOCUMENT FORMATS AND ELEMENTS

There are an almost unlimited variety of documents that you can create from personal to professional and Word gives you the tools to create almost all of the elements you may need. With such a wide variety, however, there are certain documents in the academic and professional world that you will find yourself using frequently. This section covers the layout of these documents as well as the elements you may use to enhance the presentation of these documents.

3.2.1 Formal Letter Layout

In a formal letter, the margin should be 1" on each side. If you have letterhead that specifies the sender information, you can set the top margin to 2" to place the date line beneath the letterhead information. You can see an example of a formal or business letter and components in Figure 3.6. The line spacing for the document should be 1.15 and the font size should be 10 pt. Times New Roman is the standard typeface for business letters.

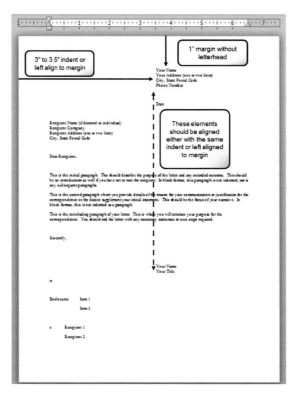

◀ **FIGURE 3.6** Formal letter example

There are several important elements to a formal letter:

• The sender information should only be entered if there is no existing letterhead with identifying information; if there is letterhead, you can begin immediately with the date line and identify the individual from the organization in the writer information at the end of the document in the writer information. If you are including sender information, you should include your name (unless it is a letter from the organization itself), organization, address, and phone number for the recipient to contact you. This element should be placed by tabbing roughly 3.5" from the left margin for standard letter size paper. There should be no paragraph spacing between these lines. You should leave a blank line before the date line.

• The date line can either be placed along the left margin or at the same location where the sender information starts, at roughly 3.5" tabbed from the left margin for standard letter size paper. You should leave a blank line beneath the date line.

• The letter addressing block is where you will detail, as specifically as possible, the intended recipient of the letter. This should be at the far left margin without space between the lines (you can accomplish this using the shift key along with the enter key to return to the start of the next line). You should detail the individual recipient (if there is one), the organization, and the organization address. This should be the same content that you place on the corresponding envelope for mailing the letter. You should add a blank line beneath this block.

- The salutation line should take the form "Dear" and then the courtesy title (such as Dr., Mr., Miss, or Mrs.) and name of the recipient followed by a comma. If you are directing it to a group or organization, it should be "Ladies and Gentlemen" followed by a comma or, if the recipients are unknown, it should be "To Whom it May Concern" followed by a colon. You should add a blank line beneath this line of text.

- The body of the letter will be composed of paragraphs just like any other document, but it should be in block paragraph format with no indentation. You should keep a blank line between paragraphs with no extra spacing between lines. You should leave one blank line beneath the last paragraph of the letter body.

- The complimentary close should typically be "Sincerely" followed by a comma. You should leave two blank lines beneath the complimentary close.

- The writer information should consist of two lines: your name and your job title. This should align with the left margin if the rest of the page does or it should be placed to align with the sender or date information if either is indented. There should be no blank space between your name and title. You should leave one blank line after the writer information.

- The reference initials are the initials of the person who typed the document. This is most important in organizations and is less important when the letter is from an individual where they most likely typed it. When this is included, you should leave a blank line beneath it.

- Enclosures denote additional documents or items that accompany the letter. You can denote enclosures with the word "Enclosure" followed by a tab and then the first enclosure item. Any additional enclosures should be on a separate line (without blank lines between them) left aligned with the name of the first item.

- Copy notation denotes the persons or organizations who received a copy of the letter. You denote copies with a lowercase letter "c" followed by the tab key. You would then add the name of the additional recipient. With multiple additional recipients, you should add each on a new line left aligned with the first additional recipient name.

NOTE

To return the cursor to the beginning of the next line without creating a new paragraph, you can hold down the shift key before pressing the enter key in Word.

3.2.2 Reports

Reports differ in layout by their use and the directions given by either an organization or professor in an academic setting, but there are general guidelines to follow for their construction. Side margins are most often either 1" or 1.5" and the bottom margin should be 1" consistently throughout the document. The first page top margin should be 2" with subsequent pages having a top margin of 1"; any header information (such as a last name and page number in an academic report) should be 0.5" from the top of the page between the top paper edge and the start of the text. The first page should not have a header. The common format for reports is either 10 pt or 12 pt font in Times New Roman typeface. The reference or bibliography page should have a 2" top margin with the header information common to the rest of the report. You can see an example report in Figure 3.7.

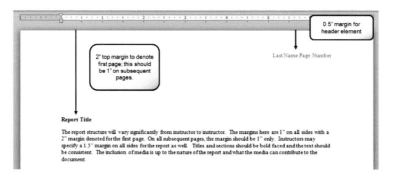

◀ **FIGURE 3.7** Business report example

3.2.3 Business Memos

Business memos are common documents to update staff of policy changes and information of which they should be aware. Physical memos are becoming less common with the ubiquitous access to e-mail, which is how most of this information is sent today. However, it is still important to understand the formatting for this document should you need to create one. It is interesting to note that the information fields in a memo are common to the standard e-mail format as well. You can see an example of a business memo in Figure 3.8.

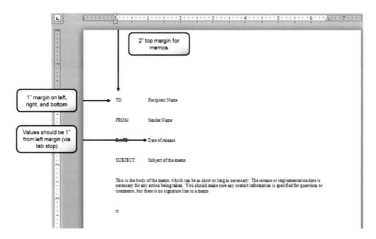

◀ **FIGURE 3.8** Business memo example

The top margin of a memo should be 2" with a 1" margin for the sides and bottom. The standard font for a memo is 10 pt Times New Roman. There are four data fields that lead a memo: TO, FROM, DATE, and SUBJECT. Each of these should be typed at the left margin in capital letters followed by a colon. The value for the field, such as your name for the FROM entry, should be indented to 1" from the left margin (accomplished via tab stops). You should have a blank line between each field.

After the initial field information, you should include a blank line and then the contents of the memo. There is typically no complimentary close or signature line in a memo, but it is common to have the reference initials of the person who typed the memo in a large organization. These should be placed beneath the memo body with a single blank line before the initials.

3.2.4 Using Headers and Footers

Headers and footers are often used in word processing documents. These allow you to maintain consistent elements on all pages of your document. A header, for example, may contain the title of the document or a last name for a report. The footer may contain the page number or copyright information. In the document you have open already, you should use the header to enter your name. Headers allow you to format the body of your document more consistently while keeping certain necessary information fixed on every page.

Activity 12 – Headers and Footers

Create a new document called *Activity12* and read how to activate headers and footers in your document. Add text to the document by practicing your typing skills. Now activate the header and footer and add text to each of these. Include a page number in the footer from the available tools in Word. Exit the header and footer and save your document.

You can activate the header of a document by double-clicking at the top of the visible document page. Similarly, you can double-click the bottom of the visible document page to activate the footer. When you do, you will get a context-sensitive Header and Footer Tools ribbon, as shown in Figure 3.9.

◀ **FIGURE 3.9** Header and Footer Tools ribbon and example in Word

From here, you can add common elements like the page number. You can also select pre-defined headers and footers from the respective *Header* and *Footer* icons. In Word 2010, these icons are also available in the Insert ribbon. When the header and footer are active, you can type text directly in the space allotted for them.

> **OFFICE 2011** In Word 2011, the header and footer are located in the Document Elements ribbon; you can also use the *View* menu and select *Header and Footer* to activate the header and footer for the document.

3.2.5 Adding a Cover Page

One of the more commonly used document elements is a cover page. A cover page for a document provides the title and author information for a document. This is an optional inclusion for a document. A title page can also provide an abstract for the document; an abstract is a short paragraph of a few sentences summarizing the document contents or contributions of the work. There are a variety of predefined cover pages available for use in Word.

To add a cover page to your report in Microsoft Word 2010, you need to activate the Insert ribbon and choose *Cover Page*. This will open the menu to select the cover page style you want to use. You can also use this menu to delete the current cover page.

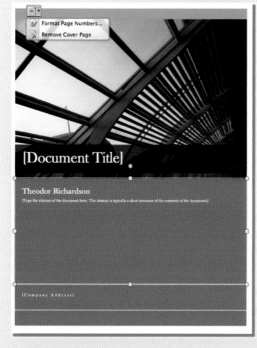

OFFICE 2011 In Word 2011, you can insert a cover page using the Document Elements ribbon and selecting Cover. When you add a cover page in Word 2011, you are given a small menu icon on that page which you can click and select Remove Cover Page. An example cover page with this icon active is shown in Figure 3.10.

▲ **FIGURE 3.10** Example cover page in Word 2011

Once you have selected the cover page you want to use, you can start entering the information in the predefined text boxes. This is similar to completing a document template in the previous section. You should at minimum include a title and the document ownership, whether it is the individual author or the company who owns the document material. Remember that a cover page should only be used when necessary. A short report would be better served with a header on the first page rather than a cover page.

3.2.6 Adding a Table of Contents

Another common element to include in your document is a *Table of Contents*. This uses the heading styles throughout your document to compile the important sections and it will include page numbers for these items automatically. The table of contents is one type of a larger class of automated table structures you can add to any document.

> A **TABLE OF CONTENTS** *is a list of chapter headings or major content divisions and the page numbers on which they are located. This allows for quick navigation of large documents to find desired elements and sections.*

To insert a table of contents into your document, you must first highlight where you want it in your document. This is typically located before any of the actual document content between the cover page and the first section of the material. In Word 2010, you can insert a table of contents by selecting the *References* ribbon and choosing the *Table of Contents* icon. This opens a dropdown menu of predefined options for your table of contents; you can also select *Insert Table of Contents* to get the dialog box shown in Figure 3.11.

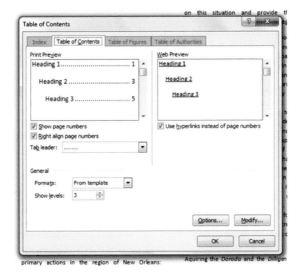

◀ **FIGURE 3.11** Table of Contents dialog box in Word 2010

This allows you to setup the number of heading levels you want to include and to adjust certain visual elements such as the character used to link between the section heading and the page number.

OFFICE 2011 The predefined options for the table of contents in Word 2011 are available from the Document Elements ribbon or you can click the *Options* icon to open the dialog box for advanced options; you can also open the dialog box to customize the table of contents by selecting the *Insert* menu, choosing *Index and Tables*, and then selecting the *Table of Contents* tab on the dialog box that appears.

If you continue to edit or develop your document after you have added your table of contents, you can update it to reflect the current headings included in the text or to adjust the page numbers correctly. In Word 2010, you can select the *Update Table* icon to perform this task on the Table of Contents panel of the References ribbon.

OFFICE 2011 In Word 2011, you can also select the *Update* icon located on the Table of Contents pane of the Document Elements ribbon.

In addition to the table of contents, there are also three other document elements of note that are similar. All of these are optional and may or may not be necessary for you to use in your document:

- *Index* – An index is a listing of key terms and concepts and where they are located throughout your document. You can add an entry to the index in Word 2010 by selecting *Mark Entry* on the References ribbon. You can then click *Insert Index* to get the Index tab of the dialog box from Figure 3.11 to customize your index display in the text. To add an entry to the index in Word 2011, select the *Insert* menu, choose *Index and Tables* and select the *Index* tab on the open dialog box; you can then click the *Mark Entry* button to enter the index entry information. You can add your index to the document from this same dialog box.

- *Table of Figures* – The table of figures is based on the captions that you add to your documents. This works similar to the table of contents by automatically determining the page number on which the captions reside. You can insert a table of figures in Word 2010 by selecting *Insert Table of Figures* on the References ribbon. You can update an existing table of figures by selecting the *Update Table* icon on the Captions panel in the References ribbon. In Word 2011, you can add a table of figures by choosing the *Insert* menu, selecting *Index and Tables*, and choosing the *Table of Figures* tab on the dialog box. The table can be updated if new captions are added by selecting the table, pressing the *Control* key and choosing the *Update* option.

- *Table of Authorities* – A table of authorities is a list of references in a legal document. For most works, you will not need to create one of these, but the option is available in Word. You can add a citation in Word 2010 using the *Mark Citation* icon on the Table of Authorities panel of the References ribbon and you can insert the table of authorities using the *Insert Table of Authorities* icon on the References ribbon. The *Update Table* icon located in the Table of Authorities panel can be used to update the table later as the document is edited. For Word 2011, you can use the *Insert* menu, select *Index and Tables*, and then choose the Table of Authorities tab on the dialog box. The options to *Mark Citation* and insert the table are on this dialog. You can update the table by selecting the table, pressing the *Control* key and choosing the *Update* option.

3.2.7 Additional Document Elements

There are a number of additional document elements you may need to include. Some of these relate more to larger publications and larger organizations, but it is beneficial to know where to access these items if you need to do so. Some of these optional document elements include an index, watermarks, borders, cover pages, blank pages, and a table of contents. Some common elements you may use to enhance your document are the following:

- *Watermarks* – A watermark is a visual element on the pages of your document to either signify ownership or a certain classification for the document (such as *Confidential* or *Do Not Copy*). You can create your own watermark or use an existing logo for an organization or business so that any document created with the watermark will be imprinted with the logo, identifying ownership. To add a watermark to your document in Word 2010, select the Page Layout ribbon and choose *Watermark*; from here you can select a predefined watermark or select *Custom Watermark* to build your own.

- *Borders* – Adding a page border may be useful depending on the type of document you are creating. Page borders are most often seen on fliers and personal memos; they are not generally used in professional publications unless they are highlighting a particular element of text like an abstract for the document. To add a border to your page in Word 2010, select the Page Layout ribbon and choose *Page Borders*. This will open a dialog box that allows you to select the type of border you want for your page and choose the width and style for it. You can add a page border in Word 2011 by selecting the *Format* menu, choosing *Borders and Shading* and then selecting the *Page Border* tab on the dialog box that opens.

- *Blank Pages* – Sometimes it is necessary to add a blank page into your document; this is commonly found behind the title page of a lengthy report. You can create a blank page in Word 2010 by selecting the Insert ribbon and choosing *Blank Page*. You can add a blank page in Word 2011 by selecting the Document Elements ribbon and choosing *Blank* under the Insert Pages panel.

- *Page Breaks* – A page break ends the current page regardless of remaining space on the page and starts a new page. This is useful if you do not want chapters or sections of a document to run together. In Word 2010, you can select *Page Break* from the Insert ribbon. In Word 2011, you can add a page break by selecting the Document Elements ribbon and choosing the *Break* icon and then selecting *Page*.

There are a number of additional media elements that can be added to a word processing document to enhance its visual display. These are covered in the next chapter which provides more detail on adding and using visual enhancements.

3.2.8 File Management Shortcuts

As you already know from the text formatting shortcuts, productivity or keyboard shortcuts are keyboard commands that can be entered quickly to save you the time of having to open a menu or ribbon to find the command you wish to use. These exist for the most common actions you perform in a software system and are common to most software programs that utilize individual documents or files to store and organize information.

You activate a shortcut command by holding down the *Ctrl* key on a Windows machine and typing the letter corresponding to the shortcut while the *Ctrl* key is held down. These shortcuts work on a Macintosh machine as well, except the *Command* key is used to activate the shortcut instead of the *Ctrl* key. The most common shortcuts with which you should be familiar for managing documents are as follows:

- *New Document* (*Ctrl-N* on Windows machines or *Command-N* on Macintosh machines)—This command opens a new blank document in the active program.

- *Open Document* (*Ctrl-O* or *Command-O*)—This shortcut is used to open an existing file. It will open a dialog box that allows you to choose the file you wish to open.

- *Save Document* (*Ctrl-S* or *Command-S*)—This is the same as selecting the *Save* command; it will save any progress in an open document that has already been saved. If the document has not yet been saved, it will act like the *Save As* command.

- *Print Document* (*Ctrl-P* or *Command-P*)—This command initiates the printing process. If the software allows you to set options before you print, it will open a dialog box; otherwise, it will attempt to use the default printer to initiate a print command.

- *Undo Last Action* (*Ctrl-Z* or *Command-Z*)—This will attempt to undo the last action you performed in the open document; not all actions can be undone with this command. Some programs maintain a buffer of actions, allowing you to undo multiple changes that you made to the document.

- *Redo Last Action* (*Ctrl-Y* or *Command-Y*)—This will reverse the effects of the *Undo* command; not all actions that are undone can be reversed by the *Redo* command. Again, there are some programs that will maintain a buffer of commands and changes, allowing you to redo multiple actions that were reversed by the *Undo* command.

- *Select All Content* (*Ctrl-A* or *Command-A*)—This command will select all of the content in the current document or document element (like a table cell) that is allowed to be selected. This is a useful command if you want to perform actions like applying formatting to everything in your document.

- *Quit* (*Ctrl-Q* or *Command-Q*)—This command will attempt to exit the currently active program.

These are in addition to the shortcuts that are used to alter text formatting and to utilize the system clipboard for transferring information quickly and easily from one document or location to another. These are valuable to learn and will save you a considerable amount of time when you are typing. Additionally, specific programs may have a unique set of shortcut commands in addition to or instead of the ones covered here.

3.3 KEYBOARDING III

In this keyboarding lesson, you will add the bottom row keys to your typing knowledge. This allows you to type using the complete alphabet, so by the time you are finished, you should be moving toward the ability to type any word without visual reference. Another important key you will learn in this lesson is the shift key; this allows you to switch between uppercase and lowercase letters as well as different punctuation marks that utilize the same key. These alternate punctuation marks are located above the character that is typed when you strike the key by default. You can see the bottom row keys highlighted in Figure 3.12.

◀ **FIGURE 3.12** Primary bottom row keys

3.3.1 Bottom Row Keys

The bottom row keys include the letters Z through M on the keyboard arrangement; they also include the comma and stop (also called the period) keys. Your fingers should move down and to the right to reach the assigned keys. Your index fingers and pinky fingers will have additional assigned keys to cover the entire row. Another important key found in this row is the shift key, which can be reached on either side of the keyboard with your pinky fingers. The movement for each finger to the assigned bottom row keys is shown in Figure 3.13.

◀ **FIGURE 3.13** Finger motion for primary bottom row keys

The Shift Key and Caps Lock

The shift key is another key that retains its name from the original mechanical functionality of the typewriter. This key would be pressed to mechanically shift the case stamp to move from lowercase to capital letters. Before the shift key, all typing was done in capital letters only. Now, the key is used to shift case or to switch to the alternate symbol on number and punctuation keys. There is a shift key located on either side of the keyboard which should be depressed by the pinky of the opposite hand while the other hand strikes the key. For example, you would use your left pinky to strike the shift key while your right hand types a capital J by striking the J key. Shift is active the entire time it is physically depressed.

The alternative to depressing the shift key and holding it while striking multiple keys is to use the caps lock key. This key acts as a toggle which performs the same function as the shift key. When the caps lock key is turned on, it acts as though the shift key is constantly depressed; in this case, pressing the shift key will revert the key that is struck back to its default symbol. When caps lock is pressed again, it toggles the functionality back off and the keyboard will function as normal. The caps lock key is only found on the left side of the keyboard and should be struck with the left pinky finger.

Keyboarding Lessons 31–45

By the time you have completed the following lessons, you will have practiced all of the bottom keys highlighted in dark blue in **Figure 3.14. You** should concentrate in these lessons on learning the hand motion necessary to reach the keys without looking at them and retaining the position of the rest of your fingers as the assigned finger stretches to another row to strike the desired key. As you practice, you are building muscle memory in your hands and memorizing key positions, so you should train your hands properly now to avoid having to retrain them to break bad form later. The more practice you have with this, the better your form will become and the more your speed will increase.

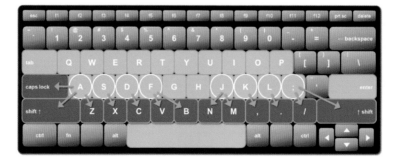

◀ **FIGURE 3.14** Keyboarding III keys and hand motion mapping

The software included with the text and available online at *www.keyboardingandbe-yond.com* will time the lessons and alert you to any mistakes made while entering the text for these exercises. Because this is practice, you should feel free to redo these lessons and activities as much as you need to improve your performance and form.

Lesson 3.1 The M Key

In this lesson, you will use your right index finger to press the M key as well as using the keys you have already learned. You should focus on your form and keep your hands positioned over the home row keys while you move only the necessary finger to strike the keys you wish to type. The software will count up the amount of time it takes for you to complete the task, so you can take as long as you need and retry the exercise to improve your time.

Type the following:

```
mmmm jjjj mmmm mmjj mjmj jmjm hmjm hjmh jmmj mjjm
mmmm jjjj mmmm mmjj mjmj jmjm hmjm hjmh jmmj mjjm
me mop mild mold memo mail lame make might
mk mo mj ml mh mg mi mu my
mokom kommok kljmop hmjikl ma am me em
me mop mild mold memory mailer maker might
```

Lesson 3.2 The Comma Key

In this lesson, you will use your left index finger to press the R key as well as using the keys you have already learned. You should focus on your form and keep your hands positioned over the home row keys while you move only the necessary finger to strike the keys you wish to type. The software will count up the amount of time it takes for you to complete the task, so you can take as long as you need and retry the exercise to improve your time.

> You only need to space once after a comma. If the comma appears in the middle of a numerical value, you do not have to space after its use.

NOTE

Type the following:

```
,,,, kkkk ,k,k ,,kk kk,, ,,kk kk,, i,i, ,kk, k,,k ik,ki
,,,, kkkk ,k,k ,,kk kk,, ,,kk kk,, i,i, ,kk, k,,k ik,ki
ike, hike, mike, like, this, that, again, kit,
may, august, april, july, perhaps, not, yes
may, august, april, july, perhaps, not, yes
ike, hike, mike, like, this, that, again, kit,
```

Lesson 3.3 The Period Key

In this lesson, you will use your right ring finger to press the period or stop (.) key as well as using the keys you have already learned. You should focus on your form and keep your hands positioned over the home row keys while you move only the necessary finger to strike the keys you wish to type. The software will count up the amount of time it takes for you to complete the task, so you can take as long as you need and retry the exercise to improve your time.

<table>
<tr><td>NOTE</td><td>When you type a full stop or period at the end of a sentence, you should add a single space before starting a new sentence. A period or decimal point inside of a value does not require space after its use. Similarly, a period signifying an abbreviation (such as "oz." for ounces or "Dr." for Doctor) requires only a single space after its use.</td></tr>
</table>

Type the following:

```
.... llll .... ..ll .l.l l.l. o.o. oo.. .ll. l..l lo.ol .ollo.
.... llll .... ..ll .l.l l.l. o.o. oo.. .ll. l..l lo.ol .ollo.
yes. end. this. that. poor. mike. try.
this is the end. that was the end. this is the start.
this is the end. that was the end. this is the start.
yes. end. this. that. poor. mike. try.
```

Lesson 3.4 The Slash Key

In this lesson, you will use your right pinky finger to press the slash (/) key as well as using the keys you have already learned. You should focus on your form and keep your hands positioned over the home row keys while you move only the necessary finger to strike the keys you wish to type. The software will count up the amount of time it takes for you to complete the task, so you can take as long as you need and retry the exercise to improve your time.

<table>
<tr><td>NOTE</td><td>When you couple the shift key with the slash key, it types a question mark (?). Similar to a period, you should add a single space after its use before starting the next sentence.</td></tr>
</table>

Type the following:

```
//// ;;;; //// //;; ;/;/ ;/;/ ;p;p; /p/p /;;/ ;//; /;pp;/
p;//;p
//// ;;;; //// //;; ;/;/ ;/;/ ;p;p; /p/p /;;/ ;//; /;pp;/
p;//;p
m/h k/s d/t p/f op/ed s/h
/;p /;l pl/ p/a s/d f/g g/h h/j k/k l/l p/p l/l
/;p /;l pl/ p/a s/d f/g g/h h/j k/k l/l p/p l/l
m/h k/s d/t p/f op/ed s/h
```

Lesson 3.5 The N Key

In this lesson, you will use your right index finger to press the N key as well as using the keys you have already learned. You should focus on your form and keep your hands positioned over the home row keys while you move only the necessary finger to strike the keys you wish to type. The software will count up the amount of time it takes for you to complete the task, so you can take as long as you need and retry the exercise to improve your time.

Type the following:

```
nnnn jjjj nnnn nnjj jjnn jnjn njnj njjn jnnj jmnnmj nmjjmn
nnnn jjjj nnnn nnjj jjnn jnjn njnj njjn jnnj jmnnmj nmjjmn
ninja hand land sand man manned unmanned unhand than pan
nano mano mana money honey launder squander fond pond
nano mano mana money honey launder squander fond pond
ninja hand land sand man manned unmanned unhand than pan
```

Lesson 3.6 The V Key

In this lesson, you will use your left index finger to press the V key as well as using the keys you have already learned. You should focus on your form and keep your hands positioned over the home row keys while you move only the necessary finger to strike the keys you wish to type. The software will count up the amount of time it takes for you to complete the task, so you can take as long as you need and retry the exercise to improve your time.

Type the following:

```
vvvv ffff vvvv vvff ffvv vfvf fvfv vffv fvvf vfrrfv rfvvfr
vvvv ffff vvvv vvff ffvv vfvf fvfv vffv fvvf vfrrfv rfvvfr
valve vast variant valiant vary vast vorpal
vanity visit visual vilify villain villainy visit solve
vanity visit visual vilify villain villainy visit solve
valve vast variant valiant vary vast vorpal
```

Lesson 3.7 The C Key

In this lesson, you will use your left middle finger to press the C key as well as using the keys you have already learned. You should focus on your form and keep your hands positioned over the home row keys while you move only the necessary finger to strike the keys you wish to type. The software will count up the amount of time it takes for you to complete the task, so you can take as long as you need and retry the exercise to improve your time.

Type the following:

```
cccc dddd cccc ccdd dcdc cdcd cddc dccd cdeedc edccde
cccc dddd cccc ccdd dcdc cdcd cddc dccd cdeedc edccde
cost calculate can cannot critical crucial crisp
chasm charm chalk chap parch chirp chip perch merchant
chasm charm chalk chap parch chirp chip perch merchant
cost calculate can cannot critical crucial crisp
```

Lesson 3.8 The X Key

In this lesson, you will use your left ring finger to press the R key as well as using the keys you have already learned. You should focus on your form and keep your hands positioned over the home row keys while you move only the necessary finger to strike the keys you wish to type. The software will count up the amount of time it takes for you to complete the task, so you can take as long as you need and retry the exercise to improve your time.

Type the following:

```
xxxx ssss xxxx xxss xsxs sxsx sxxs xssx xswwsx wsxxsw
xxxx ssss xxxx xxss xsxs sxsx sxxs xssx xswwsx wsxxsw
xerxes xerox xeroxes xanadu excelsior excellent excel
xsw xad xaf rxf xjk lxk ;xl /;x x.l x,k nxm
xsw xad xaf rxf xjk lxk ;xl /;x x.l x,k nxm
xerxes xerox xeroxes xanadu excelsior excellent excel
```

Lesson 3.9 The Z Key

In this lesson, you will use your left pinky finger to press the Z key as well as using the keys you have already learned. You should focus on your form and keep your hands positioned over the home row keys while you move only the necessary finger to strike the keys you wish to type. The software will count up the amount of time it takes for you to complete the task, so you can take as long as you need and retry the exercise to improve your time.

Type the following:

```
zzzz aaaa zzzz zzaa zaza azaz zaaz azza zaqqaz qazzaq qzqz
zzzz aaaa zzzz zzaa zaza azaz zaaz azza zaqqaz qazzaq qzqz
```

```
zero zilch wizard zipper zip zen aztec zoning
zdrf zsaw zsaq qazs zlks zkjd znmh z,/; zp;o
zdrf zsaw zsaq qazs zlks zkjd znmh z,/; zp;o
zero zilch wizard zipper zip zen aztec zoning
```

Lesson 3.10 The B Key

In this lesson, you will use your left index finger to press the B key as well as using the keys you have already learned. You should focus on your form and keep your hands positioned over the home row keys while you move only the necessary finger to strike the keys you wish to type. The software will count up the amount of time it takes for you to complete the task, so you can take as long as you need and retry the exercise to improve your time.

Type the following:

```
bbbb ffff bbbb bbff fbfb bfbf fbbf bffb bfrfb fvbbvf ftgb bgtf
bbbb ffff bbbb bbff fbfb bfbf fbbf bffb bfrfb fvbbvf ftgb bgtf
barn bark bar barstool barricade ban banner banned base
blast birth bark burst balloon blowout bassist basest
blast birth bark burst balloon blowout bassist basest
barn bark bar barstool barricade ban banner banned base
```

Lesson 3.11 Right Hand Shift Practice

For this lesson, you will use the assigned keys for your right hand along with the left shift key (struck using your left pinky). You should try to focus on tapping the keys lightly so that you strike them just hard enough to type the character and then release pressure on the key; the shift key will only modify the struck keys when it is depressed during the key strike. The software will count up the amount of time it takes for you to complete the task, so you can take as long as you need and retry the exercise to improve your time.

> **NOTE**
>
> When using a semicolon (;), you only need to space once after use. When using the shifted colon character (:), you should add a space unless it is in the middle of a numerical value such as 2:00 as a time value.

Type the following:

```
Junk Punk Link Mink Monk Limp Hunk Jump Limp
LoJp PLkj <kk> >kk< Jump? Limp? Junk: Imp
Pool; Poll; Hunk. <poll> <un> <on> ??//
JKL:jkl; NM<>? YUIOP Hjkl; ;lkjH :LKJh hJKL:
```

```
JKL:jkl; NM<>? YUIOP Hjkl; ;lkjH :LKJh hJKL:
LoJp PLkj <kk> >kk< Jump? Limp? Junk: Imp
Junk Punk Link Mink Monk Limp Hunk Jump Limp
```

Lesson 3.12 Left Hand Shift Practice

In this lesson, you will practice using your left hand to type while using the right shift key. You should keep your right hand in place over the home row keys and use only the shift, enter, and spacebar keys with it. The software will count up the amount of time it takes for you to complete the task, so you can take as long as you need and retry the exercise to improve your time.

Type the following:

```
Axe A Was War Raw Trace Vase Drag Carve
Qwer Asdf Zxcv FtGb Gbtr Gbvf REWQ VCXZ FDSA
aQx sWc dEv fRbGt tGbrFv EdC WsX QaZ
aQx sWc dEv fRbGt tGbrFv EdC WsX QaZ
Qwer Asdf Zxcv FtGb Gbtr Gbvf REWQ VCXZ FDSA
Axe A Was War Raw Trace Vase Drag Carve
```

Lesson 3.13 Both Hand Shift Practice

In this lesson, you will use all of the home row keys, top row keys, and bottom row keys that have been assigned as well as the enter key, spacebar, and shift keys. Remember that you will use the right shift key when striking keys with your left hand and the left shift key when striking keys with your right hand. The software will count up the amount of time it takes for you to complete the task, so you can take as long as you need and retry the exercise to improve your time.

Type the following:

```
This is the start
This is the start of
This is the start of a
This is the start of a long
This is the start of a long sentence.
Trust Mike to mark the map. Mike marks many maps.
Mistakes made by Bob make me look bad. Bob is my uncle.
Tell Tom to trust Tina in Italy. Tina is unsure of Tom.
Ask Mark to map the Alps. Mark maps a lot.
Give me a hand, Katie. Thanks, Billy.
```

Lesson 3.14 Caps Lock Practice

In this lesson, you will practice toggling the caps lock setting on and off by reaching your left pinky to the caps lock key. The timer for this exercise counts down, so you should try to gain enough proficiency and speed to complete the exercise in its entirety before the timer runs out. You should also focus on minimizing the errors, particularly in the correct capitalization of the letters. Because you are still learning, you should repeat this exercise as necessary until you are able to complete it with time left on the timer!

Type the following:

```
YOU SHOULD PAY attention to WHERE things start TO SHIFT and
alter your TYPING to match WHAT IS NEEDED. Sometimes, just a
SHIFT KEY will do the job when OTHER TIMES YOU WILL TYPE FOR A
WHILE IN CAPS. WHEN DO YOU USE EACH ONE? That is a good ques-
tion to ask when deciding on CAPS LOCK OR SHIFT KEY USAGE. CAPS
LOCK SHOULD BE TOGGLED and shift should just be pressed for one
or two keys at once.
```

Lesson 3.15 Typing Speed Test

In this lesson, you will practice typing all of the keys you have learned so far, including the home row keys, the bottom row keys, and the top row keys. The timer for this exercise counts down, so you should try to gain enough proficiency and speed to complete the exercise in its entirety before the timer runs out. Because you are still learning, you should repeat this exercise as necessary until you are able to complete it with time left on the timer!

Type the following:

```
Try
Try to
Try to build
Try to build this
Try to build this sentence
Try to build this sentence by
Try to build this sentence by Tom
Try to build this sentence by Tom as
Try to build this sentence by Tom as fast
Try to build this sentence by Tom as fast as
Try to build this sentence by Tom as fast as you
Try to build this sentence by Tom as fast as you can,
Try to build this sentence by Tom as fast as you can, Alice.
```

CHAPTER SUMMARY

In this chapter, you learned in detail about more complex document creation. This includes the use of templates for creating common document types. You have also been introduced to several document types that are common in the modern business environment. The page layout for these documents as well as items such as cover pages, headers, and footers can all be used to enhance the display of your documents. After completing the keyboarding lessons for this chapter, you should be able to type any word and you should concentrate on typing common and complex words to reinforce the letter locations in your mind.

CHAPTER KNOWLEDGE CHECK

1 A *template* is a preformatted placeholder document for your content; you can build your own instance of the document using the predefined areas where you can add objects and text, knowing what it will look like when you are finished.

- ○ **A.** True
- ○ **B.** False

2 The ruler in Word 2011 can be activated or deactivated by selecting the *File* menu and choosing *Ruler*.

- ○ **A.** True
- ○ **B.** False

3 In Word 2011, the *Size* icon is located in the _____ ribbon.

- ○ **A.** Home
- ○ **B.** Layout
- ○ **C.** Quick Access Menu
- ○ **D.** None of the above

4 In Word 2011, the _____ dialog box is where you will find similar settings to the Page Layout dialog box.

- ○ **A.** Page Setup
- ○ **B.** Document
- ○ **C.** Navigation pane
- ○ **D.** None of the above

5 Headers and Footers allow you to maintain _____ elements on all pages of your document.

- ○ **A.** Several
- ○ **B.** Consistent
- ○ **C.** Repetitive
- ○ **D.** None of the above

6 A table of contents is another common element you can include in your document. This uses the _____ throughout your document to compile the important sections and it will include page numbers for these items automatically.

- ○ **A.** Navigation pane
- ○ **B.** Heading styles
- ○ **C.** Styles
- ○ **D.** None of the above

7 An index is a listing of key terms and concepts and where they are located throughout your document.

- ○ **A.** True
- ○ **B.** False

8 A _____ is a visual element on the pages of your document to either signify ownership or a certain classification for the document such as *Confidential* or *Do Not Copy.*

- ○ **A.** Watermark
- ○ **B.** Quote
- ○ **C.** Comment
- ○ **D.** None of the above

9 A page space ends the current page regardless of remaining space on the page and starts a new page.

- ○ **A.** True
- ○ **B.** False

10 You activate a _____ by holding down the *Ctrl* key on a Windows machine and typing the letter corresponding to the shortcut while the *Ctrl* key is held down.

- ○ **A.** Short key
- ○ **B.** Shortcut command
- ○ **C.** Web page
- ○ **D.** None of the above

CHAPTER EXERCISES

1. A cover letter is a specific type of formal letter that accompanies a resume as a narrative explaining your interest and qualification for a potential job. This has the same structure as a formal letter. Research potential jobs in which you are interested on a Web site such as *Monster.com* and write a cover letter for the position, paying particular attention to the formatting of the document.

2. Create a memo for your company explaining that every Friday for the next month will be a half day as a reward for the hard work and productivity of the employees. You should send this to all employees as the recipient with an immediate release date. Be sure to format the letter correctly according to the guidelines for margins and font.

3. Draft a one page report on the history of either the typewriter or the QWERTY keyboard. Each paragraph should detail the significant developments and increase in mechanization or evolution to the computer environment. Add a header with your last name and format the report with 1.5" margins on the left, right, and bottom of the page.

4. Create a document with two column format and 2" margins on each side of the page. Add a header to the document with your name and the date the document was created. Now use the entire alphabet to create sentences with proper punctuation in your document. The text should be in complete sentences, but the sentences do not have to relate to each other. The key element is that you use each letter at least once in your document within a word used properly in a sentence.

5. Create a title page for a marketing proposal for a new product you want to sell to a large business. The target audience is upper management in a large organization, so it will be necessary to place an executive summary on the title page itself so the group can understand what is being covered in the report. Choosing the right kind of layout and presenting your content to your intended audience on the cover page should be the primary focus of this exercise even above the product you are proposing.

6. In Word 2011, create a new document from a template either by selecting the *File* menu and choosing *New from Template* or by clicking the *New from Template* icon in the Quick Access toolbar. This will open the Word Document Gallery. From this interface, select *Resumes* and choose one of the templates. Prepare a one page resume that includes your education, training, special skills, and an objective statement. (If you are using Word 2010 use the backstage view to access templates.)

7. Business memos are common documents used to update staff of policy changes and information of which they should be aware. Physical memos are becoming less common with the ubiquitous access to e-mail, which is how most of this information is sent today. Using the lessons learned write a one page business memo letting employees know that the building garage will be closed for one week due to repairs. Be sure to explain that they will have to park outside the building at the curbside during the repairs. Use the templates available from the backstage view in Word 2010 or the File menu in Word 2011 to select your memo format.

8. As you have learned, headers and footers are often used in word processing documents. These allow you to maintain consistent elements on all pages of your document. Develop a header and a footer that includes information for your business or organization (this can be real or fictional) that would display on the first page of a document instead of using printed letterhead paper.

9. Create a tile page for a book report you are writing for a course you are taking in school. The first page should only have the title with no page numbers. Insert a page break and insert page numbers using roman numerals. Insert a second page break and restart your numbering using standard numbers.

10. Using the lessons learned, develop a table of contents page. Look back to section 3.2.6 and follow the procedures applicable to the Word version you are using such as 2010 or 2011. You will have to come up with five headings and subheadings to properly develop your table of contents.

CHAPTER REVIEW QUESTIONS

Please answer the questions based on the Microsoft Office application version you are using (2010 or 2011).

1. Please explain and compare the advantages of using a document template versus creating a new document from scratch.

2. Please define and compare the difference between setting a layout and margins within a Word document.

3. Please list the steps needed to access the page layout options in Word 2010 or Word 2011.

4. Discuss and compare the elements needed to develop a formal business letter.

5. Please discuss the differences between a header and footer. What are the steps needed to access these options and what information is common to each?

6. Please list the steps needed to insert a cover page into your document.

7. Please discuss and explain the differences between a Table of Contents and a List of Figures. List the situations when each might be used.

8. Define and explain the idea of a Watermark. What are the steps necessary to insert one into your document and what are at least two situations that could warrant the use of this feature?

9. Please explain the relationship between page breaks and how they relate to the Table of Contents feature.

10. List the common file management shortcuts listed in this chapter. Please explain what each short cut will initiate for the user.

KEYBOARDING DRILLS

1. Type as much of the following as you can in thirty seconds; try to complete the exercise before the timer runs out if possible. You can use the included software to track your time, speed, and errors:

```
This
This is
This is a
This is a sentence
This is a sentence building
This is a sentence building exercise
This is a sentence building exercise using
This is a sentence building exercise using all
This is a sentence building exercise using all the tricks
This is a sentence building exercise using all the tricks you
This is a sentence building exercise using all the tricks you
know.
```

2. Type as much of the following as you can in thirty seconds; try to complete the exercise before the timer runs out if possible. You can use the included software to track your time, speed, and errors:

```
How many people can you fit in your car? How many people can
you fit on a bus? How many buses can you fit in your car? How
many cars can you fit on your bus? Who could fly the plane? How
can Tom swim so fast? Why can I not fly in the sky like a bird?
How can Joe go so slowly? Where is Mary when I need her? Why
are there so many questions? Who thought of these questions,
anyway?
```

3. Track your time and focus on your form to type the following with as few errors as possible. You can use the included software to track your time, speed, and errors:

```
This / is / a / broken / sentence. The / proper / way / is /
to < edit > out < the > extra < punctuation > but < then > you
, would , not , be , practicing , punctuation , in , your,
typing. It . is . better . to . learn . where . your .
punctuation ; marks ; are ; located ; and ; add ; them ;
quickly : when : you : need : to : do : so.
```

4. Track your time and focus on your form to type the following with as few errors as possible. You can use the included software to track your time, speed, and errors:

A writing test is a laughing thing that has no strings on a
paper lined with little things that stretch for miles on a
sea of white that marks it blue with lines and dots and knows
not what pencils write or when is night and who is right or
why we write with all our might to do it right when time comes
to stop our pencils from moving.

5. Type as much of the following as you can in one minute. You can use the
included software to track your time, speed, and errors:

A typing test on the other hand is a measure of knowing your
hands and where they sit when not in sight and typing on and
on all night to get it right and learn with touch instead
of eyes where keys are that you visualize in your mind and
think with hand motion where the next letter can be found and
strike it down to make the clicking sound and make the letter,
once found, pound on the screen in the digital realm where
signals fly and letters are written in the blink of an eye from
binary to the human eye.

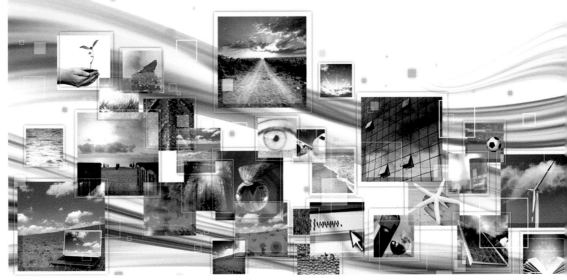

Media Elements and Number Keys

IN THIS CHAPTER

This chapter introduces you to the various media elements that can be added to a Word document to enhance the visual display of the document and create a better presentation of your content. The available media for a Word document is centered on visual elements that lend themselves to printed documents. This includes shapes, images, clip art, and screenshots. Specialized elements called SmartArt can also be included to construct professional graphics simply. Charts run by data in Excel spreadsheets can also be incorporated into a Word document. The keyboarding lesson for this chapter will introduce you to the number keys on the keyboard located two rows above the home row keys. When you have completed this chapter, you will be able to:

- Add images to your document and manipulate them to fit your display

- Insert shapes and clip art into your document to enhance the presentation of information

- Construct tables within your document to organize information

- Add charts to your document to visually present data

- Utilize the number keys on the keyboard with proper typing form

4.1 VISUALLY ENHANCING DOCUMENTS

One of the benefits of utilizing word processing software is the dramatic increase in control the software offers regarding the arrangement and display of your text and information. Word, for example, allows for the incorporation of multiple, diverse *media elements* into your document display from images to tables and charts. This allows for the creation of any number of documents with a display that matches your overall design vision.

> A **MEDIA ELEMENT** *is any tool for communicating information within the channel of communication. For example, an image added to a text document would be considered a media element because it communicates information within the document.*

However, there are issues to consider when using visual elements to enhance the presentation of any document. Most importantly, you need to consider your audience and the environment in which this document will be used. For example, clip art images may be welcome in flyers and other casual media but it should most likely be kept out of board meeting minutes.

Another issue to consider is that your document above all must be clear and readable to your audience. You should never sacrifice clarity for display because the ability for the audience to understand the information being communicated should be the primary consideration in communication. A missed or unclear message is more damaging to what you have to say than a plain-looking display. Causing your document to look too cluttered with visual elements or including visual elements that detract from the attractiveness of your document can also be detrimental.

Here are some questions you should ask to decide on whether the media inclusion will benefit your document; if you answer yes to the following questions you are probably on track with including the media element:

- Does the visual element enhance the overall message of the document?

- Does the visual element summarize or clarify information within the document in a helpful way?

- Is the visual element consistent with the tone and message of the document?
- Does the visual element fit with the audience and environment of the document?

Alternately, if you answer yes to any of the following questions, you should consider omitting the visual element or choosing another way to display the information:

- Does the visual element detract from the overall message or clarity of the document?
- Does the visual element overshadow the rest of the document content without intending to do so?
- Does the visual element clash with the display of the document?

4.2 MEDIA ELEMENTS IN WORD

Word is second only to PowerPoint® for the ability to include media elements in the Microsoft Office suite of productivity software. The media elements in Word are designed to enhance the document presentation and make it either more readable or more attractive. If the inclusion of the media does not further these goals, it should be omitted for the sake of clarity and conciseness. You should take note that visual elements added to your page will make it more visually interesting, but they will distract the viewer from the text itself. The eye will focus on the location with the most visual information, which will typically be a graphic or image; this means your audience will see a picture before they see the text of the document that goes with it. Media elements can dramatically enhance the presentation of a document beyond even attention getting typography. Often times, it is possible to summarize a complicated explanation with an image of a diagram; similarly, it may be better to use a table or chart to explain complex data results. Media elements in Word are designed to improve visual communication and they can be remarkably effective. This section introduces you to the common types of media elements that can be included in your documents and how to add and adjust them as needed.

4.2.1 Images

To insert an image into your Word document, you must first have it saved on your local machine. The typical image file formats are JPEG (Joint Photographics Experts Group) file interchange format, Graphics Interchange Format (GIF), bitmap, Portable Network Graphic (PNG), and Tag Image File Format (TIFF); any of these can be inserted into a document. To insert an image into your word processing document in Word 2010, you can select the Insert ribbon and choose *Picture*. This will open the *Insert Picture* dialog box where you can select the image you want to insert.

In Word 2011, you can insert an image from the Home ribbon by choosing the *Picture* icon and then choosing *Picture from File*. As with any text content, you must make sure you have adequate permission to use an image file if you have not created it yourself. You can see an example of an inserted image in Figure 4.1.

◀ **FIGURE 4.1** Image inserted into a Word 2010 document

Once you have added an image to your document, you can resize the image using any of the grip points that appear around its edge when it is selected. The midpoint grip points change only one dimension at a time (this can deform the image by changing the ratio between its length and width). The corner grip points change the two sides they connect at once. You can also use the context-sensitive Format ribbon for Picture Tools (which appears whenever you click on an image inside your document) to set the size of the image directly; this ribbon contains a large number of features which can be used to adjust the display of your image. You can see an example of this ribbon in Figure 4.2.

◀ **FIGURE 4.2** Format ribbon for Picture Tools

The green grip point (elevated by a short line above the image) is used to set the rotation of the image. You can click and drag this point to rotate your image in place on the page. You can also perform a specified rotation by using the Rotate menu icon in the Page Layout ribbon. You can also flip the image vertically or horizontally with the choices available.

OFFICE 2011 In Word 2011, the flip and rotate commands are located on the context-sensitive Format ribbon that extends from the Home ribbon whenever an object is selected. These commands can be found under the Rotate menu icon.

One of the features you can change for your image is how it behaves in the document, as text or as a separate object. By default, any image you add to your document will be placed in line with your text, expanding the current line size to fit the image; the image will act like another character in the text of the document in this format. You can click and drag it as you can with any other text. You can change how the image behaves by changing its *text wrapping* properties.

TEXT WRAPPING, *or text flow for an object, is the setting in a document or Web page determining how text behaves around an object. An example of this is how much space it leaves blank around the perimeter of the object and whether it treats the object as a character in the text or a separate object in the document.*

The different text wrap options are *square* (where the image is given a padded rectangle to occupy and the text will surround it), *tight* (which acts like the square setting without the padding on the rectangle), *through* (where the text will come as close as possible to the outline of the shape itself), top and bottom (which clears the horizontal space of the entire column of text around the image), *behind text* (which places the image on the layer of the document beneath the text; the text will overlap the image), and *in front of text* (this places the image on a layer of the document above the text, obscuring any text behind the image without displacing it). The use of the *square* setting tends to be the most legible in printed documents. You can also set the text wrap options in Word 2010 by selecting the image, activating the Page Layout ribbon, and choosing the *Wrap Text* icon.

OFFICE 2011 In Word 2011, you can change the text wrap settings by activating the context-sensitive Format Picture ribbon with the image selected and choosing *Wrap Text*.

To insert a caption for the image, you can right-click on the image and choose *Insert Caption* from the menu that appears. This will open the Insert Caption Dialog Box shown in Figure 4.3. You can add your caption text you want to display and how you want it labeled in the document (such as *Figure*). You can add a figure number (such as "Figure 1") to this caption as well; this is recommended if you have more than one image in your document or if it is a more formal type of document. It is also helpful to reference your figure by number in the text of the document, identifying the enhancement to the text it provides.

◀ FIGURE 4.3 Insert Caption Dialog Box in Microsoft Word 2010

There are a number of other formatting options that you have for images in Word. In addition to altering the Word Wrap properties, you can select the positioning of the image at predefined places on the page; when you use this option, it defaults to wrapping the text around the image instead of keeping the image in line with the text. You can also use the align menu to change the alignment of the image to the page or to other elements in the page. You can also send the image forward or backward on the layers of the document (similar to stacking paper clippings where the topmost element is visible in front). You can access these advanced image options from the Page Layout ribbon in Word 2010 and from the Format ribbon for Picture Tools whenever you have the image selected in the document.

OFFICE 2011 The context-sensitive Format Picture ribbon in Word 2011 is the equivalent of the Format ribbon for Picture Tools from Word 2010.

On the *Picture Styles* panel, you can select one of the predefined styles such as one that will make the image look like an old printout from a handheld instant camera. On the *Adjust* panel, you can click the *Corrections* icon to access a variety of tools to manipulate the overall display of the image content; this allows you to increase or decrease the brightness, contrast, and sharpness of the image. The original image will appear in the center of the options, and you can adjust it by clicking one of the options around it.

NOTE

There are a number of settings that can be used to correct a picture that is inserted into a document. There is a preview visualization of the effect whenever a transformation is selected, but the following list will help you understand these transformation terms:

- *Color Saturation*—This is the term for how pure the color is; the higher the saturation, the purer the color. The primary colors red, blue, and green are the purest (and most saturated) colors.

- *Color Tone*—The color tone is how light or dark the color is. Each color can produce a spectrum of tones. The tone value is relative, so the surrounding colors will affect the perception of the tone.

- *Sharpen and Soften*—This setting will vary how clear the differentiation is between neighboring pixels of the image. Sharpen will increase the differentiation by more strongly defining boundaries in the image. Soften will decrease the differentiation by blending together the colors of the image.

- *Brightness and Contrast*—Brightness is the threshold for the color level that registers as black; higher brightness means there are more colors allowed between pure white and pure black. Contrast is a measure of the spectrum of colors between pure white and pure black; higher contrast will generally show more granular detail of the image.

Selecting the *Color* icon in the *Adjust* panel (this is called *Recolor* in Word 2011) gives you options to select the color saturation, color tone, and recolor options, such as turning the image to grayscale. The Adjust panel has some other useful items as well. Along the right side of the Adjust panel are the following options:

- *Compress Picture* will reduce the file size of the Word document by sampling the picture to the necessary resolution for the screen.

- *Reset Picture* will undo all of the formatting you added since inserting the image at the beginning.

CROPPING *is the act of cutting off outer portions of an image or object. This is the digital equivalent of using scissors to cut off pieces of an image on paper.*

ASPECT RATIO *is the longer dimension of an object divided by the shorter dimension. This is the ratio that should be preserved whenever any changes are made to an object to avoid distortion. The aspect ratio of a standard 5 x 3 photograph is 5:3.*

You can also use the built-in tools to crop the image so that it focuses better on the subject. Cropping allows you to remove parts from the top, bottom, left, or right of the image that you do not want to display. When you select the *Crop* tool, you can use any of the grab points on the image and move them in toward the center to cut off portions of the image you do not want (this works like resizing the image in place when the crop tool is not active). You can see an example of the crop tool in action in Figure 4.4.

◀ FIGURE 4.4 Cropping an image

The *Crop* icon has some other useful options. For instance, you can crop your image to a drawing shape. Selecting any of these options will override your manual cropping. There are two more predefined options that you may find useful:

- *Crop to Fill* causes the entire image to be forced to the area defined by cropping. This will fill the cropped space with as much of the image as possible, cutting off only what is necessary to preserve the defined space.

- *Crop to Fit* causes the image to be forced in its entirety to the defined space. This may cause gaps in the display if no image information is available to match the space defined.

One thing you must remember with pictures is that you should always maintain the original aspect ratio of the image. Otherwise, faces and bodies will look stretched or pinched when you distort the image in only one direction. This not only looks bad, but it will also grab the attention of your audience in a negative way because their eyes will be drawn to the distortion instead of what you want them to see. To prevent this distortion, you can lock the aspect ratio. With the image selected, you can choose the *Expansion* icon in the *Size* panel of the Format ribbon for Picture Tools and make sure the Lock Aspect Ratio checkbox is selected in the Layout dialog box that appears.

OFFICE 2011 To lock the aspect ratio of an image in Word 2011, you can select the image and open the *Format Picture* ribbon that appears when the image is selected. On the *Size* panel, there is a checkbox linking the Height and Width entries; when this is checked, the aspect ratio is locked and when it is unchecked, the aspect ratio can be altered.

To add a screenshot in Word 2011, you must create the screenshot as an image (by using *Command+Shift+3* on a Mac to create a new screen capture as an image on the desktop) and then import it into Word as you would any other image file.

In Word 2010, you can also select the *Screenshot* icon on the *Insert* ribbon to place an image of the active programs and documents on your machine (other than the current document). When you see the dropdown list, you can simply select the window of which you wish to capture an image in your open document and click it with the mouse. The screenshot will act just like an image in the document itself.

Activity 13 – Screenshots and Image Editing

Create a new document and save it as *Activity13*. Insert a screen capture image from another open document into the *Activity13* document (if you do not have another document open, you can create a new one and practice your typing form to enter text into the document). Because screen captures are treated as images, you can modify your screen capture document just like an image. Use the Styles panel of the Image Formatting ribbon to frame the image. Then, crop the image so it does not contain the Word interface around the content, and turn the image to grayscale using the recolor options. Save your work.

4.2.2 Shapes

In Microsoft Word, you can add simple shapes to your document and format them as you would an image. These shapes are treated as objects within your document for which you can set the color and formatting as well as the placement and text wrap properties just as you saw with inserted images. To insert a shape in Word 2010, select the *Insert* ribbon and choose the *Shape* icon. You can see the menu of available shapes in Figure 4.5.

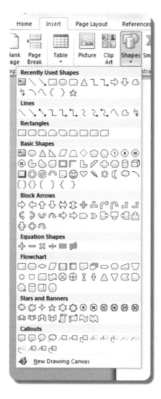

◀ **FIGURE 4.5** Shape Menu in Microsoft Word 2010

When you insert a shape, you are given a context-sensitive ribbon to adjust its format and properties. By default, the shape is set to layer above the text of your document, but you can adjust this property on the context-sensitive Format ribbon for Drawing Tools that appears whenever you select a shape. You can also change the fill, line, and any effects that you want to apply to the shape from this ribbon. In Word 2010, you can also use the Shape menu to insert a Drawing Canvas, which is configured as a document object in line with your text in which you can place multiple shapes and treat the entire canvas as a single object.

> **OFFICE 2011** In Word 2011, you can add a shape to your document by selecting the *Shape* icon on the *Home* ribbon; this is organized into categories instead of displaying all of the options at once.

In the Shape Styles panel on the context-sensitive Format ribbon for Drawing Tools, you will find options to set the shape to an existing style from the gallery, manipulate the shape fill color, change the width and style of the shape outline, or add effects to your shape similar to what can be added to text through the text effects menu. With the shape selected, right-clicking and selecting *Format Shape* will open a dialog box that lets you alter these properties for your shape; this is the same dialog box that you get by selecting the expansion icon on the Shape Styles panel in Word 2010.

Activity 14 – Adding and Formatting Shapes

For this activity, you will add three circles to your page using the shapes menu. You should format these so they are in front of the text in terms of layout, and they should fit inside of each other so that the largest is behind the middle size and the middle size is behind the smallest circle. Use the formatting ribbon for the shape objects and apply a different style to each one from the preset options. Create a shadow for each of these so that the shadow effect appears on the shape below it. Save your work as *Activity14*.

4.2.3 Clip Art

Because documents are often a visual medium for expression, it is common to add visual enhancements to attract attention to your document. The most common of these elements is clip art. Microsoft maintains an enormous repository of clip art images for you to use to enhance your documents. The handling of clip art is significantly different in Office 2010 and Office 2011, so separate sections have been provided to guide you on how to get the same results in either software suite as well as how to get additional clip art images from Microsoft online at *www.office.com*.

4.2.3.1 *Clip Art in Office 2010*

Adding clip art is fully integrated into the Word 2010 environment. You can add clip art by going to the *Images* panel in the *Insert* ribbon and selecting *Clip Art*. The Clip Art panel, shown in Figure 4.6, will appear on the side of your interface. This contains the search box and results of your keyword search for clip art images.

▼ **FIGURE 4.6** Clip Art panel in Office 2010

You can enter a keyword term in the *Search for* box and then select where you would like Word to search for the artwork. If you have just installed the program, you probably do not have too many options in your local folders, so you should include Office.com content in your searches whenever possible. Using this option requires you to be connected to the Internet. When you click on one of the results, you will see a menu of options.

The first choice is to insert the image into the document; this will place the image at the current cursor position and will treat the clip art as any other image-type object. You can also copy it to the clipboard so you can paste it into any location that accepts image data (inside the application or elsewhere) or you can select *Make Available Offline* to add it to your local media collection. If you choose this option from the list, you will be prompted to identify where you want to store the file.

4.2.3.2 *Clip Art in Office 2011*

Word 2011 has two options for directly inserting clip art into your document. The first is called the Clip Art Browser (which is shown in Figure 4.7); you can access this by clicking on the *Picture* icon on the *Home* ribbon to open the menu where you can select *Clip Art Browser*. This will open a panel of locally stored and indexed clip art images. If you want to place one of these images in the document, just click on the image and drag it where you would like for it to be placed.

◀ **FIGURE 4.7** Clip Art Browser in Office 2011

▼ **FIGURE 4.8** Microsoft Clip Art Gallery

The second option is to select *Clip Art* Gallery, which is also found on the menu under *Picture* in the *Home* ribbon. This option will launch a standalone application called Microsoft Clip Gallery, shown in Figure 4.8. Here you can search for a specific item you want or select categories. You can also configure your clip art categories, image classifications, and image tags and add new media to your collection using the Import button. To add one of the clip art items to your document at the current cursor position, select the graphic you want and click the *Insert* button.

4.2.3.3 *Getting Clip Art from Office.com*

You can download clips from Office.com (*www.office.com*) to add to your documents. Simply go to the Office.com site and select the *Images* tab. You will then be able to select a category and perform a search on existing clip art within the Office.com repository. If you do not find what you want in that category, you can use the navigation pane on the left-hand side to change the category or find results from all categories. If you visit the site using Microsoft Internet Explorer, the ActiveX® tools allow you to copy the image directly from the site to your system clipboard, as shown in Figure 4.9. You can then simply use the Paste function (or Ctrl-P) to paste the item into your document.

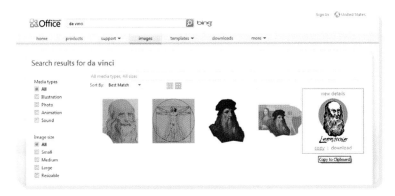

◀ **FIGURE 4.9** Clip Art options from Office.com using Internet Explorer

If you visit Office.com with an Internet browser other than Internet Explorer, you can still use the clip art that is offered, but you have to download it to a local folder on your machine to make use of it. You do this by clicking on the clip art graphic you want and selecting *Download*. You can add this image into your clip art repository by importing it into your media manager for your version of the Office suite.

4.2.4 SmartArt

SmartArt is a tool that is available in most of the Microsoft Office applications; it converts bulleted text (typically with two outline levels) into a professional looking graphic image. The styles and format for SmartArt are all predefined, but you can alter the color scheme to match your document and change certain style attributes. SmartArt graphics will expand to the size of the list that you type and most will handle multiple levels of organization and convert the list from outline to visual format.

To insert a SmartArt graphic in Word 2010, select the *Insert* ribbon and choose *SmartArt*; you can also use the SmartArt quick link within the content placeholder textbox. This will open the Choose a SmartArt Graphic dialog box shown in Figure 4.10. From here, you can select the type of graphic you want to create.

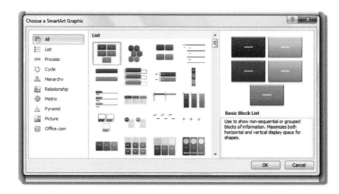

◀ **FIGURE 4.10** Choose a SmartArt Graphic Dialog Box from Word 2010

When you insert and select a SmartArt graphic, you are given a small window in which to type the text of your graphic in bulleted outline form. The outline level of the text determines where it is placed on the graphic.

OFFICE 2011 In Word 2011, you can open the SmartArt ribbon and simply choose the graphic type you want to use from the styles available.

When you select the SmartArt graphic, you will also see two context-sensitive ribbons containing tools for configuring SmartArt; these are the Design ribbon and the Format

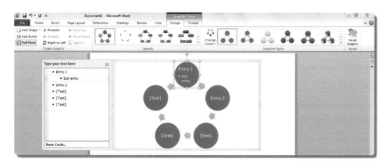

▲ **FIGURE 4.11** Example SmartArt text entry and SmartArt Tools Design Ribbon in Word 2010

ribbon. The Format ribbon is similar to the other formatting ribbons you have already seen; you can change the style of the drawing object within the SmartArt graphic selected and you can change the text formatting for any selected text. You can see an example of the active Design ribbon in Figure 4.11 (along with an example of the SmartArt text entry box).

The Design ribbon in PowerPoint 2010 contains several tools specific to SmartArt. The Create Graphic panel provides you with tools to add to your graphic or rearrange elements. The Add Shape icon allows you to insert new graphic objects for your SmartArt and select their placement (relative to the currently active bullet point or object). You can also show or hide the Text Pane (where you enter the information in the bulleted list) using the Text Pane icon. The Promote and Demote icons allow you to change the outline level of the selected bulleted text. Move Up and Move Down allow you to adjust the order of the objects (you can use these within the Text Pane as well). The Layouts panel allows you to change the SmartArt graphic within the same style you already chose for the current graphic; if you need to change your entire category, you will need to create a new SmartArt graphic.

NOTE

Some SmartArt graphics will have placeholder elements to add a picture. To add pictures, you can click the picture icon in the graphic or the picture icon next to the text in the Text Pane. You can edit the image and its properties with the same Format ribbon for Picture Tools that you use for any other image.

The Colors icon lets you adjust the color scheme of the graphic and SmartArt Styles selection allows you to make changes to the look and feel of the entire graphic at once. Reset Graphic sets the style back to the default settings. Finally, the Convert icon allows you to change the SmartArt graphic into regular drawing objects and text.

OFFICE 2011 These functions are all available in Word 2011, but the location of them is split between the SmartArt ribbon and the Text pane. The promotion, demotion, and ordering icons are all located on the Text pane while the formatting and style options remain on the SmartArt ribbon where you can change the layout of your graphic as well. The Text pane will appear as a small clickable icon beside the graphic when it is hidden so you can reactivate it from there.

4.2.5 Tables

A table is a great tool to manage information in your document. Tables do not have the computational power of the spreadsheets found in Microsoft Excel, but they can be effective for presenting a lot of information in a small space. For instance, you can use a table to present a list of values or results such as a comparison of different currencies shown in Figure 4.12. To insert a table like the one shown in Word 2010, select the *Insert* ribbon and choose the *Table* icon; this will allow you to select the number of entries you want the table to have in rows and columns. You can also select the *Insert Table* option from the submenu to get a dialog box allowing you to enter the number or rows and columns you wish to include.

▼ **FIGURE 4.12** Example Table showing Currency Comparison

World Currency Comparison (As of 5/16/2011)

Currency	In Euro (€)	Per Euro (€)
British Pound (£)	1.14	0.87
Australian Dollar ($)	0.75	1.33
US Dollar ($)	0.71	1.41
Chinese Yuan (¥)	0.11	9.21

Statistics taken from MSN Money
(http://moneycentral.msn.com/investor/market/exchangerates.aspx?selRegion=0&selCurrency=9)

When you add a table to your document in Word 2010, you will get two context-sensitive ribbons to format your table; these are the Design ribbon and the Layout ribbon for

Table Tools. You can select a style to format your table and choose whether you want to include elements like a header row from the Design ribbon. The Layout ribbon allows you to format the alignment of the text within each cell and add or remove rows.

> **OFFICE 2011** Word 2011 has a separate Tables ribbon which you can use to add tables to your document; this is available in the *New* icon where you can select the number or rows and columns or select the *Insert Table* option to define the table parameters manually. Word 2011 contains most of the formatting options on the existing Tables ribbon; when you add a table to your document, though, the context-sensitive Table Layout ribbon appears which contains commands for table cell management and alignment. The commands for adding borders and shading in Word 2011 are found on the Tables ribbon.

In the example shown, a header row is included and the table is formatted with the *Light Shading* option. Internal borders have also been added (via the *Borders* icon) to show the delineation between table cells. You can select entire rows or columns (or a combination of both) by clicking the mouse inside the starting table cell and dragging the cursor through the range you wish to select; this will leave the cells highlighted so you can easily adjust the format of all of the selected cells at once. Pressing the tab key will move the cursor from one cell to the next in a table; when the end of the table is reached, pressing the tab key will automatically create a new table row.

Activity 15 – Typing Tables

Create a new document called *Activity15*. Add a table to your document with three rows and three columns. Enter the values 1 through 9 by entering one value in each table cell. Use the tab key to move from cell to cell. What is the sequence of cells when you navigate by using the tab key? What happens when you press the tab key at the end of the table? Expand the table to accommodate the numbers from 1 to 15. Save your work.

4.2.6 Charts

Charts are another great way to present data quickly. A chart can show a lot of complex data in a single visualization that may take a significant amount of text to explain. In Word, charts are built from Excel spreadsheet documents. Do not be intimidated if you have never used Excel prior to this; everything you need for the chart is preformatted for you so all you have to do is enter the data you want to include.

You can insert a chart in Word 2010 by using the *Insert* ribbon and selecting *Chart*. This opens the Insert Chart dialog box shown in Figure 4.13. From this dialog box, you can select the overall type of chart you want to include and then choose the specific chart display you want to use in the panel on the right.

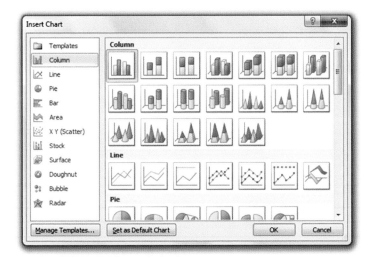

◀ **FIGURE 4.13** The Insert Chart Dialog Box in Word 2010

When you create a new chart, Word will open Microsoft Office Excel side by side with the Word document as shown in Figure 4.14. The data that will be used to construct your chart is displayed in the spreadsheet in Excel. You can resize the data used in the chart by dragging the blue indicator in Excel (which encloses the data which is used by the chart) to reduce the number of data points or increase it. Some chart types will have multiple horizontal values as well, which can also be resized in the same way.

▼ **FIGURE 4.14** Chart Data Entry

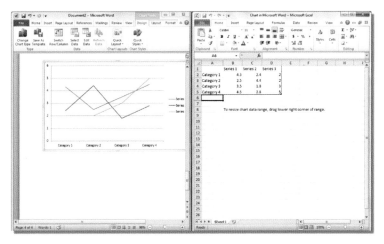

When you close the chart data, your Word document should return to its former window size and you can see the three context-sensitive Chart Tools ribbons that appear whenever the chart is selected. The Format ribbon that appears here should be familiar to you by now; this allows you to set the text effects and shape effects of the different chart elements. For instance, you can add a shadow to the data line you have created. You can also add text effects to the chart information, but you should not sacrifice clarity and readability to add effects.

The Design ribbon for Chart Tools (which is included in the standard Charts ribbon in Word 2011) allows you to set the look and feel of the chart. There are a number of preset layouts and styles that you can select to display your data from the Chart Layouts panel and the Chart Styles panel. You can also use the *Edit Data* icon of the Data panel to open the Excel spreadsheet to make any changes to the data on which the chart is based.

The Layout ribbon for Chart Tools (or the Chart Layout ribbon in Word 2011) allows you to change the display elements of the chart. You can primarily change how much visual information is displayed on the chart using this ribbon. For example, you could select the *Legend* icon and choose *None* to remove the series name from a chart.

You can alter the font size for any of the text elements of the chart using the Home ribbon. You can also change the size of the chart manually by dragging the grip points on the corners and midpoints just as you can for any other object in Word.

4.2.7 Symbols

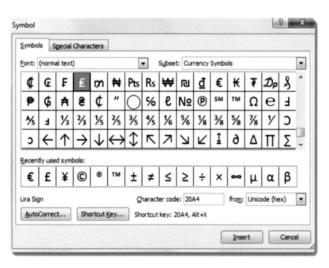

▲ FIGURE 4.15 Symbol selection in Microsoft Word 2010

Symbols are substitutions for a text character that cannot be found on a regular keyboard. Examples of this include foreign currency, copyright symbols, and symbols commonly used in mathematics. To insert a symbol in Microsoft Word 2010, you can select the *Insert* ribbon and click the *Symbol* icon. A list of the common symbols will appear, including common currency symbols. You can also select the More Symbols option to get a dialog box which allows you to select symbols from different languages. You can see an example of this dialog box being used to insert the symbol for British pounds in Figure 4.15.

In addition to currency symbols and letters from other alphabets, there are a few unique fonts that contain symbol libraries instead of text characters. These fonts include *Wingdings* and *Webdings*. You can use the font selection box to choose these symbols to see what is available from them. You can also select the subset selection box to choose technical symbols or foreign alphabets that do not have representation on your own keyboard. When you have finished selecting the symbol you want, click the *Insert* button to place it in line with your text.

OFFICE 2011 To add symbols in Word 2011, you can select the Insert menu, choose Symbol, and then open the Symbol Browser to find the symbol you wish to add.

4.2.8 Equations

Microsoft Word has a library of symbols that allow you to construct equations within your document. To add an equation in Word 2010, you can select the *Insert* ribbon and choose the *Equation* symbol. When you choose the Equation symbol, a dropdown list will appear with several common equations that you can insert and modify or you can choose *Insert New Equation* to create your own.

OFFICE 2011 In Word 2011, the icon for *Equation* is located in the Document Elements ribbon. When you select an equation, the Equation Tools ribbon which chains off of the Document Elements ribbon is used to edit and alter the equation.

When you insert an equation in Word and click within it, you will get a context-sensitive ribbon for constructing and editing equations. In Word 2010, this is the Design ribbon for Equation Tools. You can see an example of the ribbon and an example equation in Figure 4.16.

Equations are treated as a unique object in your document; by default, the equation is given its own line in the document. The context-sensitive ribbon

▼ **FIGURE 4.16** Equation example in Word 2010

for equations contains all of the common symbols associated with mathematics which you can simply click to insert. It also contains a variety of structures that can be used to format your equation such as *Fraction, Script, Radical, Integral*, etc.

If you click on any of these icons, you will see a dropdown list from which you can select the elements and formatting you need for your equation. The structures which you can select from these lists contain small boxes surrounded by dotted lines; these are the building blocks of your equation and you can think of the box as containing a set of parentheses in mathematics. Whatever you type inside of the box will become part of the structure. You can also nest structures within each other to form complex equations.

The other feature of the ribbon you should note is the ability to switch your equation from *Professional* to *Linear* format. Professional is the actual arrangement of symbols that you would see in a mathematics course or textbook; Linear is the arrangement of the symbols and elements in a single line. The Linear format will automatically add parentheses to separate elements of the equation that are implied by the structures in the Professional display. When you click the outer box around an equation, you will get a dropdown list that allows you to select the formatting you wish to use.

4.2.9   Additional Document Enhancements

In addition to the media elements you have seen so far, there are several quick enhancements you can add to your document to adjust its visual style or utilize callouts beyond the main text of your document in word processing. These include:

- *Text Boxes*–A text box in Microsoft Word is a standalone object containing keyboard entered text; it behaves inside the document similarly to the images you previously inserted. You can set the text box to have the same text wrapping properties of an image. This makes it beneficial if you want to add a quote or other note to your text to call it out to the attention of your reader; these can enhance the visual style of the document without the use of graphics. Microsoft Word 2010 has several options for text boxes that are available by choosing the *Text Box* icon on the Insert ribbon; you can choose a standard text box and format it yourself or use one of the predefined options available in the list. In Microsoft Word 2011, you can add either a horizontal text box or a vertical text box to your document from the Text Box icon on the Home ribbon. You can apply whatever formatting you like to the resulting text box, but there are no predefined options in Word 2011 as there are in Word 2010.

- *Drop Cap*–This is a visual enhancement to a paragraph of text that can apply to the heading or first line of a paragraph. It sets the first letter of the text as an independent text box with a large print size that can be resized and formatted independently of the rest of the text. It is used to call attention to the paragraph and attract the eye of the viewer to start reading the text that follows. This is sometimes used in newspaper or magazine articles as a style choice. To activate this in Word 2010, select the text you want to enhance and choose the *Drop Cap* icon on the Insert ribbon and select whether you want it dropped into the paragraph of the text or into the margin. In Word 2011, you can add this by highlighting the text to which you want the effect to apply and then selecting the *Format* menu and choosing *Drop Cap*.

• *Hyperlink*–A hyperlink is a reference to another document or external location (mostly on the Web). Whenever you type a Web address and press the spacebar at the end of it, Word will automatically create the address as a hyperlink within the document. You can right-click the hyperlink and select the *Remove Hyperlink* option if you want to get rid of the external reference. You can tell a hyperlink in Word by the blue color and underline as well as the change in the mouse pointer icon when you hover over the text. To activate a hyperlink in a Word document, you must press a modifier key (either the control key on a Windows machine or the command key on a Mac) and click the hyperlink with the mouse; if you are clicking a link to a Web site or online resource, this will open your default Internet browser to access the content. If you want to manually insert a hyperlink into your document (which is useful if you want the displayed text to be different than the address to which you are linking), you can select the Hyperlink icon (on the Insert ribbon in Word 2010). This will open a dialog box which allows you to enter the text to display and link to the resource of your choice.

Activity 16 – Hyperlinks

Create a new document titled *Activity16*. Enter five Web sites you commonly use as text in the document. When you press the spacebar after the Web address, it should automatically create the hyperlink to the site. Now add another Web site using the Hyperlink icon on the ribbon interface. Enter the title of the Web site as the text to display and the URL of the Web site as the destination for the link. How do you remove hyperlinks from text in your document? Remove every other hyperlink so that just the address or name of the Web site remains. Save your work.

4.3 KEYBOARDING IV

In this lesson, you will learn to type the number keys with proper typing form. At the end of this lesson, you will be able to type any alphanumeric value correctly. This is the first time that your fingers have to cross more than one row to reach keys, so it may take time and practice to get used to the motion and be able to return back to the proper home row keys. You should still only be moving one finger per hand at a time if you are practicing correct typing form.

4.3.1 Number Keys

The number keys are the highest row of keys on the standardized layout of the keyboard (the function keys are higher, but they are specialized keys and vary from keyboard to keyboard). Your fingers will stretch high and to the left to reach these keys. Each of the number keys also has a punctuation symbol that will be typed whenever they are depressed

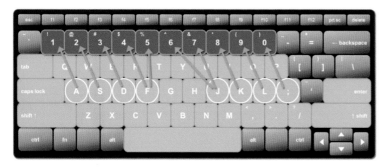

in combination with the shift key. You should note that the caps lock key does not change the number keys to their associated symbols; the shift key must be depressed to cause the number keys to type their associated symbols instead. You can see a map of the number keys and the associated finger motion necessary to reach them in Figure 4.17.

▲ FIGURE 4.17 Number key map and associated motion

4.3.2 Control and Alt Keys

The control and alt keys are called modifier keys, because, like the shift key, they do not type characters directly. Instead, they alter the behavior of the keys that are struck while they are depressed. The control key (or its equivalent, command key for Mac) is used to activate shortcuts to common tasks in combination with other keys, such as pressing both the control key and the A key to select all text in a document. A variety of control key combinations are used in formatting text and utilizing commands from the File menu. The alt key is also used to modify the behavior of the other key or keys with which it is struck. The most common application of the alt key is in the *Ctrl+Alt+Delete* combination used to access the Task Manager in the Windows environment.

4.3.3 Keyboarding Lessons 46–60

By the time you have completed the following lessons, you will have practiced all of the number keys and modifier keys highlighted in dark blue in Figure 4.18. You should concentrate in these lessons on learning the hand motion necessary to reach the keys without looking at them; you should also concentrate on keeping your hands over the home row keys and

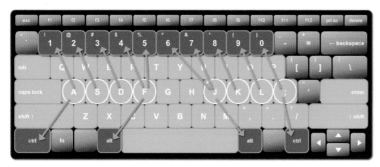

stretching your fingers individually to reach the number row. It may take some practice to reach these keys directly and skip the top row keys, but it will improve your speed and form if you can bypass the top row and strike the number keys directly. The more practice you have with this, the better your form will become and the more your speed will increase.

▲ FIGURE 4.18 Keyboarding IV keys and associated hand motion mapping

The software included with the text and available online at *www.keyboardingandbeyond* *.com* will time the lessons and alert you to any mistakes made while entering the text for these exercises. Because this is practice, you should feel free to redo these lessons and activities as much as you need to improve your performance and form.

Lesson 4.1 The 7 Key

In this lesson, you will use your right index finger to press the 7 key as well as using the keys you have already learned. You should focus on your form and keep your hands positioned over the home row keys while you move only the necessary finger to strike the keys you wish to type. The software will count up the amount of time it takes for you to complete the task, so you can take as long as you need and retry the exercise to improve your time.

Type the following:

```
7777 jjjj 7777 77jj jj77 j77j 7jj7 7&&7 &77& j7&&7j ju7j
7777 jjjj 7777 77jj jj77 j77j 7jj7 7&&7 &77& j7&&7j ju7j
7, 7, & 7 is a lot. There are 7 dwarves present here.
77 & 7 is more. There are 77 houses in this row.
777 is even more. There are 777 cents in your pocket.
7777 jjjj 7777 77jj jj77 j77j 7jj7 7&&7 &77& j7&&7j ju7j
```

Lesson 4.2 The 8 Key

In this lesson, you will use your right middle finger to press the 8 key as well as using the keys you have already learned. You should focus on your form and keep your hands positioned over the home row keys while you move only the necessary finger to strike the keys you wish to type. The software will count up the amount of time it takes for you to complete the task, so you can take as long as you need and retry the exercise to improve your time.

Type the following:

```
8888 kkkk 8888 88kk kk88 k88k 8kk8 8**8 *88* k8**8k ki8k
8888 kkkk 8888 88kk kk88 k88k 8kk8 8**8 *88* k8**8k ki8k
88 is more than 78. 888 is more than 878. 8 is more than 7.
7 * 8 is more than 8. 88 is less than 78 * 8.
88,887 is less than 88,888. 88.8 is more than 88.7.
8888 kkkk 8888 88kk kk88 k88k 8kk8 8**8 *88* k8**8k ki8k
```

Lesson 4.3 The 9 Key

In this lesson, you will use your right ring finger to press the 9 key as well as using the keys you have already learned. You should focus on your form and keep your hands positioned over the home row keys while you move only the necessary finger to strike the keys you wish to type. The software will count up the amount of time it takes for you to complete the task, so you can take as long as you need and retry the exercise to improve your time.

Type the following:

```
9999 llll 9999 9911 1199 1991 9119 9((9 (99( 19((91 lo9l
9999 llll 9999 9911 1199 1991 9119 9((9 (99( 19((91 lo9l
9 is more than 8. 99 is more than 87. 99,999 is more than 9.
9.99 is more than 9. 97 is less than 98. 998 is more than 997.
9 is less than ten and more than eight. 9 is a high digit.
9999 llll 9999 9911 1199 1991 9119 9((9 (99( 19((91 lo9l
```

Lesson 4.4 The 0 Key

In this lesson, you will use your right pinky finger to press the 0 key as well as using the keys you have already learned. You should focus on your form and keep your hands positioned over the home row keys while you move only the necessary finger to strike the keys you wish to type. The software will count up the amount of time it takes for you to complete the task, so you can take as long as you need and retry the exercise to improve your time.

Type the following:

```
0000 ;;;; 0000 00;; ;;00 ;00; 0;;0 0))0 )00) ;0))0; ;p0;
0000 ;;;; 0000 00;; ;;00 ;00; 0;;0 0))0 )00) ;0))0; ;p0;
0 is less than 7. 90 is more than 80. 9,000,000 is a lot.
09 is equal to 9. 70, 80, and 90 are even numbers.
(90) (70) (7,8) (8,9) (0,0) (0,7) (7,8,9)
0000 ;;;; 0000 00;; ;;00 ;00; 0;;0 0))0 )00) ;0))0; ;p0;
```

Lesson 4.5 The 6 Key

In this lesson, you will use your right index finger to press the 6 key as well as using the keys you have already learned. You should focus on your form and keep your hands positioned over the home row keys while you move only the necessary finger to strike the keys you wish to type. The software will count up the amount of time it takes for you to complete the task, so you can take as long as you need and retry the exercise to improve your time.

Type the following:

```
6666 jjjj 6666 66jj jj66 j66j 6jj6 6^^6 ^66^ j6^^6j jy6j
6666 jjjj 6666 66jj jj66 j66j 6jj6 6^^6 ^66^ j6^^6j jy6j
6^6 is more than 9. 67 & 8 is much less than 9^9.
6 < 7 < 8 < 9 & 9 > 8 > 7 > 6; (0,0) is left of (7,7).
67 < 68 < 69 < 76 < 77 < 78 < 80 < 99 < 909 < 979 < 9669
6666 jjjj 6666 66jj jj66 j66j 6jj6 6^^6 ^66^ j6^^6j jy6j
```

Lesson 4.6 Right Hand Numbers and Symbols

For this lesson, you will use the number keys assigned to your right hand along with their shifted symbol counterparts and the spacebar, shift, and enter keys. You should try to focus on tapping the keys lightly so that you strike them just hard enough to type the character and then release pressure on the key. The software will count up the amount of time it takes for you to complete the task, so you can take as long as you need and retry the exercise to improve your time.

Type the following:

```
6678 7789 8890 0987 0876 6670 6680 9908 9976 0998
6678 7789 8890 0987 0876 6670 6680 9908 9976 0998
(8) (9) (0) (6) (77)^(88) & (88)^7^99 * (99870)^6
6*7*8*9*0 * 0(9)(8)(7)(6) & 9(8)(7)(6)^6&7*8*(9)
6*7*8*9*0 * 0(9)(8)(7)(6) & 9(8)(7)(6)^6&7*8*(9)
(8) (9) (0) (6) (77)^(88) & (88)^7^99 * (99870)^6
```

Lesson 4.7 The 4 Key

In this lesson, you will use your left index finger to press the 4 key as well as using the keys you have already learned. You should focus on your form and keep your hands positioned over the home row keys while you move only the necessary finger to strike the keys you wish to type. The software will count up the amount of time it takes for you to complete the task, so you can take as long as you need and retry the exercise to improve your time.

Type the following:

```
4444 ffff 4444 44ff ff44 f44f 4ff4 4$$4 $44$ f4$$4f fr4f
4444 ffff 4444 44ff ff44 f44f 4ff4 4$$4 $44$ f4$$4f fr4f
$4.00 < $6.00, $4.09 < $4.90, & $7.69 < $8.99
$400,999.89, $67,998.09, $47,896.67, & $9,999,999.99
$4.00 < $6.00, $4.09 < $4.90, & $7.69 < $8.99
4444 ffff 4444 44ff ff44 f44f 4ff4 4$$4 $44$ f4$$4f fr4f
```

Lesson 4.8 The 3 Key

In this lesson, you will use your left middle finger to press the 3 key as well as using the keys you have already learned. You should focus on your form and keep your hands positioned over the home row keys while you move only the necessary finger to strike the keys you wish to type. The software will count up the amount of time it takes for you to complete the task, so you can take as long as you need and retry the exercise to improve your time.

Type the following:

```
3333 dddd 3333 33dd dd33 d33d 3dd3 3##3 #33# d3##3d de3d
3333 dddd 3333 33dd dd33 d33d 3dd3 3##3 #33# d3##3d de3d
34,000.00 #34 #78 #67 #99 (#67,#89) (3*(9*0))
#3 is the bus you want. #34 will take you to Brooklyn.
```

```
#4 will take you to New Jersey. #434 costs $3.99 for one way.
#4 is a bad pencil; half of it is a good pencil choice.
3333 dddd 3333 33dd dd33 d33d 3dd3 3##3 #33# d3##3d de3d
```

Lesson 4.9 The 2 Key

In this lesson, you will use your left ring finger to press the 2 key as well as using the keys you have already learned. You should focus on your form and keep your hands positioned over the home row keys while you move only the necessary finger to strike the keys you wish to type. The software will count up the amount of time it takes for you to complete the task, so you can take as long as you need and retry the exercise to improve your time.

Type the following:

```
2222 ssss 2222 22ss ss22 s22s 2ss2 2@@2 @22@ s2@@2s sw2s
2222 ssss 2222 22ss ss22 s22s 2ss2 2@@2 @22@ s2@@2s sw2s
tommy2@todotoday.com suzieQ@24hourmaids.com jr.richie@rich.com
#2 is a good pencil choice. The #2 train is late.
It should arrive at 2:00 PM but it is 2:22 and it is not here.
2:00 is when I take my tea. Noon is a better lunch than 2:22.
There are 200 rooms in the hotel at 22nd St. and 2nd Ave.
2222 ssss 2222 22ss ss22 s22s 2ss2 2@@2 @22@ s2@@2s sw2s
```

Lesson 4.10 The 1 Key

In this lesson, you will use your left pinky finger to press the 1 key as well as using the keys you have already learned. You should focus on your form and keep your hands positioned over the home row keys while you move only the necessary finger to strike the keys you wish to type. The software will count up the amount of time it takes for you to complete the task, so you can take as long as you need and retry the exercise to improve your time.

NOTE When using the exclamation point (!) at the end of a sentence, you should space after it as you would with a period or full stop character.

Type the following:

```
1111 aaaa 1111 11aa aa11 a11a 1aa1 1!!1 !11! a1!!1a aq1a
1111 aaaa 1111 11aa aa11 a11a 1aa1 1!!1 !11! a1!!1a aq1a
I have $1.00 in change. That is $0.10 * 10!
He said 99,999,999! That is a lot of $1.00 bills!
Meet at 1:00 sharp! There is no room for 1:01 or 1:02!
1111 aaaa 1111 11aa aa11 a11a 1aa1 1!!1 !11! a1!!1a aq1a
```

Lesson 4.11 The 5 Key

In this lesson, you will use your left index finger to press the 5 key as well as using the keys you have already learned. You should focus on your form and keep your hands positioned over the home row keys while you move only the necessary finger to strike the keys you wish to type. The software will count up the amount of time it takes for you to complete the task, so you can take as long as you need and retry the exercise to improve your time.

Type the following:

```
5555 ffff 5555 55ff ff55 f55f 5ff5 5%%5 %55% f5%%5f fr5f
5555 ffff 5555 55ff ff55 f55f 5ff5 5%%5 %55% f5%%5f fr5f
55% is a majority share! I will rake 5% of the leaves!
50% for each is 50/50. $0.05 is 5% of $1.00.
1 < 2 < 3 < 4 < 5 < 6 < 7 < 8 < 9 < 10 < 55,555
5555 ffff 5555 55ff ff55 f55f 5ff5 5%%5 %55% f5%%5f fr5f
```

Lesson 4.12 Left Hand Numbers and Symbols

In this lesson, you will practice using each of the keys assigned to your left hand. The only other keys you should use are the enter key, shift key, and spacebar with your right hand. The software will count up the amount of time it takes for you to complete the task, so you can take as long as you need and retry the exercise to improve your time. You should focus on your form and reaching the row of number keys as effectively and smoothly as possible.

Type the following:

```
1123 2244 3345 5543 5224 5112 2113 4113 5123 4123 5324
1123 2244 3345 5543 5224 5112 2113 4113 5123 4123 5324
#213 $4321 4532% 12345! 5543% 1% $2 #4 5! 345 215 4312
234 443 5543 #2 #4 5% 34% 55% 15% 3451221345 54321 54321 12354
234 443 5543 #2 #4 5% 34% 55% 15% 3451221345 54321 54321 12354
#213 $4321 4532% 12345! 5543% 1% $2 #4 5! 345 215 4312
```

Lesson 4.13 Number Key Practice and Review

In this lesson, you will practice typing all of the number keys and their shifted symbol counterparts. The timer for this exercise counts down, so you should try to gain enough proficiency and speed to complete the exercise in its entirety before the timer runs out. Because you are still learning, you should repeat this exercise as necessary until you are able to complete it with time left on the timer!

Type the following:

```
#22 77% $49999 * 77^6 * 4% (99)99(88)88(77)77(66)66
5^6 & 77*8 & (99)(11)! (11)11(22)22(33)33(44)44(55)55
998 887 776 665 554 443 332 221 110 009 @23
```

```
998 887 776 665 554 443 332 221 110 009 @23
#22 77% $49999 * 77^6 * 4% (99)99(88)88(77)77(66)66
5^6 & 77*8 & (99)(11)! (11)11(22)22(33)33(44)44(55)55
```

Lesson 4.14 Alphanumeric Typing Review

In this lesson, you will practice typing all of the keys you have learned so far. This exercise focuses on combining the use of numbers and alphabetic characters common in typing units of value and measurements. The timer for this exercise counts down, so you should try to gain enough proficiency and speed to complete the exercise in its entirety before the timer runs out. Because you are still learning, you should repeat this exercise as necessary until you are able to complete it with time left on the timer!

Type the following:

```
44 ft. 32 in. 54 qt. 3 tbsp. 67 tsp. 77 mph.
55 cm. 45 mm. 12 oz. 16 mg. 99 kph. 22 lb.
Coordinates (0,0) point to the answer!
I use 77% of my time wisely. Another 20% is wasted.
(8,8) has equal x and y. 7^6^4 * 8 is a large number.
(99.99 * 8^7)*6^3 is a lot! What is 77/11?
How much is enough? $99,999,999.98.
```

Lesson 4.15 Timed Typing Practice

In this lesson, you will practice typing all of the keys you have learned so far. The timer for this exercise counts down, so you should try to gain enough proficiency and speed to complete the exercise in its entirety before the timer runs out. Because you are still learning, you should repeat this exercise as necessary until you are able to complete it with time left on the timer!

Type the following:

```
There are 125,000 people in this town. Tuition costs roughly
$15,000.00 per year for students out of state and $7,500 for
students who reside in the state to attend one of the 17
colleges and universities present. There are 42,000 students
here, which is over a 33% student population! This is
considered a college town by most standards, but the other 66%
of the population (working and retired) disagree with that
assessment. The primary occupation here is professor or
administration within the secondary education environment!
```

CHAPTER SUMMARY

This chapter introduced you to the various media elements that can be added to a word processing document to enhance the visual appeal and clarity of the document. Images and their associated captions are common additions to reports and clip art is typically used in informal documents to attract attention. Tables and charts can be used to effectively and clearly present information that would require lengthy text to explain with the same clarity; these can be great tools for visually presenting information in a more effective manner. There are a variety of options available for modifying the presentation of a word processing document to fit its purpose and audience, and Word allows for the inclusion of these elements. When you have completed the keyboarding lessons in this chapter, you should be able to type any alphanumeric value and switch between lowercase and uppercase letters and the numeric and symbolic characters of the number keys. The only remaining keys on the common QWERTY keyboard that remain for the next lesson are a few punctuation keys.

CHAPTER KNOWLEDGE CHECK

1 Objects such as images and shapes in your document can be manipulated using the _____ of the object.

- ○ **A.** Image Color
- ○ **B.** Cross Reference
- ○ **C.** Grip Points
- ○ **D.** Clip Art

2 A chart in your document is powered by _____ and interprets the data for display in Word.

- ○ **A.** Equation Editor
- ○ **B.** PowerPoint
- ○ **C.** Access
- ○ **D.** Excel
- ○ **E.** Outlook

3 Using _____ is a way to create a professional quality image quickly by entering text in a bulleted list for visual interpretation.

○ **A.** Clip Art

○ **B.** SmartArt

○ **C.** Shapes

○ **D.** Screenshots

4 Equations are constructed by using building block patterns that equate to parts of the equation in ____.

○ **A.** Another document

○ **B.** Parentheses

○ **C.** Bullet points

○ **D.** All of the above

○ **E.** None of the above

5 You can add tables to your document in any size, but you cannot add to the number of rows in the table once it is placed.

○ **A.** True

○ **B.** False

6 The tab key will move from cell to cell in a table placed in Word.

○ **A.** True

○ **B.** False

7 The width of a column in a table in Word is fixed and cannot be adjusted once placed.

○ **A.** True

○ **B.** False

8 The two versions of displaying equations are _____.

○ **A.** Linear and Radial

○ **B.** Radial and Professional

○ **C.** Casual and Professional

○ **D.** Linear and Professional

○ **E.** None of the above

9 _____ is the process of cutting off parts of the image from view.

- ○ **A.** Sizing
- ○ **B.** Saturation
- ○ **C.** Cropping
- ○ **D.** Slicing
- ○ **E.** None of the above

10 The aspect ratio is the _____ in an image or shape.

- ○ **A.** Relationship between the height and width
- ○ **B.** Ratio of how much the dimensions are stretched
- ○ **C.** Ratio of how much the size of the image has changed
- ○ **D.** The color saturation versus the original hue
- ○ **E.** All of the above
- ○ **F.** None of the above

CHAPTER EXERCISES

1. Arrows are a kind of shape that behaves differently from most. With an arrow, you can attach one or both ends of the arrow shape to one of the grab points around the edge of the shape (that can typically be used to modify the shape). When it is attached, the grab point to which it is attached will run red and moving the shape will move the arrow with it. Create three circles in a document and attach one of the arrow types to link each of the circles to the other circles. Spread them out in a triangle formation on the document while the arrows are attached. How do the arrows behave when one end of the arrow is disconnected from the shape and the attached shape is moved? Compare the behavior of the three types of arrows.

2. Create a document containing a SmartArt graphic for organizing a list of foods you like to eat; this should include sub-entries in the diagram as well. Create a list of at least five items with two of them containing at least two sub-entries. Format the SmartArt and then use the command to break it into text boxes and shapes. How does this change the behavior of the object as a whole? Which format is easier to edit and which format gives you more control over the object?

3. Create a table within a document to track the temperature high and low for five days (you can get this information from a weather service). Format the table with a header row containing city name and the days of the week for which the temperature is tracked and choose a table style. Add the weather information for another city to your table. Merge the cells so that the city name spans both the temperature high and low for each city. What types of data are suited for display in a table?

4. Create a line chart in your document. Add at least 8 data points of money over time to plot the line. Adjust the display so the series name is not displayed but the chart title is given along with the units and measurements for the axes. When would you suggest it is better to use a chart than a table for presenting information succinctly?

5. Use *office.com* to find two pieces of clip art for the same subject (such as school or business): one should be a photograph and the other should be an illustration. Add both of them to your document and describe the process of searching for the clip art images and the differences in how your search worked to find each image. What features of Word or *office.com* allowed you to import and manage the clip art images?

6. Use the equation editor in Word to construct Einstein's equation for relating matter and energy ($E=mc^2$). Use the building blocks to create the equation and display it in both Professional and Linear format. What is the difference between the two display modes? Explain the tools you used to construct the equation.

7. *WordArt* is a special type of display for creating unique text effects in a document. Prior to the extensive Text Effects menu for formatting text, using WordArt was the only way to create professional text effects in a document. Create a document heading using the WordArt menu. Try to recreate it using the styles and text effects menus available for standard text. Are the results the same? Which of the processes is easier or are the two processes equivalent?

8. Create a new document in Word and save it to your computer as *MyObject*. Add content to your *MyObject* document and save it. Using Word's Object

insertion (on the Insert ribbon in Word 2010 and the Insert menu and Object choice in Word 2011) add the *MyObject* object to your document. How is the content added to the new document? When would this functionality be useful?

9. Create a new document and add a table to it with 7 rows and 3 columns. The columns should be: Symbol, Name, and Meaning. Now add one symbol to each row using the Symbol insertion ability in Word. For the name entry for each symbol, give the text description of the symbol name. For the meaning entry, describe its usage. Format the table using the table styles formatting commands. Add a header to the document and save your work.

10. Create a document in Word and add content to it by practicing your typing skills. In a new Word document, add a screen capture of the other document and format it for optimum printing on a black and white printer. Add a frame to the image and add a caption describing what the image displays. Crop the bottom off of the Word interface while keeping the content and the ribbon interface. In the text of the Word document, describe how you optimized the display for black and white printing.

CHAPTER REVIEW QUESTIONS

1. Give an example where a table would summarize data better than using a text explanation other than the ones presented in the chapter. Would this data also lend itself to being displayed in a chart? Which one is a better data display and why?

2. When should clip art be used in a document to enhance its display? Give two examples in which using clip art would be beneficial and two examples where it would be detrimental to the document display and purpose. What is the distinction that helps decide whether it should or should not be used?

3. What are the benefits of including hyperlinks in your document? What are two examples where hyperlinks would be a benefit and what are two circumstances in which hyperlinks would be a drawback? What is the difference that defines whether hyperlinks should be used or not?

4. Word allows you to include a special *Object* in your document, which is either an included file or a reference to another file. These files can contain any information from your operating system's file structure. When would it be a good idea to include such objects in your document? When would it be a bad idea to include them? What precautions should you take before opening a file included in a document as an object?

5. When you are referencing text from another document, you could either copy and paste the text or use a screenshot of the text in your document (assuming the content is your own and you are allowed to copy and paste the text); what are the pros and cons of both approaches to including the external text in your document?

6. The productivity software PowerPoint that is part of the Microsoft Office suite allows you to add video and sound to your documents but Word does not support this inclusion (other than Word's Object inclusion which shows only an icon and name). Why would these types of media be excluded from a Word document?

7. Drop Cap is a type of emphasis that was placed on the first letter of an article in a newspaper, but it is largely unused today. What is the history and proper usage of the Drop Cap emphasis?

8. When is the use of a cover page in a report necessary and when is it best left out of the document? Is it always wise to use a cover page template in Word or are there circumstances in which you should create your own cover page without the added graphics?

9. What are the benefits and dangers of using specific fonts as substitutions for symbols (such as Webdings or Wingdings) in a document? What are the alternatives for creating symbols in a document?

10. When would you suggest using the Hyperlink icon to add Web links to your document to give alternate text to the link instead of just using the automatic creation of a hyperlink when you press the spacebar after the end of the Web address? What are the benefits and drawbacks of this type of hyperlink inclusion? Consider the nature of the Web and links operating within documents in your answer.

KEYBOARDING DRILLS

1. Type as much of the following as you can in thirty seconds; try to complete the exercise before the timer runs out if possible. You can use the included software to track your time, speed, and errors:

```
There are 50 states here. 48 of them are joined, that is 96%
of the individual states joined together.
If only 99.99% was right, the rest would be wrong.
2^4 > 2*4 and 55% of $10.00 is greater than 500 cents.
If the train at platform #4 goes 88 mph heading east and the
train at platform #3 goes 55 mph heading west, the trains will
never cross each other.
99 > 88 > 76 > 54 > 44 > 32 > 21 > 10 > 9 > 7 > 6 > 4 > 3
```

2. Type as much of the following as you can in thirty seconds; try to complete the exercise before the timer runs out if possible. You can use the included software to track your time, speed, and errors:

```
(8,8) has equal x and y. 7^6^4 * 8 is a large number.
(99.99 * 8^7)*6^3 is a lot! What is 77/11?
998 887 776 665 554 443 332 221 110 009 @23
#22 77% $49999 * 77^6 * 4% (99)99(88)88(77)77(66)66
0 is less than 7. 90 is more than 80. 9,000,000 is a lot.
09 is equal to 9. 70, 80, and 90 are even numbers.
```

3. Track your time and focus on your form to type the following with as few errors as possible. You can use the included software to track your time, speed, and errors:

```
34,000.00 #34 #78 #67 #99 (#67,#89) (3*(9*0))
#3 is the bus you want. #34 will take you to Brooklyn.
6^6 is more than 9. 67 & 8 is much less than 9^9.
6 < 7 < 8 < 9 & 9 > 8 > 7 > 6; (0,0) is left of (7,7).
67 < 68 < 69 < 76 < 77 < 78 < 80 < 99 < 909 < 979 < 9669
2:00 is when I take my tea. Noon is a better lunch than 2:22.
```

4. Track your time and focus on your form to type the following with as few errors as possible. You can use the included software to track your time, speed, and errors:

```
234 443 5543 #2 #4 5% 34% 55% 15% 3451221345 54321 54321 12354
234 443 5543 #2 #4 5% 34% 55% 15% 3451221345 54321 54321 12354
#213 $4321 4532% 12345! 5543% 1% $2 #4 5! 345 215 4312
(90) (70) (7,8) (8,9) (0,0) (0,7) (7,8,9)
6*7*8*9*0 * 0(9)(8)(7)(6) & 9(8)(7)(6)^6&7*8*(9)
234 443 5543 #2 #4 5% 34% 55% 15% 3451221345 54321 54321 12354
```

5. Type as much of the following as you can in one minute. You can use the included software to track your time, speed, and errors:

```
999 980 098 877 766 564 342 213 435 876 567 908 809 812
122 322 455 633 733 822 933 099 899 899 799 699 599 499
$12.00 $14.50 $16.80 $18.90 $19.99 $21.99 $33.22 $55.00
33% 55% 67% 45% 21% 10% 15% 19% 33% 55% 67% 45% 21% 10%
0.01 0.03 0.05 1.02 1.05 1.09 9.09 8.12 8.15 5.76 6.78
556 764 897 901 203 456 897 678 901 202 304 507 897 987
453 378 987 654 234 098 123 456 789 901 109 987 654 321
```

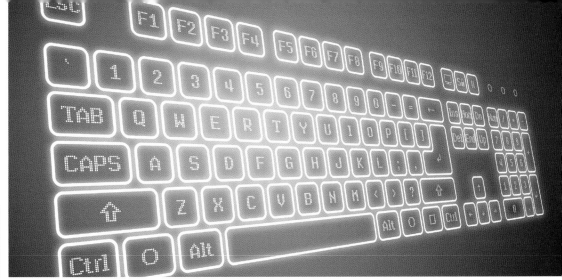

Document Editing and Punctuation Keys

This chapter focuses on managing collaborative documents and editing existing documents. This is a common practice across organizations, and Word provides several robust tools to facilitate this effort. The use of track changes and comments simplifies the process of proofreading documents or creating a single document across a group. Word also provides tools for merging different versions of a document into a single final result. In the keyboarding lesson for this chapter, you will learn the remaining punctuation keys; when you have finished this chapter, you should be able to use proper form to type on the entire standard QWERTY keyboard from touch. When you have completed the chapter, you should be able to:

- Open and modify an existing document

- Perform a spelling and grammar check on your document

- Find and replace a text string in a document

- Manage changes and comments in a document

- Type on the entire QWERTY keyboard with proper form

5.1 EDITING EXISTING DOCUMENTS

As mentioned earlier, you can use the File menu to open existing documents. This includes not only the documents you construct but also any documents that come from someone else you know or someone within your organization. The *Open* command launches a dialog box that allows you to select the document you want to review or edit. Microsoft Word has some excellent tools to edit and review documents. You can see an example of the Review ribbon in Figure 5.1. This ribbon exists in both Word 2010 and Word 2011 though the commands available on it differ slightly.

▼ **FIGURE 5.1** Review ribbon in Word 2010

In Word 2010, you can show or hide formatting marks by clicking the *Show/Hide Paragraph* icon on the Paragraph panel of the Home ribbon. On the Review ribbon, you can also select the *Show Markup* icon and select or deselect *Formatting* in the dropdown list that appears to toggle whether formatting commands appear on the page. There is also a *Display for Review* menu icon from which you can select the document markup you want to see; in general, this should either be *Final* or *Final: Show Markup*.

OFFICE 2011 In Word 2011, you can use the *Reveal Formatting* tool available from the View menu to click inside the document to view the formatting that is applied at that location. Word 2011 also allows you to manage the styles used in the document from the Toolbox available from the Quick Access Toolbar; select the Styles tab to view the styles used in the current document. You can even color code where the styles are applied by selecting the *Show Styles Guides* checkbox. You can apply styles directly from this panel or simply review the existing formatting.

Arranging and Grouping Elements

One of the tools for managing document content is the ability to group objects in a document and format them as a group. This will only apply to objects that are not in line with the document text; anything with a Text Wrap setting of *In Line with Text* cannot be combined with other elements.

> **OFFICE 2011** In Word 2011, to create a group you can select multiple objects in a document (when they are not part of the text layer) and open the context-sensitive Format ribbon which expands off of the Home ribbon. The Group menu is located on the Arrange panel of the Format ribbon.

You can select multiple objects by holding down the shift key and clicking each of them (clicking them again will deselect the object) or by dragging the mouse from one end of the objects you wish to group to the other (only objects entirely within the drag area will be selected). When you have selected all of the objects you wish to group, you can activate the Page Layout ribbon, select the *Group* menu icon on the Arrange panel, and choose *Group*. You can now manipulate the entire set of objects as a single element. The objects within the group can still be individually edited by clicking directly on the object you wish to alter. You can see an example of object grouping in Figure 5.2.

Documents in Word are organized by layers. You can visualize this by imagining a stack of paper clippings containing your elements that must be arranged so you can look down on the stack and see the visualization of the elements you desire. The standard text layer can be considered the default middle of the stack.

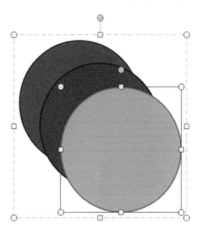

▼ **FIGURE 5.2** Example object grouping

Activity 17 – Layers and Groups

Create a new document and save it as *Activity17*. Use the shape menu to recreate the object grouping in Figure 5.2. Use the formatting commands to style each circle you add. When you have recreated the group, add another circle and place it behind the group and add another circle and place it in front of the group. Now group all five circles at once. What happens when you dissolve the group by using the Ungroup function? What happens to the new circles if you send the group of three circles to the back of the document? Ungroup all of the elements and create a single group of five circles in your document. Save your work.

When you change the Text Wrap setting on an object, you move it to a different layer within the document, whether it is in front of the text or behind it. There are two options on the Page Layout ribbon in the Arrange panel that allow you to change the layer on which your object or group resides; these are the Bring Forward and Send Backward icons.

Under the Bring Forward icon, you can choose to move the object or group a single layer forward (which will by default move it past the next object above it in the stack) or to move

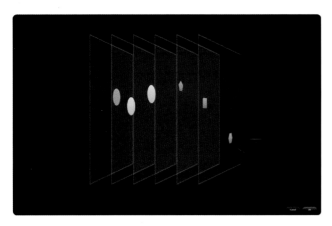

▲ **FIGURE 5.3** Layer visualization in Word 2011

it to the front, which places it on the top layer of the document (which can be seen as closest to the viewer). The Send Backward icon gives you the option to send the object or group back one layer in the document or send it to the back of the document (farthest away from the viewer). Office 2011 has a great visualization tool that demonstrates this concept visually as shown in Figure 5.3.

The other way you can change the positioning of an object or group (in addition to dragging it) is by changing the *alignment* of it. In Word 2010, you can select a predefined position from the Position menu icon from the Arrange panel of the Page Layout ribbon. You can also select one of the options from the Align menu and choose whether you want it to align to the page or align to the margin. Align to Page aligns the element to the entire page size regardless of the margin settings for the page. Align to Margin realigns the object to the orientation of the page within the margin settings.

ALIGNMENT *in terms of layout is the relative placement of an object with respect to the overall environment, which in this case is the slide.*

Spelling and Grammar Check

It is almost always useful to review your document for grammar and spelling issues. The spelling and grammar check will locate and alert you to any issues that it finds within your document regarding your word sequencing and spelling. All of the Office programs have a spelling check option. Clicking the *Spelling and Grammar* icon initiates an automated review of your document. In Word 2010, it is located in the Review ribbon.

> **OFFICE 2011** In Word 2011, select the *Tools* menu and then choose *Spelling and Grammar*. You will be prompted with any correction issues that the software locates.

An example correction prompt is shown in Figure 5.4. Any suggested alternatives are listed beneath the text field identifying the surrounding text in the document where the error was found. You can choose *Ignore* to retain what Word perceives as an error, *Ignore All* to ignore all equivalent perceived errors, and, if it is a spelling issue, *Add to Dictionary* to force Word to accept the word as a correct spelling now and in the future. If you wish to follow the suggestions for changing the perceived error, you can select *Change* to correct the highlighted instance and *Change All* to change all instances of the same type in the document.

▼ **FIGURE 5.4** Spelling and Grammar check example in Word 2010

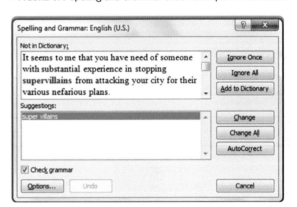

Word is not perfect when it comes to document proofreading and corrections. It may highlight items that are actually correct (called a false positive) and it will miss items that are grammatically correct and spelled correctly even if the word usage is wrong (called a false negative). You should always use the automated tool for proofing your document in case you do have easy corrections to make that you may not catch just by reading it, but you also need to make sure you (and possibly also a friend or colleague) review the document as well to find mistakes the automated system could not locate.

AutoCorrect Options

In addition to the manual tools for checking spelling and grammar, Word has several AutoCorrect features that will attempt to replace words as you type to correct common misspellings and to replace certain text entries with symbols. You can configure the AutoCorrect options if you want to add any additional rules or turn off any existing rules. Any changes you make will apply to all of Word on that computer and not just the document in which you create the rule. To reach the AutoCorrect preferences in Word 2010, select the *File* menu and then choose *Options*. This will open the Word Options dialog box. From here, click *Proofing* in the menu on the left and select the *AutoCorrect Options* button.

> **OFFICE 2011** In Word 2011, select the *Tools* menu and *AutoCorrect* to access the AutoCorrect options and rules.

The existing rules are displayed in a list at the bottom of the dialog box; you can add a rule by typing the misspelled word in the *Replace* field followed by the correct word in the *With* field and choosing *Add*. These dialog boxes are shown in Figure 5.5.

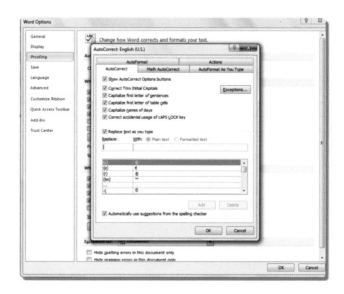

▼ **FIGURE 5.5** AutoCorrect options in Word 2010

5.1.4 Find and Replace

An additional tool that can help you with document review and editing is the find and replace functionality. Searching for repetitive terms or finding a particular word in your document is accomplished by using the Find command. This allows you to perform a simple keyword search of your document. In Word 2010, the Find icon is located on the Home ribbon; you can also access the Find command on a Windows machine using the shortcut *Ctrl-F*.

Activity 18 – Find and Replace

Create a new document and save it as *Activity18*. Enter text in your document that includes at least eight lines and make sure to type the word "hash" in at least three of the lines. Use the keyboard command shortcut to find the word "hash" in the document to practice with the interface for locating search results. Now replace each instance of the word "hash" with "sash" and repeat the use of the find command for the keyword "ash"; you should have (at least) the same results as the first search if you have done this correctly. This is because a partial match will register as a result unless the option *Find whole words only* is selected. Save your work.

The keyword entry for the Find command in Word 2010 is located on the Navigation pane. If the Navigation pane is closed when you select the Find command (by icon or by using the shortcut), the Navigation pane will be displayed on the Browse Results tab. This tab will show all instances of the keyword in the document, and you can jump to a particular location by clicking on a result.

OFFICE 2011 In Word 2011, there is an existing search box in the top-right corner of the open document window that will allow you to enter text for a keyword search of your document; you can highlight this search box using the shortcut *Command-F* or *Ctrl-F*. This will highlight all instances of the keyword (or words) in your document.

To replace the keyword with which you searched the document with another term, you use the Replace command. In Word 2010, this is located on the Home ribbon; when activated, it will open a Find and Replace dialog box where you can navigate instance by instance through the document (with the Find Next button) or simply replace every instance of the keyword with the text you enter in the Replace field. The Find and Replace dialog box is shown in Figure 5.6.

▼ **FIGURE 5.6** Find and Replace dialog box in Word 2010

In Word 2010, you can activate the Replace command using the shortcut *Ctrl-H*. You can choose whether you want to replace the current instance with *Replace*, replace every instance in the document with *Replace All*, or ignore the current instance and move to the next match by selecting *Find Next*. Clicking Cancel will stop the search.

OFFICE 2011 To open this same find and replace dialog box in Word 2011, select the *Edit* menu, select *Find*, and then choose *Advanced Find and Replace*. In Word 2011, you can also use the Search pane to perform the Find and Replace functionality. To activate the Search pane, select the *View* menu, choose *Sidebar*, and then choose *Search Pane*. This will open the side navigation pane if it is not already open; you can then utilize the Find functionality by itself or in conjunction with the Replace functionality.

5.2 DOCUMENT REVIEW AND COLLABORATION

One of the biggest mistakes you can make with a cover letter, resume, report, or any other professional document is not checking the spelling and grammar of the work before you submit it. Word has some excellent tools for checking spelling and grammar, but there are errors that it will not catch (the false negatives mentioned previously); for instance, typing the word "an" when you mean to type "and" may not register as a grammatical error and will not be flagged as a spelling error as it is a correctly spelled word. Because of this, a good practice is to have someone you trust review your important business documents before you submit or share them whenever possible. Word provides several useful tools that allow for collaboration among a team or even on a personally shared document.

5.2.1 Proofreading Marks

There are a set of established proofreading marks for correcting a printed document. When the typewriter was the common tool for typed document creation, mistakes had to be corrected by hand on the typed document. These mistakes would then be corrected when the document was typed again from the beginning. While these have largely gone out of use due to digital file editing and transfers being commonplace in most organizations and homes, it is still relevant to understand these marks if you encounter them or need to have a printed document reviewed when a digital file cannot be transferred. You can see the common proofreading marks in Figure 5.7.

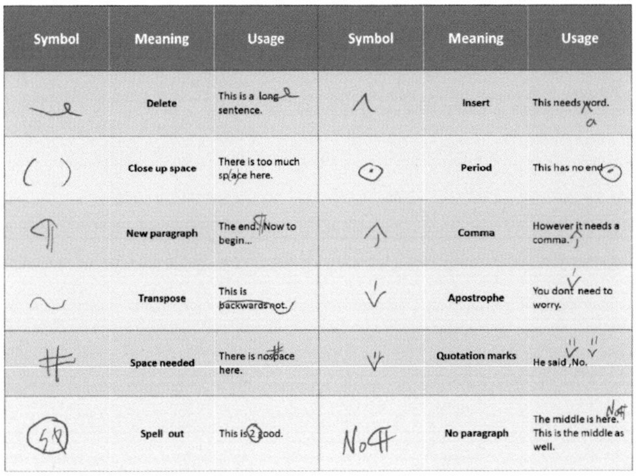

Symbol	Meaning	Usage	Symbol	Meaning	Usage
	Delete	This is a long sentence.		Insert	This needs word.
( )	Close up space	There is too much space here.		Period	This has no end
	New paragraph	The end. Now to begin...		Comma	However it needs a comma.
	Transpose	This is backwards not.		Apostrophe	You don't need to worry.
#	Space needed	There is nospace here.		Quotation marks	He said ,No.
	Spell out	This is 2 good.	No¶	No paragraph	The middle is here. This is the middle as well.

▼ **FIGURE 5.7** Common handwritten proofreading marks

Track Changes

Tracking document changes is the software approach to proofreading where you can denote changes in the document that are easily visible and easy to navigate. When you use Track Changes on a document, every change you make will be registered in a different colored (traditionally red) markup; if you have multiple contributors, each contributor will be assigned a different color for his or her changes. Words or characters that you delete will have a strikethrough effect and new words will be shown in the different color with an underline. This allows you to monitor changes or record them for someone else to review. If you are editing someone else's document, it is considered a courtesy to track changes so they can identify your edits.

To enable Track Changes in Word 2010, select the Review ribbon and choose the *Track Changes* icon; this is a toggle so it is active when it the icon is highlighted. You can use the submenu to customize your options for tracking the document changes or edit the name you wish to use for the change tracking.

> **OFFICE 2011** In Word 2011, you can enable Track Changes on the Review ribbon by moving the slide bar from *OFF* to *ON*. You can slide it back to *OFF* to disable Track Changes.

When you enable or disable Track Changes, it will not affect any prior changes made while the effect was disabled. If you were tracking changes and turned the function off, you will still need to accept or reject the changes that were tracked. Similarly, if you were not tracking changes, turning the functionality on will not affect prior alterations to the document that were made without Track Changes active.

You can navigate from one tracked change to the next using the Next and Previous icons on the Changes panel of the Review ribbon. If you want to keep the currently active change, you can select the *Accept* icon. If you want to remove the change, you can select the *Reject* icon. These icons also have submenus attached that will allow you to accept or reject all of the changes in the document without going through them one by one.

> **OFFICE 2011** Word 2011 has the accept and reject options on the Changes panel of the Review ribbon along with a toggle icon for displaying the Review pane.

5.2.3 ## Comments

Another way to mark a document for potential change when editing is to use comments. A comment in word processing is a note about the document that is written either to the author or the editor of a document for clarity. You can use comments to identify areas of the document that may need to be changed or clarified. Comments identify the person who created them either by name or by initials, so multiple people can add comments to the same document and you can still identify the source of the comment. Comments are a helpful tool for collaboration and versioning in a document. They appear in the document margin to the right so they do not impede the visibility of the main text. Unlike Track Changes, you do not accept or reject comments; instead you can simply add or remove them.

> **NOTE**
> Comments attach to a particular selection of text in the document. You can select the text to which you want the comment to apply, but if you do not select the text, it will attach to the last word before the current cursor location.

In Word 2010 and Word 2011, you can add a new comment by selecting the text on which you want to comment, activating the Review ribbon, and choosing *New Comment* (or *New* on the Comments panel in Word 2011). The *Next* and *Previous* icons in the Comments panel will allow you to move from one comment to the next in the document.

Activity 19 – Comments

Create a new document called *Activity19*. Enter at least eight lines of text to practice your typing form. By now, you should concentrate on using whole words and even forming sentences from touch typing. Select two words from your document and add a comment to them. You can type random text in the comment. What elements are contained in the comment? How can you show and hide the comment within the document and what text is highlighted for the comment? Now select a new location in the document and click the mouse to place the cursor without adding text. Add another comment to your document without any text selected. What text is highlighted for the new comment? Use the comment navigation tools on the ribbon interface to navigate between the two comments and then delete the second comment. Save your work.

To delete a comment, click on the comment you want to remove and select the *Delete* command; the submenu of the Delete command also allows you to delete all of the comments in the document, which should only be done once they have been reviewed. You can see an example of a comment in Figure 5.8.

▼ **FIGURE 5.8** Example comment in Word 2010

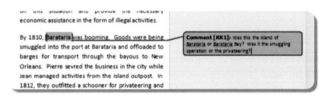

5.2.4 Document Comparison

If you have multiple versions of a document that you need to integrate, you can perform a document comparison to view the changes and decide if you want to keep them or not. These versions do not have to have the same author so you can perform a comparison after you have sent your document to someone else for editing whether they have tracked their changes or not. To perform a document comparison in Word 2010, select the Review ribbon and choose *Compare*. There are two options available here: *Compare* and *Combine*. Both of these will create a new document that merges the two versions together. Compare is used to show the differences between versions from the same author where Combine is intended for documents from multiple authors. The interface for choosing the documents is shown in Figure 5.9. This will create a new document as a result so neither of the files needs to be open at the time.

In Word 2010, the result of the comparison will display in a Reviewing pane which includes a top and bottom comparison of the documents beside the new merged document. This will automatically activate the Reviewing pane showing the document changes and the two source documents

▼ **FIGURE 5.9** Compare Documents dialog box in Microsoft Word

on the right of the interface. You can toggle the Reviewing pane from the Review ribbon and you can close the version documents in the comparison manually. You can save your file as a new document name if you wish to retain the older versions.

> **OFFICE 2011** In Word 2011, you can perform a document comparison by selecting the *Tools* menu, choosing *Track Changes*, and then choosing *Compare Documents*. Word 2011 simply creates a new document based off of the original document where the updates in the revised version are tracked as changes. The Sidebar will display the Reviewing pane which gives you a list of the changes that are included in the document. The differences between the two documents will be tracked as changes which must be either accepted or rejected no matter which version you use. This is the topic of the next section where you will learn to manage tracked changes and comments in a document.

5.3 KEYBOARDING V

In this lesson, you will learn the last of the main keys on the standard QWERTY layout, the punctuation keys. While you have learned a number of them already, this will round out the set of available keys which you will commonly use to create text. Once you have learned the layout of the keys, you should continue to practice for speed and correctness. Your goal should be to commit the keyboard layout to memory so you can reach all of the keys by touch alone. You will also learn about the backspace and delete keys, which are very useful for document editing.

5.3.1 Punctuation Keys

The final set of keys on the standard QWERTY keyboard is the remaining punctuation keys as shown in Figure 5.10 with their associated finger movement. These keys are reached with the left and right pinky respectively. These keys have both standard punctuation and alternate punctuation symbols available when using the shift key. With these keys learned, you should be able to type any text document. The next step is to concentrate on committing the layout of the keyboard to memory so you can type by touch; following that, you should focus on minimizing mistakes then increasing your speed.

▼ **FIGURE 5.10** Punctuation keys and associated finger motion

Backspace and Delete

To this point you have focused on the creation of text and typing as quickly and effectively as possible, but when you are creating documents, you will often want to make changes or erase your mistakes. This action was nearly impossible on the original mechanical typewriters; the best solution available was to move the carriage back in the line (a backspace) and use the strikethrough key to cross out the incorrect letters. Later models supported an erasure ribbon which would (imperfectly) remove the ink from the page.

Activity 20 – Backspace and Delete

For this activity, create a new document and save it as *Activity20*. Enter at least ten lines of text by practicing your typing form. Place the cursor in the center of the text without highlighting any of the actual text. What happens when you tap the backspace key? What happens when you tap the delete key (or the function key and the backspace key on a Mac)? Try holding the backspace key for a second; what happens to the pace of the text removal? What happens when you hold down the delete key? What happens when you hold the control key (or command key on a Mac) and press either the backspace or delete key? Remove all of the text you entered without moving the mouse cursor to a new position in the document.

The backspace key is part of the standard keyboard layout; the delete key is typically placed in the row of function keys but is not always located in the same place across keyboard models. The keys function almost identically, removing the last key typed. The only difference is the backspace key removes the character to the left of the cursor and the delete key removes the character to the right. You can reach the backspace key in the row of number keys with your right pinky finger; the delete key is typically placed directly above it at the far right upper end of the keyboard. If you are using a Macintosh, you may have only a backspace or a delete key and not both; holding down the function key will change the direction of deletion for the single key present on the keyboard.

When you have an object selected in Word, pressing either the backspace or delete key will remove it from the document.

NOTE

Keyboarding Lessons 61–75

By the time you have completed the following lessons, you will have practiced all of the keys highlighted in dark blue in Figure 5.11. You should concentrate in these lessons on learning the hand motion necessary to reach the keys without looking at them; this is the largest stretch of your pinky fingers that you have encountered and it will take practice and precision to strike the correct key with your right pinky because it has a range of keys for which it is responsible. By now, you should have most of the keyboard mastered and you should concentrate on keeping your form as you stretch your pinky fingers to reach the extreme keys. When you have finished and mastered these lessons, you should be able to type any standard text you encounter in a source document and type any text you wish to create with proper form and minimal error.

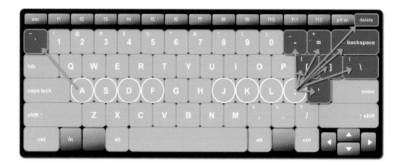

▼ **FIGURE 5.11** Keyboarding V keys and hand motion mapping

The software included with the text and available online at *www.keyboardingandbeyond* *.com* will time the lessons and alert you to any mistakes made while entering the text for these exercises. Because this is practice, you should feel free to redo these lessons and activities as much as you need to improve your performance and form.

Lesson 5.1 The Backstop Key

In this lesson, you will use your left pinky finger to press the backstop key (`) as well as using the keys you have already learned. You should focus on your form and keep your hands positioned over the home row keys while you move only the necessary finger to strike the keys you wish to type. The software will count up the amount of time it takes for you to complete the task, so you can take as long as you need and retry the exercise to improve your time.

The backstop character (`) is only used to create accented characters and should not be used in general typography. The apostrophe character should be used for single quotes and contractions.

Type the following:

```
````  aaaa  ````  ``aa aa``  a``a `aa` `~~` ~``~ a`~~`a aq`a
````  aaaa  ````  ``aa aa``  a``a `aa` `~~` ~``~ a`~~`a aq`a
~100 ~80 ~90 ~9000 `a `e `i `o `u ~44 ~88 ~0 ~789 ~1000
~100 ~80 ~90 ~9000 `a `e `i `o `u ~44 ~88 ~0 ~789 ~1000
````  aaaa  ````  ``aa aa``  a``a `aa` `~~` ~``~ a`~~`a aq`a
```

Lesson 5.2 The Hyphen Key

In this lesson, you will use your right pinky finger to press the hyphen key as well as using the keys you have already learned. You should focus on your form and keep your hands positioned over the home row keys while you move only the necessary finger to strike the keys you wish to type. The software will count up the amount of time it takes for you to complete the task, so you can take as long as you need and retry the exercise to improve your time.

The hyphen should be used for compound words. You should not space around the hyphen character when it is used to conjoin two words.

Type the following:

```
---- llll ---- --ll ll-- l--l -ll- -__- _--_ l-__-l lp-l
---- llll ---- --ll ll-- l--l -ll- -__- _--_ l-__-l lp-l
_____ _____ _____ 7-7 is 0. _____ - _____ is _____.
_____ _____ _____ 7-7 is 0. _____ - _____ is _____.
---- llll ---- --ll ll-- l--l -ll- -__- _--_ l-__-l lp-l
```

Lesson 5.3 The Equal Key

In this lesson, you will use your right pinky finger to press the equal key as well as using the keys you have already learned. You should focus on your form and keep your hands positioned over the home row keys while you move only the necessary finger to strike the keys you wish to type. The software will count up the amount of time it takes for you to complete the task, so you can take as long as you need and retry the exercise to improve your time.
```

Type the following:

```
==== llll ==== ==ll ll== l==l =ll= =++= +==+ l=++=l lp=l
==== llll ==== ==ll ll== l==l =ll= =++= +==+ l=++=l lp=l
7 + 7 = 14, 8 + 8 = 16, 9 + 9 = 18, 4 - 4 = 0, 3 - 2 = 1
7 + 7 = 14, 8 + 8 = 16, 9 + 9 = 18, 4 - 4 = 0, 3 - 2 = 1
==== llll ==== ==ll ll== l==l =ll= =++= +==+ l=++=l lp=l
```

Lesson 5.4 The Left Bracket Key

In this lesson, you will use your right pinky finger to press the left bracket key as well as using the keys you have already learned. You should focus on your form and keep your hands positioned over the home row keys while you move only the necessary finger to strike the keys you wish to type. The software will count up the amount of time it takes for you to complete the task, so you can take as long as you need and retry the exercise to improve your time.

Type the following:

```
[[[[ llll [[[[ [[ll ll[[ l[[l [ll[ [{{[ {[[{ l[{{[l lp[l
[[[[ llll [[[[ [[ll ll[[ l[[l [ll[ [{{[ {[[{ l[{{[l lp[l
[() {[() [{[(()) [{0,0,0
[() {[() [{[(()) [{0,0,0
[[[[ llll [[[[ [[ll ll[[ l[[l [ll[ [{{[ {[[{ l[{{[l lp[l
```

Lesson 5.5 The Right Bracket Key

In this lesson, you will use your right pinky finger to press the right bracket key as well as using the keys you have already learned. You should focus on your form and keep your hands positioned over the home row keys while you move only the necessary finger to strike the keys you wish to type. The software will count up the amount of time it takes for you to complete the task, so you can take as long as you need and retry the exercise to improve your time.

Type the following:

```
]]]] llll ]]]] ]]ll ll]] l]]l ]ll] ]}}] }]]} l]}}]l lp]l
]]]] llll ]]]] ]]ll ll]] l]]l ]ll] ]}}] }]]} l]}}]l lp]l
() [] {} {[()]} {7*[8*(9*9)]} {4+[3+(2+2)]}
() [] {} {[()]} {7*[8*(9*9)]} {4+[3+(2+2)]}
]]]] llll ]]]] ]]ll ll]] l]]l ]ll] ]}}] }]]} l]}}]l lp]l
```

Lesson 5.6 The Backslash Key

In this lesson, you will use your right pinky finger to press the backslash key as well as using the keys you have already learned. You should focus on your form and keep your hands positioned over the home row keys while you move only the necessary finger to strike the keys you wish to type. The software will count up the amount of time it takes for you to complete the task, so you can take as long as you need and retry the exercise to improve your time.

Type the following:

```
\\\\ 1111 \\\\ \\11 11\\ 1\\1 \11\ \||\ |\\| 1\||\1 1p\1
\\\\ 1111 \\\\ \\11 11\\ 1\\1 \11\ \||\ |\\| 1\||\1 1p\1
9\8\7\6\5\4 1|2|3|4|5|6|7|8
9\8\7\6\5\4 1|2|3|4|5|6|7|8
\\\\ 1111 \\\\ \\11 11\\ 1\\1 \11\ \||\ |\\| 1\||\1 1p\1
```

Lesson 5.7 The Apostrophe Key

In this lesson, you will use your right pinky finger to press the apostrophe key as well as using the keys you have already learned. You should focus on your form and keep your hands positioned over the home row keys while you move only the necessary finger to strike the keys you wish to type. The software will count up the amount of time it takes for you to complete the task, so you can take as long as you need and retry the exercise to improve your time.

> In Word, the apostrophe (or single quote) character and the double quote character will automatically tilt with the orientation of the text as needed.

NOTE

Type the following:

```
1111 aaaa 1111 11aa aa11 a11a 1aa1 1!!1 !11! a1!!1a aq1a
'''' 1l1l '''' 11'' ''11 '11' 1''1 '""' "''" 1'""'1 1'"'1
He said, "Yes." She said, "He said 'no.'" I said, "Hi."
can't won't don't isn't is isn't does doesn't will won't
can't won't don't isn't is isn't does doesn't will won't
He said, "Yes." She said, "He said 'no.'" I said, "Hi."
'''' 1l1l '''' 11'' ''11 '11' 1''1 '""' "''" 1'""'1 1'"'1
```

Lesson 5.8 Punctuation Practice

In this lesson, you will practice typing all of the punctuation keys you have learned so far. The timer for this exercise counts down, so you should try to gain enough proficiency and speed to complete the exercise in its entirety before the timer runs out. Because you are still learning, you should repeat this exercise as necessary until you are able to complete it with time left on the timer!

Type the following:

```
"(9,9)" '(8,8)' {"(1)"} [{2}] ((((3)))) "((("4")))"
4 + 4 = 8, 8 - 9 = -1, 7^2 = 49, 4 * 4 = 16, 4/4 = 1
There isn't a sentence that's like this, is there?
What's the matter with "obvious" usage? Nothing!
4 + 4 = 8, 8 - 9 = -1, 7^2 = 49, 4 * 4 = 16, 4/4 = 1
{[(())]} ((({{[[]]}}))) "(9,9)" '(8,8)' {"(1)"} [{2}]
```

Lesson 5.9 Sentence Typing Practice 1

In this lesson, you will practice typing all of the keys you have learned so far. The timer for this exercise counts down, so you should try to gain enough proficiency and speed to complete the exercise in its entirety before the timer runs out. Because you are still learning, you should repeat this exercise as necessary until you are able to complete it with time left on the timer!

Type the following:

```
This
This is
This isn't
This isn't a
This isn't a proper
This isn't a proper use
This isn't a proper use of
This isn't a proper use of "2"
This isn't a proper use of "2" in
This isn't a proper use of "2" in today.
```

Lesson 5.10 Sentence Typing Practice 2

In this lesson, you will practice typing all of the keys you have learned so far. The timer for this exercise counts down, so you should try to gain enough proficiency and speed to complete the exercise in its entirety before the timer runs out. Because you are still learning, you should repeat this exercise as necessary until you are able to complete it with time left on the timer!

Type the following:

```
A
A bucket
A bucket of
A bucket of 99
A bucket of 99 badgers
```

```
A bucket of 99 badgers is
A bucket of 99 badgers is not
A bucket of 99 badgers is not a
A bucket of 99 badgers is not a nice
A bucket of 99 badgers is not a nice present!
```

Lesson 5.11 Equation Building Practice

In this lesson, you will practice typing all of the keys you have learned so far. The timer for this exercise counts down, so you should try to gain enough proficiency and speed to complete the exercise in its entirety before the timer runs out. Because you are still learning, you should repeat this exercise as necessary until you are able to complete it with time left on the timer!

Type the following:

```
{9
{9 +
{9 + [8
{9 + [8 *
{9 + [8 * (3
{9 + [8 * (3 -
{9 + [8 * (3 - 1)
{9 + [8 * (3 - 1)]}
{9 + [8 * (3 - 1)]} =
{9 + [8 * (3 - 1)]} = 25
```

Lesson 5.12 Keyboard Practice 1

In this lesson, you will practice typing all of the keys you have learned so far. The timer for this exercise counts down, so you should try to gain enough proficiency and speed to complete the exercise in its entirety before the timer runs out. Because you are still learning, you should repeat this exercise as necessary until you are able to complete it with time left on the timer!

Type the following:

```
Typing is a skill needed everywhere. With everyone in every job
using more and more computers to enter data and information,
there is a growing need for proficiency in entering data and
information at remarkable rates. Over 55 words per minute is
the standard for mastering touch typing, but minimizing errors
is just as important in the equation as typing quickly!
```

Lesson 5.13 Keyboard Practice 2

In this lesson, you will practice typing all of the keys you have learned so far. The timer for this exercise counts down, so you should try to gain enough proficiency and speed to complete the exercise in its entirety before the timer runs out. Because you are still learning, you should repeat this exercise as necessary until you are able to complete it with time left on the timer!

Type the following:

```
Mechanical wheels and gears grinding fast, spokes pounding
ribbon, and ink staining white, the mechanical typewriter was
an industrial sight. Each prong with a letter and with a mighty
strike, they imprint the letter on the paper so white. The ink
of the ribbon is shifted and the carriage moves on to strike
at the next empty space. Fingers on letters and gears moving
quick, the skill of the typist is nimble and slick.
```

Lesson 5.14 Keyboard Practice 3

In this lesson, you will practice typing all of the keys you have learned so far. The timer for this exercise counts down, so you should try to gain enough proficiency and speed to complete the exercise in its entirety before the timer runs out. Because you are still learning, you should repeat this exercise as necessary until you are able to complete it with time left on the timer!

Type the following:

```
Form and precision are the best focus for typing. Speed will
come when you have the keyboard committed to memory and you
can type without looking at the keys you press. Keep your hands
still over the keyboard and move only the fingers you have to
move when you need to strike a key. Keep practicing and work
on your form until the motions are natural. Then, you should
aim for at least 55 words per minute!
```

Lesson 5.15 Keyboard Practice 4

In this lesson, you will practice typing all of the keys you have learned so far. The timer for this exercise counts down, so you should try to gain enough proficiency and speed to complete the exercise in its entirety before the timer runs out. Because you are still learning, you should repeat this exercise as necessary until you are able to complete it with time left on the timer!

Type the following:

```
Building
Building a
Building a sentence
Building a sentence (constructing
Building a sentence (constructing it
Building a sentence (constructing it really)
Building a sentence (constructing it really) takes
Building a sentence (constructing it really) takes
concentration
Building a sentence (constructing it really) takes
concentration and
Building a sentence (constructing it really) takes
concentration and skill!
```

CHAPTER SUMMARY

This chapter covers the available tools for modifying existing documents and collaborating easily among multiple authors. This includes the ability to perform keyword searches on the document to locate or replace its contents. You can also perform spelling and grammar checks to correct errors in the document as well as modify the AutoCorrect options in the document. Additionally, Word provides tools to edit documents and track the changes made to it as well as comment on the contents when you share documents across multiple authors. When you have completed the keyboarding lessons in this chapter, you should be able to type any key on the keyboard with proper typing form.

CHAPTER KNOWLEDGE CHECK

1 Creating _____ of objects in a document allows you to modify them all as a single item.

- ○ **A.** An alignment
- ○ **B.** An arrangement
- ○ **C.** A group
- ○ **D.** All of the above
- ○ **E.** None of the above

2 The _____ ribbon contains the ability to track changes and add comments to a document for collaboration and version control.

- ○ **A.** View
- ○ **B.** Review
- ○ **C.** Version
- ○ **D.** References

3 The spelling and grammar check in Word is designed to detect all errors that are possible in writing a document in English; it may detect false positives that are correct but it will not miss any mistakes.

- ○ **A.** True
- ○ **B.** False

4 Track Changes applies to a document only when it is active and any changes made while Track Changes is inactive will not be detected.

- ○ **A.** True
- ○ **B.** False

5 _____ is a way to mark a document for the author to review an issue or a question from an external editor.

- ○ **A.** An editorial
- ○ **B.** Proofreading markup
- ○ **C.** Compare
- ○ **D.** A comment

6 The options available for resolving a tracked change in a document include:

- ○ **A.** Accept
- ○ **B.** Reject
- ○ **C.** Accept all
- ○ **D.** Reject all
- ○ **E.** All of the above
- ○ **F.** None of the above

7 Custom AutoCorrect rules in Word will apply only to the document in which you defined them.

- ○ **A.** True
- ○ **B.** False

8 Using the Compare functionality in a document will create a new document from both of the existing versions instead of making changing in the existing documents.

- ○ **A.** True
- ○ **B.** False

9 Only document elements on a layer other than the text layer can be included in a group.

- ○ **A.** True
- ○ **B.** False

10 The following are all ways to control document versions and collaborate in composing a document _except_:

- ○ **A.** Comments
- ○ **B.** Track Changes
- ○ **C.** Compare
- ○ **D.** All of the above
- ○ **E.** None of the above

CHAPTER EXERCISES

1. Create two subgroups of at least two shapes each within a single grouping of document elements. Is it possible to move the subgroups within the group itself? What effect does it have on the overall group when you modify subgroups? What effect does it have on the overall group when you modify an individual element within the group? You should create a document with the original group and show the modifications for each exploration of the effects on the larger group by copying and pasting the modified group after your text explanation of the effect of the modification.

2. Create a new AutoCorrect rule for your Word software. What is the reason behind the rule and when would it be useful? Are there any instances you could find where the rule would create an error in the document? Use a screenshot in your document to show that the rule was added. You may remove the rule after completing this exercise.

3. Identify five instances where the spelling and grammar check will ignore an error (false negative) or identify an error which is actually correct (false positive). For each instance, write whether it was a false positive or a false negative. Which is the better situation to encounter and why?

4. Activate Track Changes in your document and enter at least six lines of type. Deactivate Track Changes and type another six lines. Activate Track Changes again and review the document changes using the navigation. Is there any way to detect the changes made when the Track Changes was off? How does this affect collaborative documents?

5. Create two documents and type entirely different text in each of them. Now use the document comparison functionality in Word to merge the two documents into one. Because the content is different, one of the documents will appear as new text and the other will appear as strikethrough text. Which document appeared as which type of text? Resolve the document changes to retain the maximum amount of text in the resulting document. What steps did you take for the resolution?

6. Word allows you to perform a Find procedure using regular expressions instead of standard text. A regular expression is a pattern of text recognition that will identify any specific text string that matches the pattern. One character in a regular expression is the * character; this will match any characters that come before its placement. Type three lines of text containing words that end in the same three letters (such as land and hand). Use the Find command to locate the matching results for the words you typed (in this case *and). Make sure the use of regular expressions is enabled in the *Advanced* menu for Found options. Confirm that Word located each of the instances you typed. When would this type of functionality be useful? What are the alternative ways to find these words and are they more or less accurate?

The following two activities are for Word 2010 on a Windows machine:

7. Word 2010 allows for setting editing restrictions on a document (via the Block Authors and Restrict Editing icons on the Review ribbon). Create and save a new document and limit the type of editing that can be performed by others making changes to the document. What options are available with Restrict Editing and which ones would be most useful for a collaborative document? What would be most useful for a Word form distribution to multiple employees in an organization?

8. Microsoft OneNote is an additional piece of productivity software included in the Office 2010 suite of programs. Word includes a link to OneNote called Linked Notes (available as an icon on the Review ribbon). Similar to using Excel for chart entry, this opens OneNote side by side with Word so you can add notes about your document as shown in Figure 5.12. To add a note in OneNote, simply click in the OneNote document and type your note; it will automatically link back to the Word document. Try this for yourself with a document you have saved and then write a summary of the feature and how it could be used to assist in creating a business or educational report.

◀ **FIGURE 5.12** OneNote linked notes with Word 2010

The following two exercises are for Word 2011 on a Macintosh machine:

9. The Reviewing pane in Word 2011 is used to show a summary of changes to the document in a more organized manner than simply navigating through them one at a time. Create a new document and immediately turn on the Track Changes function. Add at least eight lines of content and include a header and footer in your document. Activate the Reviewing pane (from the Review ribbon) and describe the summary information that it provides and how this is useful when reviewing a document that has multiple contributors.

10. The Publishing Layout view is unique to Word 2011. It attempts to provide an interface for desktop publishing activities in Word. Create a new document in Publishing Layout and compare and contrast the ribbons and features available in this unique layout compared to the standard layout for a normal Word 2011 document.

CHAPTER REVIEW QUESTIONS

1. From a software design perspective, why would it be a bad decision to allow objects treated as text in the text level to be added to free floating groups on different layers of the document?

2. Another means of editing documents with a mechanical typewriter was the use of strikethrough to cross out letters or words that no longer belonged in the document. What are the benefits and drawbacks of using this kind of system to make document edits?

3. Tracking changes and using comments are two common ways in which collaboration is handled in word processing documents. Are either of these sufficient by themselves or do the two techniques complement each other in use? Justify your answer with examples.

4. Identify circumstances in which you may still encounter handwritten proofreading marks. When would these be useful in a modern, computer-driven society?

5. Defining AutoCorrect rules that are too specific can lead to allowed errors in other documents because they are a systemic setting. State whether you agree or disagree with that statement and justify your position with examples.

6. What is the potential downside of using Replace All in a find and replace procedure without looking at each instance that was found? Explain your position with examples.

7. Give at least three examples of documents used in business or education where you would need to collaborate among different authors. What would you suggest as a strategy for sharing the document and keeping control of the versioning among authors making changes to the document?

8. Word 2010 allows you to add Ink Comments (drawn with the mouse as shapes over your document) to your document as well as the standard comments. What is the benefit of using Ink Comments? Would this type of comment be useful for utilizing the handwritten proofreading symbols? Justify your answer with examples.

9. In addition to just tracking changes in the text of a document, Word also tracks changes to formatting and other modifications to the document. You must accept or reject these changes as well. What are the different areas of document modification which can be tracked in Word (you can find these under the Show Markup menu on the Review ribbon) and why would each of them be useful?

10. What are the benefits and drawbacks of the *Accept All Changes* and *Reject All Changes* options for resolving different versions of a document? Justify your answer with examples.

KEYBOARDING DRILLS

1. Type as much of the following as you can in thirty seconds; try to complete the exercise before the timer runs out if possible. You can use the included software to track your time, speed, and errors:

```
"(9,9)" '(8,8)' {"(1)"} [{2}] ((((3)))) "((("4")))"
4 + 4 = 8, 8 - 9 = -1, 7^2 = 49, 4 * 4 = 16, 4/4 = 1
7 + 7 = 14, 8 + 8 = 16, 9 + 9 = 18, 4 - 4 = 0, 3 - 2 = 1
7 + 7 = 14, 8 + 8 = 16, 9 + 9 = 18, 4 - 4 = 0, 3 - 2 = 1
() [] {} {[()]} {7*[8*(9*9)]} {4+[3+(2+2)]}
"(9,9)" '(8,8)' {"(1)"} [{2}] ((((3)))) "((("4")))"
```

2. Type as much of the following as you can in thirty seconds; try to complete the exercise before the timer runs out if possible. You can use the included software to track your time, speed, and errors:

```
He said, "Yes." She said, "He said 'no.'" I said, "Hi."
can't won't don't isn't is isn't does doesn't will won't
4 + 4 = 8, 8 - 9 = -1, 7^2 = 49, 4 * 4 = 16, 4/4 = 1
4 + 4 = 8, 8 - 9 = -1, 7^2 = 49, 4 * 4 = 16, 4/4 = 1
{[(())]} (({{[[]]}}))"(9,9)" '(8,8)' {"(1)"} [{2}]
can't won't don't isn't is isn't does doesn't will won't
```

3. Track your time and focus on your form to type the following with as few errors as possible. You can use the included software to track your time, speed, and errors:

```
11 22 345 66 77 890 120 239 458 676 9900 100 10 15 25 1000
11 22 345 66 77 890 120 239 458 676 9900 100 10 15 25 1000
glass sass dad add glad fad lass lad had has
glass sass dad add glad fad lass lad had has
will pill chill call hall fall mall till skill fill full
will pill chill call hall fall mall till skill fill full
as the an as of for from to were it is was will be has had
as the an as of for from to were it is was will be has had
```

4. Track your time and focus on your form to type the following with as few errors as possible. You can use the included software to track your time, speed, and errors:

```
Vast oceans and land fill the planet. 360 degrees of light rock
and water swirl on a constant bases and we feel nothing of
the movement of the planet. The planets and stars fill a vast
universe and this small world is but a small tiny speck in the
vastness of space, yet it is so large and complete to a human
being. Every country is more land than one man needs and the
country is a small part of the world as a whole.
```

5. Type as much of the following as you can in one minute. You can use the included software to track your time, speed, and errors:

```
99
99 words
99 words are
99 words are
99 words are a
99 words are a lot
99 words are a lot for
99 words are a lot for one
99 words are a lot for one sentence
99 words are a lot for one sentence, but
99 words are a lot for one sentence, but Billy
```

```
99 words are a lot for one sentence, but Billy said,
99 words are a lot for one sentence, but Billy said, "Yes
99 words are a lot for one sentence, but Billy said, "Yes, you
99 words are a lot for one sentence, but Billy said, "Yes, you
can
99 words are a lot for one sentence, but Billy said, "Yes, you
can do
99 words are a lot for one sentence, but Billy said, "Yes, you
can do it!"
```

Document References and Typing Tests

This chapter introduces you to the reference tools that are available in Word to assist you in managing document sources, adding footnotes or endnotes, and managing automated tables and indexes. These tools are part of the References ribbon which allows you to structure such items as an index, a table of contents, and citation styles. Additional tools in Word allow you to identify research materials from reference books and perform searches on the Internet for related articles. The keyboarding section of this chapter focuses on the measurement of typing speed and enhancing your words per minute (WPM) average through typing tests. When you have completed this chapter, you will be able to:

- Utilize the research options available in Word

- Insert and modify document sources and citations

- Manage Footnotes and Endnotes in a document

- Create and maintain a Bibliography

- Identify and enhance your typing speed using the QWERTY keyboard

DOCUMENT RESEARCH

Microsoft Word offers an array of tools to produce quality business and academic documents. Word enables students, authors, and publishers the ability to easily produce high quality professional documents. Part of this functionality is the use of research tools to identify sources for your document. It is important to understand some background on what constitutes professional quality research prior to using the tools that are provided by Word. Research is an important skill that is not only used as academic and research institutions but also throughout the business world. The term research can mean many things, but it involves more than simply going online and finding any information and paraphrasing it into a document. Dictionary.com defines research as "diligent and systematic inquiry or investigation into a subject in order to discover or revise facts, theories, applications, etc." In simpler terms this means that you must evaluate the information that you find in order to apply it to the problem you are attempting to address. This information that you evaluate can be collected from surveys, notes, interviews, articles, Web sites, or other sources.

It is always important to determine the *credibility* of a source you are using for your work as part of your analysis of the source. Textbooks, conference papers, and journals often go through rigorous peer review and technical editing, so they tend to be more trustworthy sources than something published online. You can find reviews of the textbook, conference, or journal to evaluate whether it meets these criteria. Anything you find on the Web is a different matter; it is easy to create a personal Web site and post any information you want.

> *Credibility is the trustworthiness of information. Information with high credibility may have concurrence among a group of experts or explicit and convincing proof of truth.*

Anything posted on the Web does not have to be true information or researched information for it to be published. Just about anyone can post anything on the Web, no matter where or how the information was collected. The Web is available to anyone for access or contribution. The multitude of articles available from the Web offer both very credible documents and ones which should be ignored as false. For instance, Wikipedia (*www.wikipedia.org*) allows users to contribute to articles published on its site; there is a substantial effort for oversight of the articles it presents, but there is no absolute for determining if the information posted is correct or not. Therefore, you must carefully evaluate the credibility of the information you read from Wikipedia; it can be a great starting point for learning about a topic, but you cannot assume all of the information it contains is true.

Whenever you encounter an online source, there are some things you should consider in deciding whether you can trust what it has to say. Here are a few questions to ask of a potential Web site source before you use it as a source:

- *Who is the author of the site?* If the author is a reputable organization or an individual with expertise in the area, it is more likely to be a credible source.

- *What are the site extension and the domain name of the site?* Once again, a company or organization site is generally more credible than an individual unless that individual is an expert in the field. A professional versus an unprofessional domain name can also indicate the level of trust that should be placed in the source. The site extension is also telling; a site extension of *.gov* for example means it is a government publication.

- *Does the site use references and cite other sources?* This can indicate whether the author has researched the subject sufficiently. Looking at any references used and evaluating them will help determine if the page is credible.

- *Is the site modern?* You should be able to check the last updated date to determine if the document is current or not.

- *Is the site objective with its information or is there another motivation?* You should try to use objective sources in your work and evaluate the reliability of the source when there is another motive for the author to influence the reader in creating the document.

Writing professional documents requires that you write from sources that are credible in nature. However, not all sources are easily identified as credible. Sources may be either opinion pieces or based on data from a research study. For example, if you heard about an incident on the news about a crime that had been committed, can you take what the reporter says to be true? Although the public relies on media reporting, the news reporters are certainly not always credible witnesses or investigators. They most often seek the best information they feel they can get and then write opinion pieces based upon that information. Another example of this is a report of personal experience, which must be carefully considered for validity.

Other sources are much easier to evaluate such as academic journals which have a peer review process. An academic journal which publishes research articles from authors conducting research usually have a blind review process where several reviewers from the academic field look at an article and examine all of the data collected to assure credibility prior to acceptance.

Research Task Pane

The Research Task pane is a tool that allows you to find sources by keyword search. Accessing the research pane provides access to resources like the Encarta encyclopedia and the Bing search engine as long as you have an active connection to the Internet. To access the Research Task pane in Word 2010, you must first activate the Review ribbon. On the Review ribbon, click the *Research* button inside the *Proofing* pane. This will open the Research Task pane on the right side of the current open document; you can see an example of the Research Task pane in Figure 6.1.

▲ **FIGURE 6.1** The Research Task pane in Word 2010

By clicking inside the *Search for* text box, you can type a keyword used to find articles or results on a particular subject. You can also select which resources you would like to use by choosing one of the options in the drop down menu beneath the keyword entry box. You could select the default value *All Reference Books* or you can select an individual resource from the list. This includes the option to select the Microsoft search engine Bing® to conduct a general Web search on a particular topic. The results of your search will appear in the pane beneath your selection parameters. Once you have completed your search you can simply close the Research pane window by clicking once on the top right corner of the pane.

OFFICE 2011 If you are using Word 2011 for Mac, then the process for accessing the research tools is different. There is no Research Task pane in Word 2011; instead you have the Reference Tools, as shown in Figure 6.2, which has Web search, Thesaurus, Dictionary, and Translation options. You can access the Reference Tools by selecting the *Toolbox* button or selecting *Reference Tools* from the View menu. The Toolbox contains Styles, Citations, Scrapbook, and Reference Tools options. The Reference Tools selection requires an active Internet connection to access the Web.

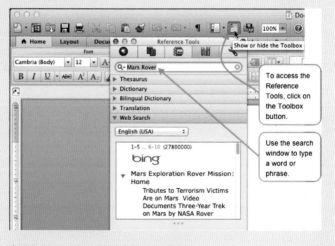

▲ **FIGURE 6.2** Word 2011 Reference Tools

Using the example in Figure 6.2, you can see that the keywords "Mars rover" have been inserted for a Web search. By entering the words and pressing the enter or return key, you can view the information returned from the search in the results window. If you wanted to use any of the other tools available within the reference tools window, you would simply type a new word and select the drop down menu for the required tool such as Dictionary.

6.1.2 Managing Document Citations and References

The Word application gives you the ability to store and manage your list of sources in order to cite them properly in your document. It is very important to keep track of your *citations* as you construct a document; these are sources whose information you are actively using or referencing in your own document. You should add a citation whenever you are using information from a source that is not common knowledge or your own conclusion. It is necessary to manage your sources so you can include citations easily.

A **CITATION** *is a reference to an external source you used to gather information, text, or content for your work.*

Microsoft Word makes this task easier by giving you the ability to add and store references in conjunction with your document. The functionality for this is located in the References ribbon of Microsoft Word 2010. You can see the References ribbon for Microsoft Word 2010 in Figure 6.3.

◀ **FIGURE 6.3** References ribbon for Microsoft Word 2010

You can add new sources or edit existing ones using the *Manage Sources* icon. This will open the Source Manager (shown in Figure 6.4). From this dialog box, you can add new citations by clicking *New*. This opens a new source creation dialog box; you can select the source type from the dropdown list; this will adjust the fields needed to accurately cite the source. You should try to complete as many of these fields as you can to give the most complete citation possible.

Once you have entered your sources, you can insert a citation in your text to any of the existing sources. These citations are linked to the original citation entry, so if you edit your source information, it will update any citations in the document. This makes it more convenient to manage your sources and keep your citations current.

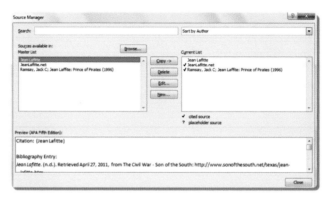

▲ **FIGURE 6.4** Source Manager for Microsoft Word 2010

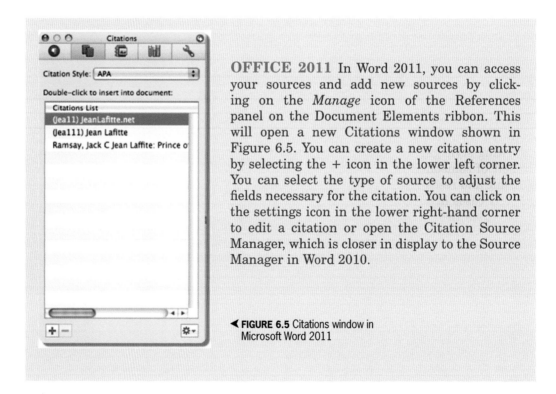

OFFICE 2011 In Word 2011, you can access your sources and add new sources by clicking on the *Manage* icon of the References panel on the Document Elements ribbon. This will open a new Citations window shown in Figure 6.5. You can create a new citation entry by selecting the + icon in the lower left corner. You can select the type of source to adjust the fields necessary for the citation. You can click on the settings icon in the lower right-hand corner to edit a citation or open the Citation Source Manager, which is closer in display to the Source Manager in Word 2010.

◀ **FIGURE 6.5** Citations window in Microsoft Word 2011

Completing a document for an academic or research institution, or even a business, will more than likely require a citation or bibliography style. There are three common styles used in the academic setting; these are the American Psychological Association's (APA) Style, the Manual Language Association's (MLA) Style, and the Chicago Manual of Style (Chicago).

Any of these three styles can be found in the university setting or adopted as a writing standard in an organization for formatting a paper. Below you will find the sites associated with each of these three styles. Although it is recommended that you acquire a style guide for the style of choice, these sites do provide some general guidance. Your instructor or facilitator in an academic setting may also prove you with other Web sources and guides that will help you format you papers using these styles.

- APA: *http://www.apastyle.org/index.aspx*
- MLA: *http://www.mla.org/*
- Chicago: *http://www.chicagomanualofstyle.org/home.html*

These styles each define the preferred method for using sources in a paper and provide guidance on how and when to use a source in a paper for that style. These guides also provide helpful hints on paraphrasing and using quoted material and how to properly give credit for material where it is due. You should remember that you are not allowed to simply copy and paste material from the Web or other sources that has been written; you must give credit to the source of the original material.

NOTE

If you are writing a paper for academic purposes, you can use a source so long as you give credit to the original author of the publication. If you simply copy an author's work for your own use without giving proper credit and following proper writing style guidelines you are committing an act of plagiarism. Plagiarism is theft of someone else's written ideas and is a serious ethical violation. All academic and research institutions have specific guidelines for this offence which in many cases involves suspension or expulsion from a program. In business organizations these violations can lead to copyright infringement that can lead to criminal and civil liabilities.

To add a citation in your document in Word 2010, select the Reference ribbon, choose the format for the citation (such as APA), and click the *Insert Citation* icon and select the source you want to use. The reference to the source in correct format for the citation style will be added to your document. You must also be sure to add either a bibliography or works cited section to your document in order to properly complete any added citation.

6.1.3 Footnotes and Endnotes

Footnotes are used to add explanation to an element of a document without interrupting the writing flow. Whether to use footnotes or *endnotes* is a stylistic choice. The main difference between them is the placement within the text.

> A **FOOTNOTE** *is an additional comment aside from the main point of a text document that is placed at the bottom of the page and indicated by a reference mark in the main text. This is typically used to clarify a point or provide an explanation that would detract from the content of the document if left in line with the main text. An* endnote *is the same thing as a footnote except it is placed at the end of the document instead of on the same page with the reference mark.*

A footnote will be placed on the page to which the notation is added; the text will have a superscript number placed beside it and the footnote explanation will be placed in a separate section at the end of the page. To place a footnote in Word 2010, click on the References ribbon and choose *Insert Footnote*; your cursor should be placed beside the text you are annotating with the footnote.

The current number of the footnote for that page (beginning with the number one) will be added at the current cursor location and you will be taken to the section at the bottom left corner of the page where you can add the footnote text. An example of this is shown in Figure 6.6. The numbering for the footnotes will be adjusted as text is moved; a link exists within the document connecting the mark in the text and the note.

foreign port. This made life difficult for merchant
vessels and denied the population foreign goods and

¹ Sources disagree on the origin of Jean Lafitte and
his brother Pierre. Different sources place them in
French territories from Haiti to Saint-Domingue.

ORLEANS

The War of 1812 would bring a new chapter to the
life of Jean Lafitte. Lafitte was contacted by the

◀ **FIGURE 6.6** Footnote placement in Microsoft Word 2010

An endnote is placed at the end of the entire document. By default, endnotes start with Roman numerals
(beginning with lowercase *i*) and accumulate throughout
the text. Adding an endnote is similar to adding a footnote. The annotation will be placed where the cursor is
located in the document and you will be taken to the endnote section to enter the text describing the annotation.
You can add an endnote in Word 2010 by selecting the
References ribbon and choosing *Insert Endnote*. While
the default properties are sufficient for most documents,
you can customize characteristics of your footnotes and
endnotes from the dialog box shown in Figure 6.7.

You can access the advanced properties for footnotes and endnotes shown in Figure 6.8 by selecting the
expansion icon on the Footnotes panel of the References
ribbon in Word 2010. This allows you to change the settings for both footnotes and endnotes, including placement of the notes, the starting value for the annotations,
and the numbering format used.

▲ **FIGURE 6.7** Footnote and Endnote Dialog dialogbox in
Microsoft Word 2010

6.1.4 Creating a Bibliography

In the new versions of Microsoft Word, adding elements like an index, table of contents,
and bibliography is almost a one click action. If you have prepared your references correctly
and added them to the Source Manager correctly, you can click on the Bibliography icon in
the References ribbon in Word 2010 and insert a fully formatted *bibliography* (with the predefined options of using either the heading Bibliography or Works Cited).

A **BIBLIOGRAPHY** *is a list of sources used in a document and typically located towards the bottom of the authored file.*

This will add the references formatted according to the citation style you have selected in the formatting defined for your document. You can see a completed example and the selection menu in Figure 6.8.

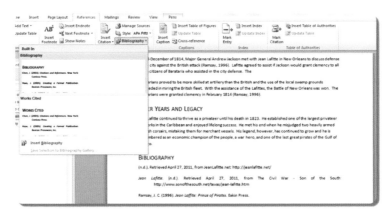

◀ **FIGURE 6.8** Example Bibliography and Selection menu in Microsoft Word 2010

If you click on the *Bibliography* icon, you will get a dropdown menu showing a preview of the built-in *Bibliography* and *Works Cited* options; you can click on either of these to insert the formatted result (arranged in the citation style you selected beside the icon such as *APA* used in the example) in your document wherever your cursor is placed. For the example project, the *Bibliography* entry was chosen and it was placed at the very end of the document.

> **OFFICE 2011** In Word 2011, the Bibliography icon is located in the References panel of the Document Elements ribbon.

6.2 ADDITIONAL PROOFING TOOLS

Word contains a number of tools for document review in addition to the tools for references and managing tables and citations already mentioned. The most common tool you will likely use is the Spelling and Grammar tool. You may also use Word Count for determining the number of words in your document; this is useful in business or academic settings where limitations may be placed on the length of a document in terms of the number of words allowed. Other tools that you may need to use are the thesaurus and the language and translation tools provided in Word.

6.2.1 Thesaurus

A thesaurus is a tool for finding words with a similar meaning (called synonyms) as a word you want to replace. This is a useful tool if you are using a word too much in your writing and want to vary it throughout. If you have used the same term too often in a document, you probably need to find an alternative word to keep your audience from getting bored of the repetition; if this happens, the audience may start to skim your writing instead of reading every word of it.

You can access the Thesaurus in Word 2010 by opening the *Review* ribbon and choosing *Thesaurus*. This will open a Research pane to the right side of your document. Type the word for which you want synonyms in the *Search for* field and select the correct Thesaurus from the drop-down menu. Hitting the enter key (or pressing the *Start searching* icon) will populate the text area beneath it with potential replacement terms. An example is shown in Figure 6.9.

If you are unsure of the exact meaning of the word you are substituting into your document, it is always a good idea to look it up and make sure you are using it correctly. You can use online dictionaries like Dictionary.com (*www.dictionary.com*) to do this or you can use any built-in dictionaries or even a Web search

▲ **FIGURE 6.9** Thesaurus example in Word

OFFICE 2011 In Word 2011, select View from the menu bar and choose *Thesaurus* or you can simply access your reference tools by selecting the Toolbox button.

6.2.2 Document Translations and Languages

Microsoft Word 2010 possesses the ability to translate words and phrases. From the Review ribbon you can access the Language panel which has two options available called Translate and Language. Using these options, you can change the language you use to type and proof a document; you can even translate documents such as email messages. It is important to realize that you must have the language pack installed that you want to use. For example, if you using Word in English language and you received an e-mail message with the Spanish language, you could translate the message to English, but you must have the Spanish language pack installed. You can see an example of the translator in Figure 6.10.

Figure 6.10 shows the process for activating the mini-translator. It is important to note you will be given the opportunity the first time you use the option to set your language translation preferences. If you are working with several languages, you can change the language preferences by selecting the Language option from the Language group. Furthermore,

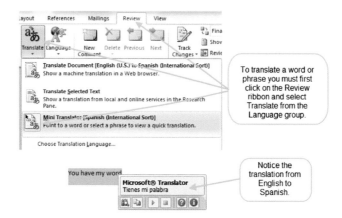

To translate a word or phrase you must first click on the Review ribbon and select Translate from the Language group.

Notice the translation from English to Spanish.

◄ FIGURE 6.10 Accessing the Word 2010 Translator

looking at the bottom of Figure 6.10 you can see a snippet from Word with the phrase "you have my word." By highlighting the phrase and holding the pointer over the highlighted area, you can see the Spanish translation of the phrase.

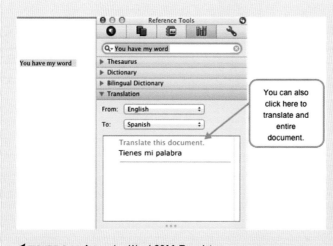

◄ FIGURE 6.11 Accessing Word 2011 Translator

OFFICE 2011 In Word 2011 on the Macintosh you can use the Reference Tools to access the Translation option. You can use the instructions demonstrated earlier in this chapter to access the reference tools or you can also select the View menu and choose *Translation*.

To translate a phrase in Word 2011, you can select the text you would like to translate as shown in Figure 6.11 and open your Reference Tools as previously demonstrated. When the Reference Tools window appears, you should immediately see the phrase you entered translated to the language you selected. You will notice in Figure 6.11 that you also have the option *Translate this document*; this option is used to translate an entire document. Just be sure to keep in mind that translating an entire document is done on the Web and the document will leave your computer unencrypted. This means you should be careful in sending documents that you want to keep confidential as there is always the possibility it could be intercepted by a computer hacker in transmission over the Internet.

6.3   KEYBOARDING VI

At this point, you should have already completed all of the prior lessons and you should now be proficient with the entire QWERTY keyboard. The remaining lessons will focus on typing speed and accuracy. You will be using the typing application you have used throughout the book to test yourself on typing speed while minimizing your number of errors.

6.3.1   Typing Tests

The typing tests are composed of sample passages of text that you should be able to type in less than one minute. Remember that you should be using good hand position on the keyboard and good posture while typing. You should also strive for accuracy and technique first, including touch typing where you are not looking at the keys on the keyboard. Remember that a smooth typist is always faster when good technique and posture is used. While the goal of touch typing is above 50 words per minute (WPM), your target speed for the practice lessons below should be to get above 30 or 40 WPM.

6.3.2   Words per Minute (WPM) Targets and Averages

The formula for words per minute (WPM) is the number of individual words typed in the time frame minus the number or errors times sixty over the number of seconds tested. The equation form of this is WPM = (words typed – number of errors)*(60/number of seconds tested). A professional data entry clerk or legal assistant usually types at about 50–80 WPM. Many jobs test for typing speed so it is critical that you complete and practice these typing exams to increase your speed and accuracy. One profession where typing exams are given is emergency dispatchers, sometimes referred to as 911 dispatchers. There are some dispatcher positions that can require 80–95 WPM and near-perfect accuracy is required. Just imagine what might happen if you were a dispatcher and you received a call for distress from a crime victim and you failed to type all of the offender description or the address correctly. This could create a hazardous situation for all involved. A new typist with practice might start out at 30–40 WPM and with practice this speed should increase relatively quickly.

6.3.3   Keyboarding Lessons 76–90

For each of these exercises, you should try to type the entire passage of text in less than a minute. Once you have completed these exercises, you should not repeat them excessively or you will start to memorize the text and compromise the results. After you have completed these example typing tests, you can select text at random and use the blank typing exercise to time your input and increase your speed. You should concentrate on form and accuracy and simply attempt to complete the exercise as quickly as possible.

Lesson 6.1 Practice Exam

Type as much of the following as you can in about one minute; try to complete the exercise before the timer runs out if possible. There are about 40–60 words in each passage. You can use the included software to track your time, speed, and errors. The goal of touch typing is to reach and repeatedly attain at least 50 WPM.

```
The need for information sharing in the criminal justice
community is evident and appears to be gaining momentum as
agencies invest in new technologies and software to
increase their crime fighting abilities. The new Global
Justice extensible markup language (XML) Data Model (Global
JXDM) developed by the Department of Justice will allow law
enforcement agencies throughout the United States
```

Lesson 6.2 Practice Exam

Type as much of the following as you can in about one minute; try to complete the exercise before the timer runs out if possible. There are about 40–60 words in each passage. You can use the included software to track your time, speed, and errors. The goal of touch typing is to reach and repeatedly attain at least 50 WPM.

```
The need for information sharing in the criminal justice community
is evident and appears to be gaining momentum as agencies invest
in new technologies and software to increase their crime fighting
abilities. As we enter the knowledge age, new technologies are
needed to help capture knowledge and spur innovation.
```

Lesson 6.3 Practice Exam

Type as much of the following as you can in about one minute; try to complete the exercise before the timer runs out if possible. There are about 40–60 words in each passage. You can use the included software to track your time, speed, and errors. The goal of touch typing is to reach and repeatedly attain at least 50 WPM.

```
Similarly, criminal justice administrators realize that the
emergence of mobile technologies, crime mapping, and system
integration have caused a new transition in the law enforcement
profession that allows officers to spend more time working the
neighborhoods in town and spending less time on administrative
duties (Skogan et al., 2002, 1).
```

Lesson 6.4 Practice Exam

Type as much of the following as you can in about one minute; try to complete the exercise before the timer runs out if possible. There are about 40–60 words in each passage.

You can use the included software to track your time, speed, and errors. The goal of touch typing is to reach and repeatedly attain at least 50 WPM.

```
New computer information systems are quickly replacing paper
based record systems throughout the nation. Many medium to
large size police departments are making these systems available
to their personnel but have been unable to implement the
resources required to transfer knowledge across jurisdictional
lines. Many criminals know that a lack of communication exists
at this level and they use this deficiency to their advantage
(Chen et al., 2002, 272).
```

Lesson 6.5 Practice Exam

Type as much of the following as you can in about one minute; try to complete the exercise before the timer runs out if possible. There are about 40–60 words in each passage. You can use the included software to track your time, speed, and errors. The goal of touch typing is to reach and repeatedly attain at least 50 WPM.

```
One of the most frequent examples of this situation can be
seen when a police officer encounters a suspicious vehicle on a
dark night and is presented with many tactical challenges. The
officer checks the vehicle's registration on approach and likely
might want to know other pieces of information, such as whether
the vehicle is stolen or has been involved in a crime in an
adjacent jurisdiction. The data requested could be difficult to
acquire specifically if the vehicle involved in an incident is
kept in an incompatible system in an adjacent jurisdiction.
```

Lesson 6.6 Practice Exam

Type as much of the following as you can in about one minute; try to complete the exercise before the timer runs out if possible. There are about 40–60 words in each passage. You can use the included software to track your time, speed, and errors. The goal of touch typing is to reach and repeatedly attain at least 50 WPM.

```
XML exchange technologies are already showing promise in the arena
of information sharing among dissimilar systems in the corporate
world. The U.S. Department of Justice's (DOJ) has developed a
new initiative to facilitate the exchange of criminal justice
information among agencies worldwide. The Global Justice XML
data model (GJXDM) involves an object-oriented data model, a data
dictionary, and XML schema specification (Toon, 2004).
```

Lesson 6.7 Practice Exam

Type as much of the following as you can in about one minute; try to complete the exercise before the timer runs out if possible. There are about 40–60 words in each passage. You can use the included software to track your time, speed, and errors. The goal of touch typing is to reach and repeatedly attain at least 50 WPM.

```
GJXDM was developed using external schema's as defined by the
World Wide Consortium (W3C) using approximately 16,000 law
enforcement related data elements. The entire code table used for
the National Incident-Based Reporting System (NIBRS) was used as
a schema, which will make it easier for agencies to fulfill annual
reporting requirements. GJXDM has other problems of its own
primarily the security issues involved (Miller, 2005).
```

Lesson 6.8 Practice Exam

Type as much of the following as you can in about one minute; try to complete the exercise before the timer runs out if possible. There are about 40–60 words in each passage. You can use the included software to track your time, speed, and errors. The goal of touch typing is to reach and repeatedly attain at least 50 WPM.

```
The GJXDM is extremely large and complex which also brings
concerns over performance of the systems involved. The DOJ also
understands the critical importance of criminal justice systems
integration towards the reduction of law suits traceable to poor
data quality, data redundancy, untimely access to information,
which can also lead to poor decision making (Roberts, 2004).
```

Lesson 6.9 Practice Exam

Type as much of the following as you can in about one minute; try to complete the exercise before the timer runs out if possible. There are about 40–60 words in each passage. You can use the included software to track your time, speed, and errors. The goal of touch typing is to reach and repeatedly attain at least 50 WPM.

```
The mapping of law enforcement systems is long overdue and cur-
rently there is not one national database for sharing knowledge
among law enforcement agencies. There are many factors that
have prevented the mapping of police information systems. One
of those reasons tends to be the fact that since the inception
of records management systems most law enforcement systems have
been created by software companies with dissimilar systems and
vendor specific proprietary software that makes other systems
incompatible (Kurtlander, 2005).
```

Lesson 6.10 Practice Exam

Type as much of the following as you can in about one minute; try to complete the exercise before the timer runs out if possible. There are about 40–60 words in each passage. You can use the included software to track your time, speed, and errors. The goal of touch typing is to reach and repeatedly attain at least 50 WPM.

```
The Department of Justice (DOJ) advancement of the GJXDM
appears as if it will change the way knowledge and information
is transferred between agencies globally. The GJXDM contains
a massive Global Justice XML Data Dictionary version (GJXDD
3.0.2) that is paving the way new information systems will be
developed in the law enforcement communities. The GJXDD or
data dictionary provides a common language which entities can
structure and disseminate information.
```

Lesson 6.11 Practice Exam

Type as much of the following as you can in about one minute; try to complete the exercise before the timer runs out if possible. There are about 40–60 words in each passage. You can use the included software to track your time, speed, and errors. The goal of touch typing is to reach and repeatedly attain at least 50 WPM.

```
In order to understand the Justice XML data model it is probably
important to have a basic understanding of object-oriented
concepts. Object-oriented programming has been around since the
sixties. The biggest reason that the DOJ decided to go with an
object-oriented model was object reuse.
```

Lesson 6.12 Practice Exam

Type as much of the following as you can in about one minute; try to complete the exercise before the timer runs out if possible. There are about 40–60 words in each passage. You can use the included software to track your time, speed, and errors. The goal of touch typing is to reach and repeatedly attain at least 50 WPM.

```
It is important to understand a few concepts before going any
further in this discussion. The first concept to learn is the
object. An object can be compared to a car. The registration,
size, shape, and color are the attributes of the vehicle. In
object-oriented programming a class is the designer's plan that
defines the behaviors and attributes of the object. The classes
are organized and sorted into common classes using a concept
```

```
called inheritance. Inheritance allows classes to inherit the
attributes of other classes (U.S. Department of Justice-Office
of Justice Programs, 2005).
```

Lesson 6.13 Practice Exam

Type as much of the following as you can in about one minute; try to complete the exercise before the timer runs out if possible. There are about 40–60 words in each passage. You can use the included software to track your time, speed, and errors. The goal of touch typing is to reach and repeatedly attain at least 50 WPM.

```
Many law enforcement systems that have been developed in the
past have been developed hastily and piecemealed without any
long-term goals in place. This has resulted in the creation
of inconsistent standards that have led to incompatible systems
(Tyworth and Sawyer, 2005). The data model also consists
of properties and types. The types are representations of
real-world objects such as a vehicle or boat.
```

Lesson 6.14 Practice Exam

Type as much of the following as you can in about one minute; try to complete the exercise before the timer runs out if possible. There are about 40–60 words in each passage. You can use the included software to track your time, speed, and errors. The goal of touch typing is to reach and repeatedly attain at least 50 WPM.

```
Accurate exchange of knowledge requires that the semantics be
clearly defined. XML tags or delimits portions of a document.
This document could be the results of some transaction or query.
XML represents the hierarchy of a document. The elements of an
XML document such as registration number, make, model, color
are the child component or a parent structure. The World Wide
Consortium (W3C) in hopes of developing ways to exchange seman-
tically correct data developed the XML Schema Definition (XSD).
```

Lesson 6.15 Practice Exam

Type as much of the following as you can in about one minute; try to complete the exercise before the timer runs out if possible. There are about 40–60 words in each passage. You can use the included software to track your time, speed, and errors. The goal of touch typing is to reach and repeatedly attain at least 50 WPM.

```
An XML schema creates an instance that determines what content
will be allowed a document. XSD defines the semantics and
structure of an XML document. Another part of the XML document
```

is the Metadata or "data about data" which allows indexing and retrieval to occur. Metadata allows information systems to build data from several sources (U.S. Department of Justice-Office of Justice Programs, 2005).

Lesson 6.16 Practice Exam

Type as much of the following as you can in about one minute; try to complete the exercise before the timer runs out if possible. There are about 40–60 words in each passage. You can use the included software to track your time, speed, and errors. The goal of touch typing is to reach and repeatedly attain at least 50 WPM.

Understanding what the dictionary is can easily be described by the simple concept that each object has its own vocabulary. The idea behind the dictionary is that it allows agencies to create their own dictionary within their systems so that documents can be exchanged easily without the expense of purchasing new proprietary systems (Newcombe, 2005). The GXJDM is massive in size and this fact worries database administrators.

Lesson 6.17 Practice Exam

Type as much of the following as you can in about one minute; try to complete the exercise before the timer runs out if possible. There are about 40–60 words in each passage. You can use the included software to track your time, speed, and errors. The goal of touch typing is to reach and repeatedly attain at least 50 WPM.

The data dictionary is required to provide common semantics and structure. The XML establishes the standard syntax and the semantics are kept in the data dictionary. Object-oriented concepts were applied in the construction of the dictionary developing re-useable objects in an inheritance hierarchy. One of the most difficult aspects of the development of the data dictionary was the compromise and compromise (U.S. Department of Justice-Office of Justice Programs, 2005).

Lesson 6.18 Practice Exam

Type as much of the following as you can in about one minute; try to complete the exercise before the timer runs out if possible. There are about 40–60 words in each passage. You can use the included software to track your time, speed, and errors. The goal of touch typing is to reach and repeatedly attain at least 50 WPM.

The DOJ has established a process for development of the GXJDM. The process was developed during several test projects, such as

the national Amber Alert, Field Interview, and Incident Report
projects. The process is a five step development system that
has been used to help in the planning of exchange development
projects at the state and local levels of government. The
process includes five phases that include the inception phase,
domain modeling phase, domain mapping phase, schema building
phase, and the packaging phase.

Lesson 6.19 Practice Exam

Type as much of the following as you can in about one minute; try to complete the exercise before the timer runs out if possible. There are about 40–60 words in each passage. You can use the included software to track your time, speed, and errors. The goal of touch typing is to reach and repeatedly attain at least 50 WPM.

The planning phase is similar to any other initial project
management planning phase. This first level requires initial
meetings with a facilitator, project initial planning occurs for
requirements, technology requirements, and personnel. The second
phase requires planning for structure and exchange content
requirements. This phase can last a few days and subject matter
experts as well as administrators must be present for input.

Lesson 6.20 Practice Exam

Type as much of the following as you can in about one minute; try to complete the exercise before the timer runs out if possible. There are about 40–60 words in each passage. You can use the included software to track your time, speed, and errors. The goal of touch typing is to reach and repeatedly attain at least 50 WPM.

The next process phase is called domain mapping phase. During
this phase domain structures are associated with types and
elements, this association process is called mapping. The
fourth step of this process involves using the results from
the mapping process and further constraining and identifying
top-level structures of the document. The fifth step is the
packaging phase; you include a sample instance to validate
the schema. During this phase it is possible to locate missing
elements and types. The final part of the packaging phase
requires that a document be produced with all the results
(U.S. Department of Justice-Office of Justice Programs, 2005).

Lesson 6.21 Practice Exam

Type as much of the following as you can in about one minute; try to complete the exercise before the timer runs out if possible. There are about 40–60 words in each passage. You can use the included software to track your time, speed, and errors. The goal of touch typing is to reach and repeatedly attain at least 50 WPM.

```
The first thing to understand about the GJXDM concerning infor-
mation systems security is that they do not contain any options
for enforcing security. Enforcing security requirements entails
using other standards depending on the architecture of the
exchange.
Security standards are applied using the Web services interoper-
ability organization using a standard from OASIS (U.S. Department
of Justice-Office of Justice Programs, 2005).
```

Lesson 6.22 Practice Exam

Type as much of the following as you can in about one minute; try to complete the exercise before the timer runs out if possible. There are about 40–60 words in each passage. You can use the included software to track your time, speed, and errors. The goal of touch typing is to reach and repeatedly attain at least 50 WPM.

```
The security issue is quite complex because when organizations
share data they may not know who is on the other end. This
reason is cause for concern. This is why juvenile records have
not been added to the GJXDD. Specific rules will have to be
added using the SAML to prevent data security violations.
Memorandums of understanding will also be needed between
agencies to help organizations establish standards for data
security (Miller, 2005).
```

Lesson 6.23 Practice Exam

Type as much of the following as you can in about one minute; try to complete the exercise before the timer runs out if possible. There are about 40–60 words in each passage. You can use the included software to track your time, speed, and errors. The goal of touch typing is to reach and repeatedly attain at least 50 WPM.

```
According to Sawyer and Tyworth (2005) the federalist model
naturally draws jurisdictional lines between federal, state, and
local government. This type of system can cause issues when
attempting to integrate systems (Sawyer and Tyworth, 2005).
Interoperability within the same continent is challenging
```

enough when taking into consideration all of the policies and jurisdictional issues. Other challenges that new terrorist threats have brought about are the existent need to share intelligence and law enforcement information with other countries. These issues will have to be addressed as well as security concerns (Howard and Kanareykin, 2006).

Lesson 6.24 Practice Exam

Type as much of the following as you can in about one minute; try to complete the exercise before the timer runs out if possible. There are about 40–60 words in each passage. You can use the included software to track your time, speed, and errors. The goal of touch typing is to reach and repeatedly attain at least 50 WPM.

Law enforcement information systems have evolved in the last decade. The emergence of the knowledge age requires that law enforcement organizations learn new ways to capture knowledge and share information. The GJXDM is a great accomplishment towards developing standards in the exchange of criminal justice information. Timely, accurate, and reliable information is needed and the GJXDM continues to evolve in the right direction (U.S. Department of Justice-Office of Justice Programs, 2005).

Lesson 6.25 Practice Exam

Type as much of the following as you can in about one minute; try to complete the exercise before the timer runs out if possible. There are about 40–60 words in each passage. You can use the included software to track your time, speed, and errors. The goal of touch typing is to reach and repeatedly attain at least 50 WPM.

There were several other best practices and research suggestions but the ones listed here seemed to be the most critical. The GJXDM exchange is a developing standard that will continue to evolve. The research suggests that although much work is still needed in the security area as well as other research topics; the GJXDM standard is here to stay and will improve the way knowledge and information is exchanged between law enforcement agencies globally. The future continued effective use of the GJXDM will require additional performance testing, optimization, and security standards to be further developed.

CHAPTER SUMMARY

This chapter covers the available tools for using the reference tools and document resources with the Word application. This includes the ability to conduct research using available research tools with the Word application. You can also perform document translation or simply highlight selected words or phrases for a quick translation. Additionally, Word provides tools to insert and manage citations and bibliographies. When you have completed the keyboarding tests in this chapter, you should be able to type a complete document at an acceptable rate of speed.

CHAPTER KNOWLEDGE CHECK

1 _____is the process of gathering data to solve a problem.

- ○ **A.** Web search
- ○ **B.** Research
- ○ **C.** Writing
- ○ **D.** None of the above

2 Credibility is defined as "the quality of being believable or worthy of trust."

- ○ **A.** True
- ○ **B.** False

3 An article based on the author's experience with very little verifiable data could be considered a:

- ○ **A.** Research article
- ○ **B.** Opinion piece
- ○ **C.** Professional article
- ○ **D.** None of the above

4 A qualitative study is also referred to as:

- ○ **A.** Social science research
- ○ **B.** Numerical analysis
- ○ **C.** Interactive
- ○ **D.** None of the above

5

A peer reviewed process helps to establish:

○ **A.** Credibility

○ **B.** Results

○ **C.** Outcomes

○ **D.** All of the above

6

Plagiarism is theft of someone else's _____ and is a serious ethical violation.

○ **A.** Ideas

○ **B.** Books

○ **C.** Money

○ **D.** None of the above

7

The Research Task pane is a tool that provides tools that include _____.

○ **A.** Web research

○ **B.** Dictionary

○ **C.** Thesaurus

○ **D.** All of the above

8

A *citation* is a _____ you use to gather information, text, or content for your work.

○ **A.** Bibliography management

○ **B.** Reference to an external source

○ **C.** Written paragraph

○ **D.** None of the above

9

_____are used to add explanation to an element of a document without interrupting the writing flow.

○ **A.** Footnotes

○ **B.** Paragraphs

○ **C.** Research task

○ **D.** None of the above

10

A _____ is a list of sources used in a document inserted towards end of the authored document.

○ **A.** Bibliography

○ **B.** Endnotes

○ **C.** Footnotes

○ **D.** All of the above

CHAPTER EXERCISES

The following five questions apply to the Windows version of Microsoft Word 2010. For the following five exercises you will utilize the same Word document as your answer sheet to submit to your instructor:

1. For this exercise, using Word 2010 locate the Research Task pane. Use the Research Task pane to research the topic "Mars rover" on all research sites available. Please write a properly formatted short essay explaining all of the current results.

2. Locate the Thesaurus, conduct a search on the following two words to include, research and quantitative. Please write the results by developing a properly formatted paragraph using five of the resulting words.

3. Using the mini translator, translate the paragraph you just wrote for the previous question.

4. Locate five sources using professional magazines in a field of interest to you. This could be a business magazine, computer magazine, or other professional topic. Using the Source Manager insert five sources that you will then use for the next questions.

5. Using the previous five sources you entered into your Source Manager to develop a bibliography using the APA format setting.

The following five questions apply to the Macintosh version of Microsoft Word 2011:

6. For this exercise, using Word 2011 on the Macintosh locate the Reference Tools. Use the search window to research the topic "Mars rover" using the Web search option. Please write a properly formatted short essay explaining all of the current results.

7. Using the Reference Tools, locate the Thesaurus, conduct a search on the following two words to include, research and quantitative. Please write the results by developing a properly formatted paragraph using five of the resulting words.

8. Using the Reference Tools, type the phrase "The key to fast typing is good posture and technique" and select translation.

9. Locate five sources using professional magazines in a field of interest to you. This could be a business magazine, computer magazine, or other professional topic. Using the Toolbox and the Citations option insert five sources that you will then use for the next question.

10. Using the previous five sources you entered into your Citation option develop a bibliography using the APA format setting.

CHAPTER REVIEW QUESTIONS

1. Please explain the difference between qualitative and qualitative research. Please be sure to include how research differs from just writing an article review.

2. Using either the Reference Tools within Word 2011 or the Research Task Pane within Word 2010, locate five sources from the Web. Using the techniques from this chapter to determine if a source is credible or not, analyze each source and explain why each source is credible.

3. What techniques are used to assure the research that scientists produce in a real-world environment is credible?

4. Using the research techniques you have learned in this chapter investigate the term "peer review process" and write an essay using credible sources you have found on the subject. Be sure to integrate a complete bibliography and end notes using the techniques you have learned in the chapter.

5. Using any of the essays you have developed, translate one complete document using the options available on either the Windows or Macintosh platform.

6. Locate the Encarta encyclopedia and find the term "Event Horizon." Use the dictionary on either the Windows or Macintosh platform to define each of the terms within the paragraph that explains this phenomena.

7. Locate the Help file within Word. Locate and explain the steps required to update your language settings or add a new language pack to your application.

8. Investigate and develop an article on a subject relating to the U.S. space program using the research and document tools found within Word. Evaluating five articles find data that supports your position on why or why not this program is important. Please include a bibliography and footnotes using the skills learned in this chapter.

9. Using the document resources located in this chapter use the Web to search for the writing standard organization your school follows. Using one of the sources located during the previous exercises; use the standards available on the Web to determine if the citation Word just formatted for you is correct according to the governing body.

10. Using the document resources located in this chapter use the Web to search for the writing standard organization your school follows. Once you have located the site write a short essay on the steps used to determine when you should use footnotes, endnotes, and a bibliography.

KEYBOARDING DRILLS

1. Type as much of the following as you can in about one minute; try to complete the exercise before the timer runs out if possible. There are about 40–60 words in each passage. You can use the included software to track your time, speed, and errors. The goal of touch typing is to reach and repeatedly attain at least 50 WPM.

```
Jean Lafitte is known as a pirate and a hero. He resented the
title of pirate since he saw his activities as serving an eco-
nomic purpose in the fledgeling United States; he titled himself
a privateer and would duel to the death if called a pirate.
```

2. Type as much of the following as you can in about one minute; try to complete the exercise before the timer runs out if possible. There are about 40–60 words in each passage. You can use the included software to track your time, speed, and errors. The goal of touch typing is to reach and repeatedly attain at least 50 WPM.

```
Lafitte was charismatic and handsome as well as tall for the
time, and the goods he brought into the local economy were
```

prized by rich and poor alike. He organized a large economy
of black market goods that were aquired by theft, piracy, and
smuggling, and he brought them into the hands of those who
could pay for them.

3. Type as much of the following as you can in about one minute; try to complete the exercise before the timer runs out if possible. There are about 40–60 words in each passage. You can use the included software to track your time, speed, and errors. The goal of touch typing is to reach and repeatedly attain at least 50 WPM.

By 1810, Barataria was booming. Goods were being smuggled into
the port at Barataria and offloaded to barges for transport
through the bayous to New Orleans. Pierre served the business
in the city while Jean managed activities from the island
outpost. In 1812, they outfitted a schooner for privateering and
started to acquire goods directly from piracy (Ramsay, 1996).

4. Type as much of the following as you can in about one minute; try to complete the exercise before the timer runs out if possible. There are about 40–60 words in each passage. You can use the included software to track your time, speed, and errors. The goal of touch typing is to reach and repeatedly attain at least 50 WPM.

According to the legend, they decided never to attack an
American vessel, preferring British pounds to American dollars
from their captured prizes. Despite having no country of
loyalty, it is rumored that the Lafittes admired the United
States Constitution and wished to emulate it in their own
growing network of operations.

5. Type as much of the following as you can in about one minute; try to complete the exercise before the timer runs out if possible. There are about 40–60 words in each passage. You can use the included software to track your time, speed, and errors. The goal of touch typing is to reach and repeatedly attain at least 50 WPM.

Aquiring the *Dorada* and the *Dilligent*, the Lafittes amassed
one of the largest privately owned corsair fleets of the time
(JeanLafitte.net). They would sail the ships into New Orleans

and load them with outgoing provisions, but maintain a list of smuggled goods on the manifest for the official signature of the customs agent who was generally unconcerned with outgoing cargo.

6. Type as much of the following as you can in about one minute; try to complete the exercise before the timer runs out if possible. There are about 40–60 words in each passage. You can use the included software to track your time, speed, and errors. The goal of touch typing is to reach and repeatedly attain at least 50 WPM.

The British planned an attack on a small smuggling ship which ended with the British officials surrounded on Barataria; the British wanted to offer the privateers amnesty and landholdings in the British colonies in exchange for their assistance to the British Navy in the war.

7. Type as much of the following as you can in about one minute; try to complete the exercise before the timer runs out if possible. There are about 40–60 words in each passage. You can use the included software to track your time, speed, and errors. The goal of touch typing is to reach and repeatedly attain at least 50 WPM.

When Lafitte warned the United States government about the impending plan of attack in the hope of getting the same offer from the United States, the government responded instead by destroying the operations at Barataria (Ramsay, 1996). Lafitte, however, managed to escape.

8. Type as much of the following as you can in about one minute; try to complete the exercise before the timer runs out if possible. There are about 40–60 words in each passage. You can use the included software to track your time, speed, and errors. The goal of touch typing is to reach and repeatedly attain at least 50 WPM.

The real legend of Jean Lafitte and his brother Pierre begins in Barataria Bay. Barataria is a small secluded island off the coast near the barrier islands of Grande Terre and Grande Isle in Barataria Bay. It was far from the United States naval base, so it made a good location for smuggling.

9. Type as much of the following as you can in about one minute; try to complete the exercise before the timer runs out if possible. There are about 40–60 words in each passage. You can use the included software to track your time, speed, and errors. The goal of touch typing is to reach and repeatedly attain at least 50 WPM.

```
The United States instituted the Embargo Act of 1807 which
specified that no United States ship could dock at a foreign
port. This made life difficult for merchant vessels and denied
the population foreign goods and luxuries. The Lafitte brothers
decided to capitalize on this situation and provide the neces-
sary economic assistance in the form of illegal activities.
```

10. Type as much of the following as you can in about one minute; try to complete the exercise before the timer runs out if possible. There are about 40–60 words in each passage. You can use the included software to track your time, speed, and errors. The goal of touch typing is to reach and repeatedly attain at least 50 WPM.

```
Baratarians proved to be more skilled at artillery than the
British and the use of the local swamp grounds succeeded in
miring the British fleet. With the assistance of the Lafittes,
the Battle of New Orleans was won. The Baratarians were granted
clemency by Andrew Jackson in February 1814 (Ramsay, 1996),
making legitimate citizens out of the gentlemen outlaws that
ruled the commerce of the region.
```

Spreadsheets and Typing Tables and Numbers

In this chapter, you will learn about data entry in spreadsheets. Spreadsheet software is another class of productivity software that is useful for organizing and managing lists, numbers, and calculations. Spreadsheet software is robust in its ability to manipulate numbers and perform complex numerical calculations. This is a good tool for managing lists of text or numerical results, such as accounting. For the keyboarding lesson in this chapter, you will practice typing tables of information as text. You will also learn to use the ten-key keypad that is common to full sized keyboards which is used to enter numerical data quickly. Once you have completed the chapter, you will be able to:

- Navigate the spreadsheet software interface

- Add and format text and numerical data in a spreadsheet

- Add simple formulas to a worksheet for performing calculations

- Organize data into tabbed tables

- Use the ten-key keypad for entering numerical data quickly

7.1 INTRODUCTION TO SPREADSHEET SOFTWARE

Spreadsheet software is used to manage and process large amounts of data. A spreadsheet is organized into a grid of rows (indicated by number) and columns (indicated by letter). The intersection of these rows and columns is called a *cell*; a cell is identified by letter and number, so A1 would be the first cell of the spreadsheet. A spreadsheet document is not delimited by printed pages as you have previously seen with word processing software. Instead, it is organized as individual spreadsheets or worksheets (identified by the tabs at the bottom of the interface in the common spreadsheet applications); the entire file is called a *workbook*. A worksheet can contain many printed pages worth of material. In fact, a worksheet can contain thousands of rows or columns that would be infeasible to print; the maximum size of a worksheet in Excel contains rows up to row 1048576 and columns up to column XFD. The power of spreadsheets is in the use of *formulas*, which are capable of complex calculation using the individual values in the cells of the sheet or even from other spreadsheets.

A **ROW** *in spreadsheet software is the horizontal grouping of data that is divided by columns; rows are signified by numbers.*

A **COLUMN** *in spreadsheet software is the vertical grouping of data that is divided by rows; columns are signified by letters.*

A **CELL** *in spreadsheet software is the intersection of a row and a column, containing a single piece of data, which can be text, a number, a formula, or an object; cells are signified by the letter of the column and the number of the row.*

A **FORMULA** *in spreadsheet software is a mathematical calculation that results in a data value; the value is displayed in the cell in which the formula is typed.*

Cells are not intended for large amounts of text; you should ideally include one piece of data or information per cell. Spreadsheets are best for organizing data and calculating results. If you want the results to accompany text, you should produce your results in a spreadsheet and export the relevant data to a word processing document. There are an enormous number of applications for spreadsheets across disciplines such as accounting and mathematics. This chapter provides you with an introduction to spreadsheet software and its functionality, but the practical applications of this technology go far beyond the scope of this text. Some general uses that you may find for spreadsheet software are formatting information in large tables, creating charts to display a visualization of data, and performing complex mathematical calculations.

The spreadsheet software application in Microsoft Office is called Excel. To get started using Excel, you should open the software just like you open Word and use the *File* menu to save your new open document. The native file type in Excel is Excel Workbook (.xlsx), which is the file type you should use unless you are exporting the data elsewhere.

7.1.1 Anatomy of Excel

Excel uses the ribbon interface with which you should now be familiar. Beneath the ribbon interface is the Formula bar, which is used for naming cells and defining calculations. The main pane of the document window looks very different from the word processing applications you have seen so far; it displays the rows, columns, and cells of the document. The bottom of the interface contains tabs for you to select the worksheet that is active in the document pane. Depending on the version of Excel you are using, the ribbons and shortcuts available will be slightly different. You can jump to the section that is relevant to you.

7.1.2 Microsoft Excel 2010

The interface for Excel 2010 has the same ribbon structure and general layout with which you should be familiar from the other Office applications. You can see an example of the interface for Excel 2010 in Figure 7.1. The Formula bar, located beneath the ribbon interface, identifies the current cell that you have selected and displays the contents of the cell. When you begin using functions, the Formula bar will become much more relevant. It allows you to perform a formula lookup and will help identify any possible errors in your formula construction.

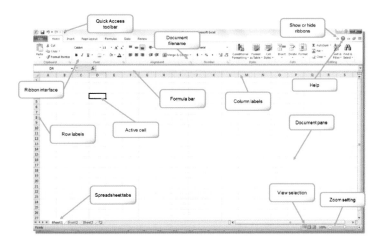

◀ **FIGURE 7.1** Anatomy of Excel 2010

You may notice that there is a significant departure in the construction and navigation of the document pane of the interface. The document is divided into cells. You can use the arrow keys to navigate from one cell to the next or you can click on a cell to activate it. The current cell is called the active cell and the row and column in which it resides will also be highlighted for you to identify them quickly. You can hold the *Shift* key to select multiple cells. Each cell acts like a text box in which you can type information.

The bottom of the interface has a set of tabs, each of which identifies an individual spreadsheet within the overall workbook (the file itself). You can navigate to these spreadsheets by clicking on the tabs or by using the directional arrows to the right of the tabs. The bottom of the interface also contains the view options, which allow you to see the page breaks in your document in either a Page Layout view or a Page Break Preview; the Normal view tends to be the most helpful for document creation. When you have numeric values selected, the bottom of the interface will also display an automatic calculation of the average of the values, the sum of the values, and the number of values you have selected (omitting white space). This is a nice feature for quickly assessing statistics on a list.

The available ribbons and functions are quite different from the interface for Word. The Home ribbon contains the Number panel for formatting numeric values (either as direct text input or as the result of formula calculations), as well as commands for style formatting and for adding and deleting cells. Of particular note are the Fill icon, which is used to replicate values or predict entries in a series, and the Sort and Filter icon, which is used for list management. The Insert ribbon, shown in Figure 7.2, contains several entries of note, particularly the Chart creation functionality, single-cell charts called Sparklines, and the icon to create a PivotTable, which is one of the more advanced features of Excel.

◀ **FIGURE 7.2** Insert ribbon in Excel 2010

The Page Layout ribbon, shown in Figure 7.3, is used to manage the spreadsheet into printable regions. You can add a background, insert manual page breaks, and set the printable region size for your spreadsheet. If printing is a concern, it may be helpful to preview the print regions to keep your document confined within the desired page delineations. This is especially important if you are using this as a printed supplement to a Word document or report.

◀ **FIGURE 7.3** Page Layout ribbon in Excel 2010

The Formulas ribbon contains categories of formulas from which you can select to insert into your document. This ribbon also contains the functionality to trace dependencies among cells in your spreadsheet and provides manual links to set calculation options for your spreadsheet; by default, all calculations are updated immediately when a value on which they depend is changed. The Formulas ribbon is shown in Figure 7.4.

◀ **FIGURE 7.4** Formulas ribbon in Excel 2010

The Data ribbon, shown in Figure 7.5, contains several useful commands, including the Remove Duplicates command to make sure no identical values are repeated in your list and the Text to Columns command to convert continuous text into multiple columns based on a delimiter character. This ribbon also contains commands to manage external sources, perform a What-If Analysis (for goal seeking), validate data, and perform advanced filtering for lists.

◀ **FIGURE 7.5** Data ribbon in Excel 2010

The Review ribbon gives you the ability to add comments to your spreadsheet. Unlike Word, Excel places comments in a triangle icon in the upper-right corner of the cell to which they are attached. The Review ribbon also gives you options for protecting your document from changes or sharing your document on a network location for others to edit. You can also select the Start Inking icon to use your mouse as a pen to mark up your document. The Review ribbon is shown in Figure 7.6.

◀ **FIGURE 7.6** Review ribbon in Excel 2010

The View ribbon, shown in Figure 7.7, allows you to change the view of the document as usual, but it also allows you to manage your workspace. The views in Excel are primarily the Normal view and views to preview page layouts for printing, such as Page Break Preview.

The Page Layout view is not recommended for constructing or working with your document. You can show or hide various document elements from this ribbon as well, such as the gridlines and the Formula bar. The Freeze Panes functionality allows you to preserve your headings as you scroll through your document. The Split function lets you set up multiple viewing panes of your document so you can view disjoined elements side by side. You can also use the Save Workspace icon to store the configuration of multiple document windows so you can view different workbooks at the same time on your monitor.

◀ **FIGURE 7.7** View ribbon in Excel 2010

Microsoft Excel 2011

The interface for Excel 2011, shown in Figure 7.8, is very similar to what you have encountered with the other Office applications, Word, for Macintosh computers. The interface contains the standard menu and ribbons where most of your functionality is located. In addition, you have a Formula bar that is used to construct calculations in the spreadsheet and edit information in the cells of the document. The main document is divided into cells, which can be navigated with the arrow keys on the keyboard. The columns are labeled by letters across the top, and the rows are labeled with numbers down the left side. The tabs at the bottom are the individual spreadsheets within the workbook (the overall document).

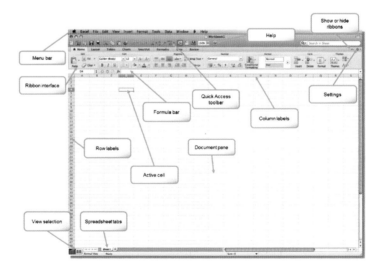

◀ **FIGURE 7.8** Anatomy of Excel 2011

Clicking with the mouse on a cell in the document makes that cell the active cell; this action outlines the cell in a thick border and highlights the row and column labels for quick reference. The cell reference will also appear on the left side of the Formula bar. Options in the Quick Access toolbar include a toggle that allows you to show or hide the Formula bar and links to common functions like SUM (which is discussed later in this chapter). The bottom of the interface contains the view selection where you can alternate between the Normal view and a preview of the page breaks in your document for printing.

> **OFFICE 2011** When you start Excel 2011, it will present you with a similar template gallery to Word 2011. You can select a template on which to base your document or you can choose Cancel on the gallery interface to get a standard spreadsheet document.

The Home ribbon contains the standard text formatting options, along with a panel for formatting numeric values. This is necessary for effectively managing and displaying data in the spreadsheets. The Home ribbon also contains icons for inserting and deleting rows and columns and for using special preset formatting options.

The Layout ribbon, shown in Figure 7.9, contains view settings and print options and is primarily used for establishing print regions and previewing the print area. This ribbon can also be used to set up a workspace where you can open multiple workbook documents on the screen for use at the same time.

◀ **FIGURE 7.9** Layout ribbon in Excel 2011

The Tables ribbon is used to format cells in the document as a table; this is useful for managing and maintaining lists of information. This ribbon also lets you select whether you want to include specific elements in your table formatting, such as a header row. The Charts ribbon is where you create a visual data representation to include in your spreadsheet. There are a number of chart types available for different types of data and different presentations of information. The SmartArt ribbon is similar to what is found in Word and PowerPoint; you can use this ribbon to add graphics to your document to convey information visually. These three ribbons are shown in Figure 7.10.

◀ **FIGURE 7.10** Tables, Charts, and SmartArt ribbons in Excel 2011

The Formulas ribbon is where you can access the available formula library in Excel. This ribbon contains an icon for quick access to formulas for summations and averaging, as well as the Formula Builder icon for creating more advanced calculations. You can also control the recalculation options for your formulas from this ribbon (by default, the recalculation is immediate whenever a value is changed) and trace the cells used in your calculations. The Formulas ribbon is shown in Figure 7.11.

◀ **FIGURE 7.11** Formulas ribbon in Excel 2011

The Data ribbon, shown in Figure 7.12, contains the functionality for managing information in your spreadsheet. You can sort and filter data from this ribbon, manage external data sources, remove duplicate values in a list, and convert the existing text into separate columns. Data validation and grouping is also performed from this ribbon.

◀ **FIGURE 7.12** Data ribbon in Excel 2011

The Review ribbon, shown in Figure 7.13, is primarily used for document collaboration and markup. You can add or address comments from this ribbon, and also share your document or set document protection so it cannot be altered.

◀ **FIGURE 7.13** Review ribbon in Excel 2011

USING SPREADSHEETS

Now that you are familiar with the interface of the software, the next step is to start creating spreadsheet documents to explore the features of the software. Spreadsheets allow you to create and organize text but also provide you with the ability to utilize text-based numbers in calculations. Formatting numbers is the first significant departure you will encounter from using word processing software. The first tab (labeled *Sheet1*) at the bottom of the interface is the initial default worksheet in the workbook. You can rename these worksheets by right-clicking on the sheet name, and selecting *Rename* from the menu. Be sure to save your work often when you have made changes so you do not lose them accidentally, just as you should in any other software program.

7.2.1 ## Adding and Formatting Text

You can type in any of the cells in your document by clicking inside of them and simply typing keys on the keyboard. The formatting options for text are very similar to what you have seen in Word. The exception to this is that the Highlight function will apply to the entire cell instead of just the highlighted text and there are no Text Effects options as Word provided. In place of this is a new ability to add borders to your cells to highlight the contents.

In addition to the changes in the Font panel of the Home ribbon, there is a new Alignment panel which contains functionality for placing your text inside of the cell. You can see the Alignment panel from the Home ribbon in Figure 7.14. You should be familiar with the justification options presented: Left, Center, and Right. The row of icons above these provides the vertical alignment capability, where you can align the text with the top of the cell (Top Align), the vertical center of the cell (Middle Align), or the bottom of the cell (Bottom Align).

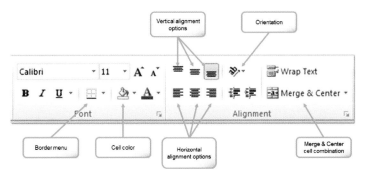

▲ **FIGURE 7.14** Font and Alignment panels of the Home ribbon in Word 2010

In addition to the vertical and horizontal alignment options, the Alignment panel also gives you the option to angle your text across the cell via the Orientation menu; this allows you to set the angle and direction of your text in the cell. Changing the orientation can make the contents of the cell more difficult to read so you should keep that in mind when using this modification. The Alignment panel also allows you to increase or decrease the indentation of the text in the cell.

There are two additional settings on the Alignment panel which should be considered: Wrap Text and Merge and Center. The Wrap Text option determines how text will behave in the cell. In Excel, any text by default will overflow into the next neighboring cell to the right if that cell does not have its own contents. When you enable Wrap Text, you allow the contents of the cell to spread over multiple lines in the cell.

NOTE To manually add a line break in Excel, you must hold down the modifier alt key along with the enter key; otherwise pressing the enter key will move you to the next cell in the document. Press the enter key twice to add a blank row between categories.

Finally, the Merge and Center functionality is used to combine the contents of neighboring cells into a single cell. When you use this, you must have the cells highlighted which you want to combine. By default, the merged contents will be centered in the result, but you can use the text formatting commands to alter this placement.

Activity 25 – Creating a Spreadsheet

Using Figure 7.15 as a guide, create a new spreadsheet and save it as *Activity25*. Recreate the formatting and display of Figure 7.15 but include yourself and either your friends or family in the list. Try to get the display of your formatting to resemble the example as closely as you can.

	A	B
1		**Naughty/Nice**
2	KK Kennedy	*Naughty*
3	RJ Malatin	*Nice*
4	M Tkach	*Naughty*
5	T DaCosta	*Nice*
6	W Mills	*Nice*
7	CD Yorkshire	*Naughty*
8	M Sliderson	*Nice*
9	K Pratt	*Nice*
10	S "L" Gomez	*Naughty*
11	FB Kennedy	*Naughty*
12	B Roberts	*Nice*

▲ **FIGURE 7.15** Example spreadsheet

If you need more room in a column for text you have entered, you can resize its width by selecting the line separating it from the next column and dragging it to expand or shrink the column width; for example, you can select the line dividing column A from column B and drag it to the right to expand column A. You can see an example of a formatted spreadsheet in Figure 7.15 demonstrating all of the elements that have been described so far.

You can apply formatting to an entire row or column by clicking on the row or column label, respectively, and then selecting the formatting commands you wish to apply. If you want to apply the formatting to the entire spreadsheet, select the small unlabeled area to the left of column A and above row 1 and select the formatting commands.

Formatting Values

One of the most significant differences between spreadsheet software and word processing software aside from the display is the management of numerical data. You may notice that if you add numbers to your spreadsheet, they will align to the right of the cell by default; text, on the other hand, aligns to the left. This is because the numerical data is being processed differently. The Number panel in the Home ribbon, shown in Figure 7.16, is where you find the formatting commands specific to the display of numerical data. The text formatting commands are all available for use on numeric values as well.

On the Number panel, you can select the formatting you want to use from the predefined list which includes Currency, Percentage, and Scientific. You can also choose *More Number Formats* from the Number Format selection box to customize your own number formatting style. This will open the Number tab of the Format Cells dialog box, which is also shown in Figure 7.16. In Excel 2010, you can also open this dialog box by selecting the expansion icon on the Number panel.

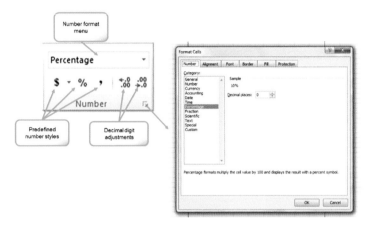

▲ **FIGURE 7.16** Number panel and Format Cells dialog box in Excel 2010

Activity 26 – Numerical Display

Create a new spreadsheet called *Activity26* (or open your work from *Activity25* and resave it as *Activity26*). In this version of the spreadsheet, you will either replace the column for "Naughty/Nice" with "Value of Presents" (you can also add a new column beside the original "Naughty/Nice" column). In this column, you will populate monetary values alongside your friends or family. You should format the values such that they are in currency with two digits past the decimal point. Make sure to save your work.

The additional commands available from the panel include the Accounting Number Format for currency values; this is a drop-down list of common world currencies. You can also use the Percent Style and Comma Style formats to adjust the cells quickly. The Increase Decimal and Decrease Decimal icons are used to increase or decrease the number of significant digits displayed for the value; this does not affect the value itself that is stored in the cell, just the manner in which that value appears.

7.2.3 Using Sequences

Excel can use two cells to predict simple series like counting numbers, days of the week, and months of the year. When you select both cells (from which the prediction will occur) with your cursor, you will see them surrounded by a thick border with a grip point at the lower-right corner of the selection; click and drag this grip point in the direction of the series entry (either horizontally or vertically) to extend the sequence. In the example shown in Figure 7.17, the grip point was drug out until a complete cycle of months from January to December was formed from the cells containing January and February.

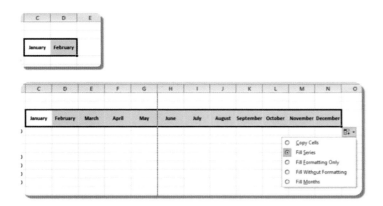

▲ **FIGURE 7.17** Series example in Excel 2010

You can use the automatic series generator in Excel to create headings for months, days, or years and to create an index for data values. The series can be extended vertically or horizontally, but the direction depends on the adjacency of the example cells you select; you can continue the sequence only in that direction. Excel will attempt to predict the sequence as an additive series; you must be sure the pattern you are attempting to have Excel predict is simple and you must verify that the values you get in response are correct. If you have only a single value highlighted, Excel will repeat that value in the adjacent cells.

7.2.4 Formatting Cells

In addition to formatting the text contents of the cells, you can also modify the cell color, dimensions, and borders for a single cell or a group of cells (when you have them selected). To set the cell dimensions you wish to have, you can use the *Format* command on the *Home* ribbon. For example, selecting *Column Width* from the drop-down list that appears allows you to choose the value for the width you want each column selected to have. You can do the same for the height as well.

You can add formatting to the cells by using the Fill Color menu and the Border menu on the Home ribbon. The Fill Color icon gives you the standard selection of theme colors (which can be selected from the Page Layout ribbon in Excel 2010 and from the Home ribbon in Excel 2011) and standard colors. The Border menu allows you to add specific borders (such as a Bottom Border or Outside Borders) from the default selections. You can also select the line styles from this menu in Excel 2010 or choose *More Borders* to access the advanced options for customizing the border. The selections you make will apply only to the cells that are highlighted when you choose the various options.

OFFICE 2011 The advanced options for border selection are available in Excel 2011 by choosing *Border Options* from the *Border* menu.

You can access all of these options from the *Format Cells* selection on the right-click menu. You must first select all of the cells to which you want the formatting to apply, right-click, select *Format Cells*, and then choose the tabs for Fill or Border as necessary. You can see an example of this dialog box in Figure 7.18.

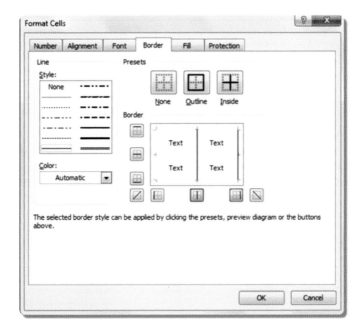

◀ **FIGURE 7.18** Border tab of Format Cells dialog box in Excel 2010

7.2.5 Freezing Panes

Using the Freeze Panes option allows you to keep your headings visible on the page no matter where you scroll within your spreadsheet. You can choose to freeze columns, rows, or both. The only caveat as to what can be frozen is that you must freeze the contents of the upper-left corner of the spreadsheet to the cell you choose for enabling the freeze. The cell you highlight when you choose the Freeze Panes option will define the border of what is frozen; any cells above and to the left of the selection (but not including the selected cell itself) will remain in place as you scroll the document.

In Excel 2010, the Freeze Panes icon is on the View ribbon; in Excel 2011, the Freeze Panes icon is on the Layout ribbon. For the example, if you click cell *C4* and select *Freeze Panes* to lock your headings in place, it will allow the remaining cells from C4 to the right and A4 down to scroll; this delineation is shown in Figure 7.19. To remove the Freeze Pane effect, select the *Freeze Panes* icon again and choose *Unfreeze Panes*.

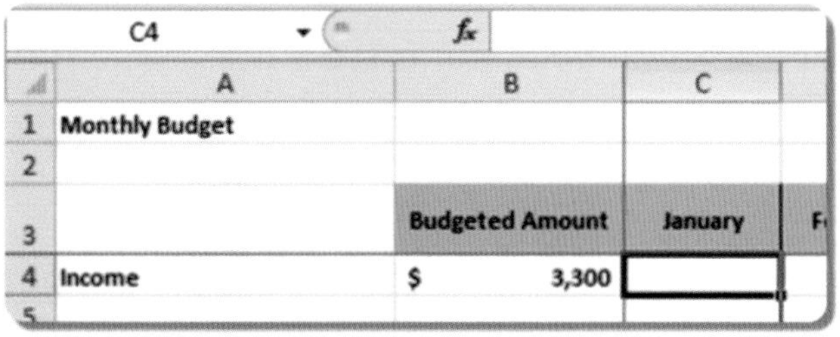

▲ **FIGURE 7.19** Example cell selection for Freeze Panes effect

7.2.6 Adding Basic Formulas

Formulas are an excellent way to perform calculations on the data within your spreadsheet. In fact, a large portion of the power of using spreadsheets is the ability to automate complex calculations. The formulas in your spreadsheet will operate just like equations, with the cells occupying the position of variables. Whenever you place your cursor in a cell and type the equals symbol (=), it signifies a calculation. You can then use the cell names as values; for the example, if you type *=B1+B2+B3+B4* into cell B5, the result of the sum from B1 to B4 will be placed as a value in cell B5. The example formula is shown in Figure 7.20.

As you type a formula, you will see your formula entry in the Formula bar along with two new symbols for Enter and Cancel; you can use these to finish your formula or you can just press the enter key. You can add any formatting to the cell that you want applied to the resulting value.

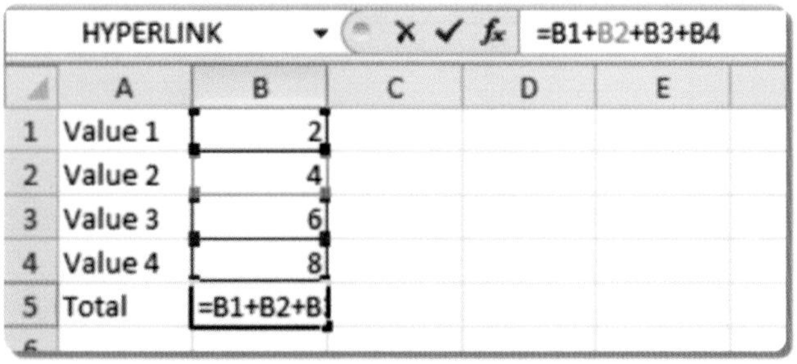

▲ **FIGURE 7.20** Example formula in Excel 2010

Activity 27 – Equations

For this activity, you will create a new spreadsheet document and save it as *Activity27*. In column A you will add the numbers 1 through 3 in cells A1 to A3. Place the numbers 4 through 6 in cells B1 to B3 and then place the numbers 7 through 9 in cells C1 through C3. Now, you will add formulas to calculate sums in column D and row 4. In cell A4, you should add the formula =A1+A2+A3. Now repeat the pattern in cells B4 and C4. Do the same in column D to calculate the sums of the row entries. As a final step, in cell D4, you should calculate the sum of all of the cells from A1 to C3. Save your work.

7.2.6.1 *Mathematical Calculations*

You can perform standard mathematical calculations in Excel in addition to entering formulas. The order of operations hierarchy in mathematics is upheld in Excel, where division and multiplication are ranked above addition and subtraction in performance order. Using parentheses will supersede any operation such that whatever is added inside of the parentheses will be performed first in the operation order.

Activity 28 – Mathematic Formulas

For this activity, you will practice with entering mathematic formulas into a spreadsheet. Create a new spreadsheet document and save it as *Activity28*. In column A, you should enter the numbers 2, 4, and 6 in cells A1 to A3. In cell B1, you should enter the equation =A1*A2. In B2 you should enter =A1/A2. In cell B3, you should enter =A3–(A1/A2). You should get the results 8, 0.5, and 7.5 as the results in cells B1 through B3. Save your work.

7.2.6.2 *Freezing Cells in Formulas*

When you copy and paste cells or when you duplicate cells, the cell values will automatically update based on the position of the formula. For instance, if you copy the example formula for sums in Figure 7.20 from cell *B5* to cell *C5*, the cell references that previously included cells in column B (cells *B1* to *B4*) will now refer to the equivalent cells in column C (cells *C1* to *C4*). To prevent this type of automatic update, you can use the dollar sign in your formula to fix a certain value.

As an example of this, consider the following:

- $B4 will preserve the column reference as column B when copied but will allow the row reference (row 4) to change.

- B$4 will preserve the row reference to row 4 but will allow the column reference, currently column B, to change.

- B4 will preserve the exact reference to column B and row 4, retaining this fixed value no matter where the formula is copied and placed.

7.2.6.3 *The SUM Formula*

In addition to standard mathematical operations, Excel has a library of existing formulas that you can use to perform complex calculations within your spreadsheet. One of the common formulas is SUM, which computes the numeric sum of the cells listed as its argument. An example of using SUM would be to replace the formula for calculating the total in Figure 7.20 (*=B1+B2+B3+B4* from the example) with the SUM formula operating on those cells; the formula would then be *=SUM(B1,B2,B3,B4)*. The term SUM is the name of the formula and the entries in the parentheses are the arguments, or values on which the formula is operating. The result of both of these calculations would be the same.

You can use the colon symbol (:) as a shortcut to include adjacent cells in an argument of a formula. Entering *B1:B4* in a formula means all of the cells from cells *B1* through *B4*, inclusive. The SUM function in the previous example can therefore be rewritten as *=SUM(B1:B4)* to produce the same result. You can only use the shortcut if you want to include all of the cells in an adjacent range. An example of this is shown in Figure 7.21.

◀ **FIGURE 7.21** Example use of the SUM formula

7.2.7 Using Directional Fill

When you want to duplicate a value or repeat a formula in a spreadsheet, you select the value you want to repeat, highlight the direction in the spreadsheet to which you want to repeat the value, and use the Fill menu to repeat it. The Fill menu, found on the Home ribbon, contains entries for the four primary directions. For example, *Fill Right* will select the leftmost value (which should be the one you want to repeat in the adjacent cells) and copy it to all of the highlighted cells to the right.

NOTE   You may get an error message (which appears as a small green triangle in the upper-left corner of the cell in Excel 2010) when you use formula fills or duplication. This happens when you omit adjacent cells in your formula. You should check whether this is a valid concern and use the error menu options to ignore the error if the adjacent cells should not be included.

7.2.8 Navigating the Spreadsheet

There are several shortcut commands on the keyboard that will allow you to move through your spreadsheet quickly. The arrow keys can be used to move one step for each key press in any of the cardinal directions. You can also hold down the shift key to select the cells between your starting location and where you end (if you move your cursor in two directions, it will select the rectangular set of cells between the starting location and the ending location just as it does when you click and drag the cursor).

The shortcut commands on the keyboard that are coupled with the Control (Ctrl) key can be used for quick navigation as follows (the Command key on a Macintosh is substituted in these examples for the Control key on a Windows machine):

- *Ctrl-a directional arrow*—This will jump the cursor to the last entry in the direction of the arrow key before a blank space in the current selection; if the cursor is already at a blank space, it will jump to the next location in line with content or, if there is no content, the cursor will jump to the end of the spreadsheet.

- *Ctrl-Shift-a directional arrow*—This has the same effect of moving the cursor as the shortcut command for Ctrl-a directional arrow, but it also highlights/selects the cells between the starting and ending location.

- *Ctrl-Home*—This returns the cursor to cell A1 regardless of the current cursor location.

- *Ctrl-End*—This sends the cursor to the farthest cell to the right and down on the spreadsheet where content has been added.

- *Ctrl-Page Down (Pg Dn)*—This command advances to the next worksheet in the workbook (just like clicking the tab to the right of the current worksheet).

- *Ctrl-Page Up (Pg Up)*—This command opens the previous worksheet in the work-book (just like clicking the tab to the left of the current worksheet).

- *Ctrl-A*—The Select All command in Excel will select only the cells that contain infor-mation that are adjacent to the current cell. Pressing *Ctrl-A* again with the adjacent information selected will select the entire worksheet.

NOTE

Pressing the tab key in a spreadsheet will move to the next cell in the document to the right of the current cell, just as it does in a table in Word.

7.2.9 Adding Charts

Charts are great tools for visualizing information. Because human beings are generally able to process visual information more quickly than text, charts are a great way to express the overall idea or trend of data in a single image rather than either a lengthy text explana-tion or large amounts of data that must be read. At this point, you should have some idea of how charts work from inserting them into your Word documents; Excel is the program that actually manages chart data whenever you add a chart to any Office document.

To create a chart in Excel, select the data range you want to include in the chart. With these cells selected, choose the chart type you want to insert. In Excel 2010, you can add a chart to your document by selecting the type of chart on the Insert ribbon; for example, you can select the *Line* icon and choose *Line* beneath the *2-D Line* heading to create a simple line chart for one or more data points that should be connected in individual lines. You can see an example of this type of line chart for a monthly budget in Figure 7.22.

OFFICE 2011 In Excel 2011, you can find the options for inserting charts in the Charts ribbon. When you have selected the option you want, a new chart will be added to your document.

In Excel, you can change the source data to automatically update the chart display. You can also change the range of cells used for the source data. To change the data selection used to generate your chart, you need to edit the chart data. In Excel 2010, you can find the *Select Data* icon in the context-sensitive Design ribbon for Chart Tools; in Excel 2011, the *Select* icon is located on the Charts ribbon. When you click this icon, a dialog box will appear from which you can edit the cell locations that determine the chart. In Excel 2010, click on the name of the series you want to alter and choose *Edit* to open a dialog box where you can select your data.

OFFICE 2011 In Excel 2011, you can edit series data by simply clicking on the name of the series; the source data fields will display on the right side of the pane.

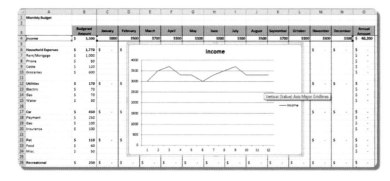

▲ **FIGURE 7.22** Example line chart

You can either enter the information (as you would for a formula) or click the data selection icon and use your mouse to highlight the correct cells in the document (press the enter key when you have selected the correct cells). You can also add a new data series to your charts. To do this, activate the data selection dialog box just as you would to edit the series. This time, you would choose the *Add* button to create a new series.

Once you have created a chart, you should format the chart so it is more readable and representative of its contents. One step in this process is adding a chart title. In Excel 2010, select the *Chart Title* icon on the context-sensitive *Layout* ribbon for Chart Tools and select *Above Chart*.

> **OFFICE 2011** In Excel 2011, select the *Chart Title* icon on the context-sensitive *Chart Layout* ribbon. Clicking the icon will add a default chart title that you can rename by clicking inside the text box and typing the name.

There are a variety of other elements you can add to your charts from the context-sensitive ribbons for designing and formatting charts. One of the more useful features with which you may want to become familiar is the use of trend lines. In Excel 2010, the trend line commands are located in the Layout ribbon for Chart Tools; in Excel 2011, these are found on the Chart Layout ribbon. To add a trend line, select the *Trendline* icon and choose one of the options available, such as *Linear Forecast Trendline*. In the dialog box that opens, select the series for which you want to predict the trend past the current cycle.

Another useful function is to adjust the labels of your axes. To do this, activate the data selection dialog box for your chart. For the horizontal axis, in Excel 2010 you will select the *Edit* button beneath *Horizontal (Category) Axis Labels*. This allows you to select a data range for your axis labels just as you can for the series data in your chart. You can do the same thing for the vertical axis as well.

> **OFFICE 2011** In Excel 2011, the series data for the horizontal axis is called *Category (x) axis labels*, which allows you to type a direct reference or use the selection icon to choose the cells you want to use as labels for your data.

7.3 KEYBOARDING VII

Now that you have practiced using the entire standard keyboard, you can concentrate on improving your speed as well as organizing your data. One of the common uses of typing in addition to word processing is entering information into data tables. This can be text data, numerical data, or a combination of both. In this lesson, you will focus on data organization into text-driven tables and learning the side keypad called a ten-key keypad that is common with full sized keyboards. This side keypad is used for quick numerical data entry and is common to many professions such as accounting.

7.3.1 Organizing Text into Tables

When you are using spreadsheet software or a table in word processing software, you have control over the alignment of your text. You can also move from one table cell to the next one to the right using the tab key. However, in cases where you do not have the ability to format tables using a pre-constructed document element, you may need to organize text into table form using only the keyboard as input. To do this, you need to figure out how long the longest element in each column will be and use the tab stops to space out the rest so your data aligns properly. This may mean examining the entire table and even counting for the longest element. To tab past the longest element, you can estimate the number of tab stops by dividing the length by 5 and adding 1 to the integer part of the result.

For example, in the text table shown, you must tab twice to accommodate the name column because Alice has five letters, so 5/5+1 = 2 tabs. The longest entry for WPM is 3 letters, so 3/5+1 = 1 because the integer result of 3/5 is 0. You can calculate the results for the Errors and Adjusted WPM columns; you should get 2 and 3 respectively if you have calculated correctly.

```
          WPM    Errors   Adjusted.WPM
Bob       22     2        20
Alice     44     3        41
Eve       122    87       35
Jeff      56     0        56
```

There is no defined standard for these types of tables and you may encounter different rules in different professions. For example, in accounting, some columns require the elements to align vertically along the decimal point in a column, which requires careful use of the spacebar along with the tab key to get the entries to align. You may also encounter cases in which you will use the vertical pipe character (|) and either the hyphen or underline character to provide borders on these tables. The lessons in this section are varied to expose you to different varieties of table data entry you may encounter.

7.3.2 Keyboarding Lessons 91–100

In the following keyboarding lessons, you should focus on constructing the tabbed tables properly. The timer counts up for all of these exercises, but you should try to complete them as quickly as possible while retaining your form and learning to spot check the number of tabs you will need to space out the table and accommodate all of the text needed in the column entries. While a lot of your typing will take place in the context of a software environment, efficient data entry is necessary in almost all professions.

7.1 Table Entry 1

For this exercise, you will focus on entering the tabbed table information presented in the text. You should learn to spot check the number of tab key presses you will need to properly organize the data into the columns needed. Note that not all of the columns will have the same width in some of these exercises. Maintain your typing form and do your best to touch by type without looking at the keys.

Type the following text:

```
Flight  Departure  Status
1123    2:00       On Time
2233    2:45       Delayed
3312    3:15       On Time
4410    4:00       10 Min
1212    4:25       On Time
110     5:00       On Time
```

7.2 Table Entry 2

For this exercise, you will focus on entering the tabbed table information presented in the text. You should learn to spot check the number of tab key presses you will need to properly organize the data into the columns needed. Note that not all of the columns will have the same width in some of these exercises. Maintain your typing form and do your best to touch by type without looking at the keys.

Type the following text:

```
Item  Account  Value
H45K  2231-09  $34.00
G55N  2231-10  122.50
G55S  2232-07  1200.00
N65J  2231-08   99.50
F32A  2231-04  110.00
F32B  2231-04   10.10
```

7.3 Table Entry 3

For this exercise, you will focus on entering the tabbed table information presented in the text. You should learn to spot check the number of tab key presses you will need to properly organize the data into the columns needed. Note that not all of the columns will have the same width in some of these exercises. Maintain your typing form and do your best to touch by type without looking at the keys.

Type the following text:

```
P1   P2   P3   (P1 AND P2) AND P3
 T    T    T    T
 T    T    F    F
 T    F    T    F
 T    F    F    F
 F    T    T    F
 F    T    F    F
 F    F    T    F
 F    F    F    F
```

7.4 Table Entry 4

For this exercise, you will focus on entering the tabbed table information presented in the text. You should learn to spot check the number of tab key presses you will need to properly organize the data into the columns needed. Note that not all of the columns will have the same width in some of these exercises. Maintain your typing form and do your best to touch by type without looking at the keys.

Type the following text:

```
Name:          Bill Williams
Account:       7788901-9976
Address:       1010 St. Louis Ln.
City:          St. Louis
Postal Code:   63109
Phone:         333-555-9980
```

7.5 Table Entry 5

For this exercise, you will focus on entering the tabbed table information presented in the text. You should learn to spot check the number of tab key presses you will need to properly organize the data into the columns needed. Note that not all of the columns will have the same width in some of these exercises. Maintain your typing form and do your best to touch by type without looking at the keys.

Type the following text:

Val.A		Val.B		Sum
23	|	23	|	46
10	|	5	|	15
11	|	22	|	33
8	|	8	|	16
2	|	2	|	4

7.6 Table Entry 6

For this exercise, you will focus on entering the tabbed table information presented in the text. You should learn to spot check the number of tab key presses you will need to properly organize the data into the columns needed. Note that not all of the columns will have the same width in some of these exercises. Maintain your typing form and do your best to touch by type without looking at the keys.

Type the following text:

```
Name           |  Address          |  Invited
B  Mills          44  Battlefield      Yes
S  Wave           14  Noise Ln         No
O  Primus         10  Leadership       Yes
B  Wasp           11  Yellow St        No
M  Weaver         21  H Ave            Yes
C  Danner         6 Redwood Dr         Yes
```

7.7 Table Entry 7

For this exercise, you will focus on entering the tabbed table information presented in the text. You should learn to spot check the number of tab key presses you will need to properly organize the data into the columns needed. Note that not all of the columns will have the same width in some of these exercises. Maintain your typing form and do your best to touch by type without looking at the keys.

Type the following text:

```
Make      Model      Year
Do        Strata     2005
Po        Prix       1983
Ho        Accor      2007
Do        Charge     2011
Ni        Stanza     1993
Su        P44        2005
```

7.8 Table Entry 8

For this exercise, you will focus on entering the tabbed table information presented in the text. You should learn to spot check the number of tab key presses you will need to properly organize the data into the columns needed. Note that not all of the columns will have the same width in some of these exercises. Maintain your typing form and do your best to touch by type without looking at the keys.

Type the following text:

```
Name              Category    Winner
L Neeson          Actor       -
J Depp            Actor       X
E McGregor        Actor       -
J Gyllenhaal      Actor       -
K Winslet         Actress     -
N Kidman          Actress     -
S Johansson       Actress     X
N Portman         Actress     -
```

7.9 Table Entry 9

For this exercise, you will focus on entering the tabbed table information presented in the text. You should learn to spot check the number of tab key presses you will need to properly organize the data into the columns needed. Note that not all of the columns will have the same width in some of these exercises. Maintain your typing form and do your best to touch by type without looking at the keys.

Type the following text:

```
Candidate         Poll Rank        Party
CD Yorkshire      23%              Independent
S Colbert         17%              Republican
I McKeller        10%              Democrat
R O'Rand           8%              Republican
E Cummings         6%              Democrat
S Poole            4%              Republican
R Parke            2%              Republican
```

7.10 Table Entry 10

For this exercise, you will focus on entering the tabbed table information presented in the text. You should learn to spot check the number of tab key presses you will need to properly organize the data into the columns needed. Note that not all of the columns will have the same width in some of these exercises. Maintain your typing form and do your best to touch by type without looking at the keys.

Type the following text:

	A	B	C	D	E	F	G	H
1		X				X	.	
2		.						
3	.				.			
4			X	X				
5			.		X			
6				.	.	.	X	X
7							.	
8	X							.

Ten Key Typing

The ten-key keypad is commonly included on the right hand side of a full sized keyboard. You can see an example of this in Figure 7.23. When using the ten-key keypad, you will move your right hand off of the keyboard and place it over the ten-key keypad with a new set of home row keys and finger motion. The home row keys on the ten-key keypad are numbers 4, 5, and 6, which correspond to your right index, middle, and ring fingers respectively. The 5 key has the tactile ridge so you can detect it with your finger without looking at it.

The top row keys are the 1, 2, and 3 keys which will be reached by moving the respective fingers straight up to strike the keys. Similarly, the bottom row keys are the 7, 8, and 9 keys

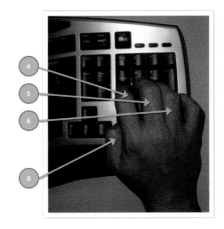

◄ FIGURE 7.23 Ten-key keypad, home row keys, and finger motion

which are struck by moving the respective fingers straight down to strike the key. The 0 key is struck with the right thumb. This keypad takes practice like a regular keyboard, but the industry standard for entering digits on this keypad is 250 digits per minute; the average speed for most people is roughly 200 digits per minute.

The keys surrounding the standard ten-key keypad will vary, but they typically include the common mathematical symbols for addition, subtraction, multiplication, and division as well as an enter key and the period or decimal point. This allows for rapid use of a computerized calculator where the enter key is equivalent to typing the equals sign. Num Lock is the lock on numerical symbols; it acts as a toggle, so when it is active, you will be typing the numbers only. When it is inactive, you will type any alternate symbols or functions on the number keys on the ten-key keypad; these could be the arrow keys or additional functions (like *home* to go to the start of a row or *end* to go to the end of a row). To reach the keys above and below the number configuration, you should use the finger that vertically lines up with the key. The keys to the right of the numbers should be typed using the right pinky (such as the plus and enter keys in the example layout).

NOTE

The intention of the ten-key keypad is to enter numeric data where you do not need spaces. However, you can easily incorporate spaces by using the spacebar on the standard keyboard with your left thumb in proper position.

7.3.4 ## Keyboarding Lessons 101–110

The following lessons all use the ten-key keypad. You can attempt these using the standard keyboard, but the speed of the standard keyboard is expectedly less than the practiced use of the ten-key keypad. The industry expectation is at least 250 digits per minute, which takes practice and repetition to achieve. There is no spacing in these exercises, but there are equation symbols. You can assume that any line break is the enter key on the ten-key keypad, which acts the same as the enter key on the standard QWERTY keyboard.

7.11 Ten Key Typing Home Row

For this exercise, you should focus on accuracy and speed. The timer for this exercise counts down, so you should try to enter the data as quickly as possible. You also need to concentrate on quick finger motion with minimal mistakes; this will take practice and you should feel free to repeat these exercises as often as necessary. Maintain your typing form and do your best to touch by type without looking at the keys.

Type the following text:

```
444+555+666
444+555+666
666+555+444+55+44+66+444+555+666
666+555+444+55+44+66+444+555+666
456654445566554445 6654
```

7.12 Ten Key Typing Top Row

For this exercise, you should focus on accuracy and speed. The timer for this exercise counts down, so you should try to enter the data as quickly as possible. You also need to concentrate on quick finger motion with minimal mistakes; this will take practice and you should feel free to repeat these exercises as often as necessary. Maintain your typing form and do your best to touch by type without looking at the keys.

Type the following text:

```
111+444+111+444+111+44+11+1441
222+555+222+555+222+55+22+2552
333+666+333+666+333+66+33+3663
111+222+333+444+555+666
111+444+222+555+333+666
```

7.13 Ten Key Typing Bottom Row

For this exercise, you should focus on accuracy and speed. The timer for this exercise counts down, so you should try to enter the data as quickly as possible. You also need to concentrate on quick finger motion with minimal mistakes; this will take practice and you should feel free to repeat these exercises as often as necessary. Maintain your typing form and do your best to touch by type without looking at the keys.

Type the following text:

```
111+444+777+111+444+777+111+44+77+44+11+147741
222+555+888+222+555+888+222+55+88+55+22+258852
333+666+999+333+666+999+333+66+99+66+33+369963
111+222+333+444+555+666+777+888+999
111+444+222+555+333+666
444+777+555+888+666+999
111+777+222+888+333+999
```

7.14 Ten Key Typing 0 Key

For this exercise, you should focus on accuracy and speed. The timer for this exercise counts down, so you should try to enter the data as quickly as possible. You also need to concentrate on quick finger motion with minimal mistakes; this will take practice and you should feel free to repeat these exercises as often as necessary. Maintain your typing form and do your best to touch by type without looking at the keys.

Type the following text:

```
111+444+777+000+111+444+777+111+44+00+77+44+11+147741
222+555+000+888+222+555+888+222+55+00+88+55+22+258852
333+000+666+999+333+666+999+333+00+66+99+66+33+369963
000+111+222+333+444+555+666+777+888+999
111+000+444+222+555+333+000+666
444+777+000+555+888+666+999+000
111+777+222+000+888+333+999+000
```

7.15 Ten Key Typing Equation Symbols

For this exercise, you should focus on accuracy and speed. The timer for this exercise counts down, so you should try to enter the data as quickly as possible. You also need to concentrate on quick finger motion with minimal mistakes; this will take practice and you should feel free to repeat these exercises as often as necessary. Maintain your typing form and do your best to touch by type without looking at the keys.

Type the following text:

```
111+444+777+000+111+444+777+111+44+00+77+44+11+147741
222-555-000-888-222-555-888-222-55-00-88-55-22-258852
333*000*666*999*333*666*999*333*00*66*99*66*33*369963
000/111/222/333/444/555/666/777/888/999
111/000*444+222-555-333+000*666/000
444+777-000+555-888+666-999+000
111/777*222/000*888/333*999/000
```

7.16 Ten Key Typing Decimal Notation

For this exercise, you should focus on accuracy and speed. The timer for this exercise counts down, so you should try to enter the data as quickly as possible. You also need to concentrate on quick finger motion with minimal mistakes; this will take practice and you should feel free to repeat these exercises as often as necessary. Maintain your typing form and do your best to touch by type without looking at the keys.

Type the following text:

```
232.33+334.55+556.77+999.11
2445.22+5567.01+3456.91
565.23-678.90-11.12-34.23-1.01
```

```
3445.91-9011.45-5678.41
7768.71*1123.98*9012.61
9011.45/1011.11/4566.99
```

7.17 Ten Key Typing Practice 1

For this exercise, you should focus on accuracy and speed. The timer for this exercise counts down, so you should try to enter the data as quickly as possible. You also need to concentrate on quick finger motion with minimal mistakes; this will take practice and you should feel free to repeat these exercises as often as necessary. Maintain your typing form and do your best to touch by type without looking at the keys.

Type the following text:

```
555-888-9999
333-222-7889
212-232-5665
777-999-3445
212-565-9880
909-808-7889
330-667-8899
212-252-7334
123-456-7890
345-678-9012
```

7.18 Ten Key Typing Practice 2

For this exercise, you should focus on accuracy and speed. The timer for this exercise counts down, so you should try to enter the data as quickly as possible. You also need to concentrate on quick finger motion with minimal mistakes; this will take practice and you should feel free to repeat these exercises as often as necessary. Maintain your typing form and do your best to touch by type without looking at the keys.

Type the following text:

```
111.11-222.22-333.33-444.44-555.55-666.66-777.77-888.88-999.99
111.11+222.22+333.33+444.44+555.55+666.66+777.77+888.88+999.99
111.11*222.22*333.33*444.44*555.55*666.66*777.77*888.88*999.99
111.11/222.22/333.33/444.44/555.55/666.66/777.77/888.88/999.99
010203040506070809001002003004005006007008009
010203040506070809001002003004005006007008009
```

7.19 Ten Key Typing Practice 3

For this exercise, you should focus on accuracy and speed. The timer for this exercise counts down, so you should try to enter the data as quickly as possible. You also need to concentrate on quick finger motion with minimal mistakes; this will take practice and you should feel free to repeat these exercises as often as necessary. Maintain your typing form and do your best to touch by type without looking at the keys.

Type the following text:

```
1221-2332-3443-4554-5665-6776-7887-9889-0110
1221-2332-3443-4554-5665-6776-7887-9889-0110
11.22.33.44.55.66.77.88.99.00.44.55.66.11.22.33.77.88.99.00
09.08.07.06.05.04.03.02.01+12.13.14.15.16.17.18.19.10
90.80.70.60.40.30.20.50.10.20.30+1+2+3+4+5+6+7+8+9
1221-2332-3443-4554-5665-6776-7887-9889-0110
1221-2332-3443-4554-5665-6776-7887-9889-0110
```

7.20 Ten Key Typing Practice 4

For this exercise, you should focus on accuracy and speed. The timer for this exercise counts down, so you should try to enter the data as quickly as possible. You also need to concentrate on quick finger motion with minimal mistakes; this will take practice and you should feel free to repeat these exercises as often as necessary. Maintain your typing form and do your best to touch by type without looking at the keys.

Type the following text:

```
111.444+111.444+111.4477+11+147.741
222.555+222.555+222.5588+22+258.852
333.666+333.666+333.6699+33+369.963
333.666+333.666+333.6699+33+369.963
222.555+222.555+222.5588+22+258.852
111.444+111.444+111.4477+11+147.741
1221-2332-3443-4554-5665-6776-7887-9889-0110
1221-2332-3443-4554-5665-6776-7887-9889-0110
```

CHAPTER SUMMARY

This chapter introduced the basic functionality of spreadsheet software. You learned how to add text and format standard text and numerical data. You also learned how to add basic equations and use basic formulas with standard or frozen cell referenced. There is a much larger level of functionality for spreadsheet software and it can be a very powerful tool in business when used correctly. You have also been introduced to the ten-key keypad in the keyboarding lesson for this chapter; using this side keypad, you can achieve remarkable speed at entering numbers and calculations, but, like the regular keyboard, it takes a lot of practice to learn to use it efficiently and effectively. When you have completed the keyboarding lessons in this chapter, you should be on the way to proficiency at both tabbed table creation and ten key typing.

CHAPTER KNOWLEDGE CHECK

1 A spreadsheet document is organized into _____.

- ○ **A.** Columns
- ○ **B.** Rows
- ○ **C.** Cells
- ○ **D.** All of the above
- ○ **E.** None of the above

2 Columns are labeled with _____ and rows are labeled with _____.

- ○ **A.** Numbers, Letters
- ○ **B.** Evens, Odds
- ○ **C.** Letters, Numbers
- ○ **D.** Decimals, Integers
- ○ **E.** None of the above

3 By default, text is aligned to the _____ and numeric data is aligned to the _____.

- ○ **A.** Top, Bottom
- ○ **B.** Right, Left
- ○ **C.** Left, Center
- ○ **D.** Margins, Middle
- ○ **E.** None of the above

4

The following is a valid cell reference for a formula:

- ○ **A.** B3
- ○ **B.** $B3
- ○ **C.** B$3
- ○ **D.** B3
- ○ **E.** All of the above
- ○ **F.** None of the above

5

In Excel, no calculation is performed unless you begin the cell contents with an equal (=) sign.

- ○ **A.** True
- ○ **B.** False

6

By default, all calculations in Excel are performed immediately when the enter key is struck in the cell where the formula is entered.

- ○ **A.** True
- ○ **B.** False

7

In Excel, the data used to create a line, column, or other data-dependent element in a chart is called a _____.

- ○ **A.** Set
- ○ **B.** Series
- ○ **C.** Dataset
- ○ **D.** Sequence
- ○ **E.** None of the above

8

Directional fill can be used in eight different directions including the primary and diagonal compass directions.

- ○ **A.** True
- ○ **B.** False

9

Excel can predict a sequence off of at least _____ or more cells and expand it across additional cells.

- ○ **A.** 4
- ○ **B.** 3
- ○ **C.** 8
- ○ **D.** All of the above
- ○ **E.** None of the above

10   Freeze panes will prevent the cells to the left and above the cell in which it is activated from scrolling with the rest of the document; this is used primarily to keep headers for data in place.

   ○ **A.** True

   ○ **B.** False

CHAPTER EXERCISES

1. Use the data example in Figure 7.24 to construct an example account management spreadsheet. You should apply the formatting techniques you have learned for spreadsheet data to format the amount column as numbers and format the transaction date column as date values. Make sure to mark debits as negative numbers and credits as positive numbers. Calculate the value for the total using the SUM formula.

	A	B	C
1	**Item**	**Transaction**	**Amount**
2	Deposit	13-Aug	$1,000.00
3	Electric	14-Aug	-$120.00
4	Phone	14-Aug	-$50.00
5	Water	15-Aug	-$40.00
6	Groceries	16-Aug	-$200.00
7	Sewage	16-Aug	-$50.00
8		**Total:**	**$540.00**

◀ **FIGURE 7.24** Example account spreadsheet

2. Using Figure 7.24 as a guide, construct a balance spreadsheet for a checking account. Use the Conditional Formatting function in Excel to define a rule for how positive numbers (credits) and negative numbers (debits) display in the amount column. You should format the debit values in red and the credit values in green.

3. Use the list example in Figure 7.25 as a guide to construct an address list in Excel with your own data (either real or fictional). Add headers to your data and format the result as a table using one of the preset table styles available in Excel. How do these styles differ from the styles used in Word?

	A	B	C	D	E	F
1	Steven Bassmaster	202 Ocean Drive	Gulfport	MI	34087	314-435-9770
2	Kat Kennedy	1 Crazy Circle	Port Royal	Jamaica	10001	770-664-3355
3	Cal Carter	33 Mechanic Lane	Brooklyn	NJ	19104	553-228-9909
4	Penelope Pastry	11 Shortcake Lane	Candlyland	SC	19219	218-272-6653
5	Clive Cleaver	1 Green Mile	Denver	CO	45607	777-555-4478
6	Matthew Lane	4 Songbird Lane	New York	NY	56647	112-505-5005
7	Lea Princess	44 Darth Drive	Yavin	PA	27789	545-343-1441
8	Sam Saruman	8 Uruk Hai Crossing	Mordor	VA	91909	447-446-4445
9	Steven Bassmaster	202 Ocean Drive	Gulfport	MI	34087	314-435-9770
10	Carmen Ketchup	3000 Mustard Maker Circle	Washington	DC	20007	112-555-7778
11	Dan Dogmeister	12 Sausage Way	New York	NY	11101	212-212-2222

◀ **FIGURE 7.25** Example address list

4. Using Figure 7.25 as an example, construct an address list in Excel using your own data (real or fictional). Add a row of headers to your data. Use the Filter function available for formatting lists in Excel; select only the rows and columns you want to include in the result before applying the filter. Define a custom rule for the state/country value to narrow down the entries to a single state.

5. Using Figure 7.26 as a guide, prepare a spreadsheet to use as a monthly budget for a year. Format the cells and columns with the correct headings and add the SUM formula to calculate totals. Use the Excel command to freeze the pane in the cell directly beneath the entry for January in the income line so the headers stay in place.

◀ **FIGURE 7.26** Example budget spreadsheet

6. Based on the spreadsheet in Figure 7.26, create a budget example and populate the income row. Use this information to create a line chart in your document. Replace the default axis labels on the x-axis with the months of the year and give your chart a title.

7. Explore the template options available in Excel and compare them to the types of documents that are available from Word. What do the template documents reveal about the purpose of each software program? Write a comparison document in Word with at least three template examples supporting each software package.

8. Write a summary of the different categories of charts available in Excel (this is best suited to a Word document). Describe one example of the type of dataset that would be best represented by each specific chart type.

9. Using Figure 7.27 as an example, create a pie chart in a spreadsheet document and format it as shown. You can change the information for the candidates as you see fit, but you should match the formatting used for the data and the chart. Change the data type to percentages using the number formatting options.

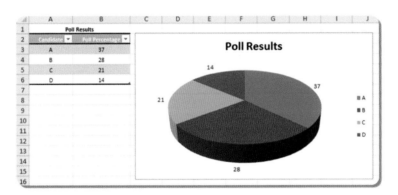

◀ **FIGURE 7.27** Example pie chart and data

10. Create a pie chart like the one shown in Figure 7.27, but change the data set type to multiple choice results where the total is a number instead of a percentage. When you have placed it in your document, add additional data to the data set. What happens to the chart when you expand the data set? What steps do you have to take to refresh of reset the chart data?

CHAPTER REVIEW QUESTIONS

1. What are the main differences between using a table in a word processing document and using a spreadsheet document for organizing information? List at least six tools available with spreadsheets that are not available in tables.

2. Give two examples of when you would need to use a fixed cell reference in a spreadsheet. Give a brief explanation in your own words on how to freeze a cell reference.

3. SUM is just one example of a formula that is commonly used in Excel. Find at least two more formulas from the list and explain in your own words how to use them and give an example of their use (you do not have to have actual data used in the examples).

4. Choose three of the number formatting styles available in Excel; write a short description of how they format the data and when they would be used.

5. What is the difference between using series prediction and the Fill command in Excel? Give two examples where each of these functions would be used.

6. Choose two of the chart categories available in Excel and identify an example of a data series that would work well when displayed in that type of chart. What makes that data set ideal for the chart type and what visual information does the chart convey which would take a lot of text to explain?

7. What considerations should you have when printing an Excel spreadsheet to include with a business report? Include elements like the paper size as well as considerations of the data being presented.

8. Excel documents allow for the use of headers and footers in the document; give at least two reasons why these would be necessary. Cite examples in your analysis. Why would this information be placed in a header and not in an existing row in the document?

9. Media elements like images and SmartArt can be placed in Excel spreadsheets as well. Why would this be an option for inclusion and when would you suggest using such elements in your document?

10. Conditional Formatting is a function that will analyze the data range on which it is applied and will format the cells differently depending on their value. When would this be useful in a spreadsheet and what visual information does it provide? Give at least three examples in your explanation.

KEYBOARDING DRILLS

1. Type as much of the following as you can in thirty seconds; try to complete as much of the exercise before the timer runs out if possible. You can use the included software to track your time, speed, and errors:

```
111.444+111.444+111.4477+11+147.741
222.555+222.555+222.5588+22+258.852
333.666+333.666+333.6699+33+369.963
1221-2332-3443-4554-5665-6776-7887-9889-0110
1221-2332-3443-4554-5665-6776-7887-9889-0110
333.666+333.666+333.6699+33+369.963
222.555+222.555+222.5588+22+258.852
111.444+111.444+111.4477+11+147.741
1221-2332-3443-4554-5665-6776-7887-9889-0110
1221-2332-3443-4554-5665-6776-7887-9889-0110
```

2. Type as much of the following as you can in thirty seconds; try to complete as much of the exercise before the timer runs out if possible. You can use the included software to track your time, speed, and errors:

```
111+444+777+000+111+444+777+111+44+00+77+44+11+147741
222-555-000-888-222-555-888-222-55-00-88-55-22-258852
333*000*666*999*333*666*999*333*00*66*99*66*33*369963
000/111/222/333/444/555/666/777/888/999
111/000*444+222-555-333+000*666/000
444+777-000+555-888+666-999+000
111/777*222/000*888/333*999/000
11.22.33.44.55.66.77.88.99.00.44.55.66.11.22.33.77.88.99.00
09.08.07.06.05.04.03.02.01+12.13.14.15.16.17.18.19.10
```

3. Track your time and focus on your form to type the following with as few errors as possible. You can use the included software to track your time, speed, and errors:

```
Val.A    |   Val.B     |    Difference
25       |   23        |    2
10       |   5         |    5
55       |   44        |    11
16       |   8         |    8
 9       |   5         |    4
```

4. Track your time and focus on your form to type the following with as few errors as possible. You can use the included software to track your time, speed, and errors:

	A	B	C	D	E	F	G	H
I	2	3	5	4	6	7	1	8
II	6	8	2	4	3	5	7	1
III	8	3	6	5	4	7	8	1
IV	3	1	5	4	2	7	8	6
V	1	8	6	7	4	5	3	2
VI	8	7	6	5	4	3	2	1
VII	2	7	4	5	3	1	8	6
VIII	4	5	6	1	8	4	3	2

5. Type as much of the following as you can in one minute. You can use the included software to track your time, speed, and errors:

```
111222333444555666777888999000102030405060708090 00
101+202+303+404+505+606+707+808+909+004+006+007+004+006
```

```
001+002+003+008+009+209+305+601+781+997+290+234+564+889
1112223334445556667778889990001020304050607080900
101-202-303-404-505-606-707-808-909-004-006-007-004-006
001-002-003-008-009-209-305-601-781-997-290-234-564-889
1112223334445556667778889990001020304050607080900
101*202*303*404*505*606*707*808*909*004*006*007*004*006
001*002*003*008*009*209*305*601*781*997*290*234*564*889
1112223334445556667778889990001020304050607080900
101/202/303/404/505/606/707/808/909/004/006/007/004/006
001/002/003/008/009/209/305/601/781/997/290/234/564/889
1112223334445556667778889990001020304050607080900 ●
```

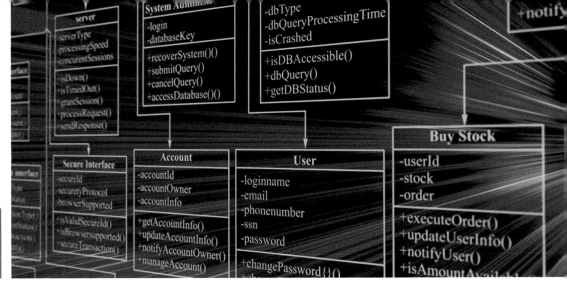

Databases and Data Entry

This chapter introduces you to data entry and how modern computer information systems are used in most organizations. You will be introduced to the differences between a spreadsheet and a database. You will learn about database management systems and how they help to convert data into useful information. You will also learn about one of the most common database management systems, which is the Access software program that comes with Microsoft Office Professional 2010. The keyboarding lessons in this chapter focus on the area of data entry in forms, a common task in data processing. Once you have completed the chapter, you will be able to:

- Understand the differences between data and information

- Start the Access database application and navigate the interface

- Save and backup a database file using the Access application

- Utilize the compact and repair function within Access

- Efficiently enter data into a form or database application

MODERN INFORMATION SYSTEMS

Most of the successful modern organizations have learned how to harness the data they have throughout the organization to transform it into useful information. Typing skills are important on an individual basis, but another element of typing is the process of data entry, which is a significant task in managing an organization's volume of data. Most jobs in an organization require at the very least some form of data entry into a computer information management system.

Correct and efficient data entry is very important to the organization. Entering false data or inaccurate records can lead to mistakes which can have negative effects on the organization as a whole. You might have heard of the saying "garbage in, garbage out." An information management system is really only as good as the data that is entered by the data entry specialist; any errors will propagate throughout the organization and can lead to significant repercussions.

There are some terms with which you should be familiar in data entry such as data and information. *Data* in its most basic form can be defined simply as raw facts. Data is what is typically entered into a database which the database system processes into something usable. The data elements by themselves may be meaningless, even to the person entering them in the database.

> **DATA** *is defined as raw facts; these have no context for meaning. The number 8 by itself is data; not knowing the context means it has limited usefulness.*

An example of data entry in an organization could be a collection of cards with some customer information from a delivery; all of the similar cards with customer data may need to be entered into an electronic database system. At the end of the month, if the manager wants to do follow up calls to all of the customers who received deliveries and if the data entry was performed with no errors, then a report can be generated to associate customer names to the correct phone numbers in the database system. This association gives the information context; now the numbers have a meaning as the phone number of customers. The data entered is now considered useful *information* which can be manipulated in all sorts of ways to provide feedback to the organization.

INFORMATION *can be defined as data combined with context, which gives it meaning and value. The series of numbers with the context as your best friend's phone number is an example of information.*

If the person doing the data entry made a mistake entering the customer records, then a few people might not receive phone calls from the manager, which could affect customer service in the future. The manager that made all of the phone calls to the customers more than likely pulled some sort of report from the information system. The report would look nothing like the original cards, and it is only as good as the data that was entered into the system. This same data can be compiled into information providing sales information on the particular products that were purchased or maybe even a report that produces metrics on how many customers take deliveries at home versus those who pickup items at the warehouse for the store. Any error in any of the data will negatively affect all of these reports.

Bad data entry can actually lead to more serious consequences. For example in the medical field, how many times do you hear about a patient receiving the wrong procedure? What if you are a data entry clerk working for the doctor at a very busy clinic and you inadvertently select the wrong procedure from a drop down list? Bad data can lead to poor outcomes that can cost an organization millions of dollars in liabilities and even negatively affect individuals or families.

Modern information systems are extremely complex and require many people with expertise in many technical specialty areas to properly develop and maintain in order to maximize their benefits to the organization. An organization's information management system is built based on the business requirements of the organization. Business requirements include user needs, business processes used in the organization, size of the organization, and the number of users just to name a few. The heart of the information management system is the database management system and there are many brands of these available which include IBM®, Oracle®, and Microsoft's SQL® Server environment. Smaller companies may use Access, which is part of the Microsoft Office suite of applications for Windows. The rest of this chapter focuses on an introduction to Access and how to use these systems for efficient data entry using the typing techniques you have already learned.

8.2 INTRODUCTION TO ACCESS

The Access database application is a relational database management system (RDBMS) that is primarily designed to meet the data management needs of small to medium businesses. Access can store all types of data to include text, numbers, and pictures. You can even import Excel data that can then be queried to produce useful information. Access 2010 also has the ability to be used as a single desktop instance or be shared within an organization's network.

One of the nicest enhancements is the ability to upgrade a database to the industrial-strength Microsoft SQL Server® platform. You can also use Access as the front end to an SQL Server engine, which means you can develop the user interface using Access 2010 and have SQL Server on the back end.

You might be wondering what exactly an RDBMS is. A relational database management system is a database management platform based on the relational theory formulated by E.F. Codd in the 1970s. E.F. Codd established the theoretical foundation of developing relationships between tables in a database using algebraic set theory. A *database* is simply a collection of data structures that are organized to serve the particular needs of an organization or person. These organized structures are commonly known as tables. The RDBMS can have more than one database instance open at once. For example, you might have an inventory database and a customer contacts database that use the same RDBMS. One of the first questions a student might ask in an Access course is "What is the difference between Access and the Excel application?" This question is a common one because Excel also stores and organizes records.

Imagine you work at a local police department that has a serious problem with evidence management. In the department's early years, there were fewer crimes and a small amount of items in the evidence room. The evidence room is the location where police agencies store items used in a crime for later use in prosecution. Evidence rooms might also store items that have been found and are awaiting recovery by their rightful owner. Matthew, the administrative officer, is quite handy at working with Microsoft applications and decides to use Excel to manage the inventory in the evidence room.

Matthew knows that Access is a superior application for this task but at the time did not have Access available. As the years go by, the evidence list log continues to grow, and Matthew begins to struggle to keep up with the log he maintains in the Excel file. Every time officers add new items, he must make changes to the file, which can be a tedious process. The other compounding problem is that much of the evidence must leave the evidence room temporarily at times to be sent to the crime lab or court and accurate records of each of these transactions must be kept. Using the Excel spreadsheet requires a manual search using filtering to search through the records. This is why many refer to Excel as a flat file database system. The disadvantage to using Excel for a project such as managing inventory is that there are no relationships between data and no ability to query the data.

In Matthew's case, on the most recent check the evidence inventory had grown to more than 10,000 items and he was beginning to think that maybe he truly needed a database management system. A relational database management system would give Matthew a more user-friendly interface in which to enter and remove pieces of evidence from the system and the ability to pull detailed reports on evidence availability and inventory levels. It is also possible to query the dataset on specific criteria, such as a case number, and produce within seconds the exact location of the item, important dates, names of individuals handling the evidence, and detailed item descriptions.

8.2.1 Working with the Interface

The Access 2010 user interface is quite user friendly; even though it is packed with many options, you can easily master the application with patience and practice. To start Access, you must first make sure you have the correct version of Microsoft Office Suite. There are six editions of Office 2010, but only three of them include Access; these are:

- Microsoft Office Professional 2010
- Microsoft Office Professional Plus 2010
- Microsoft Office Professional Academic 2010

> A **RECORD** is a collection of data grouped together in an organized fashion contained in a table. For example you might have a table called customer which contains many fields such as first and last name, phone number, and address. A table can contain many records for your customer base.

Note that Access is not available in the Office 2011 suite for the Macintosh operating system.

Starting Access is as easy as clicking the *Start* menu button and selecting *All Programs*. Once you have made this selection, you will notice a program menu with a listing of all applications available for use. Find and click *Microsoft Office*; all of the programs available appear as shown in Figure 8.1.

Now simply click on *Microsoft Access 2010* to open the user interface, shown in Figure 8.2.

The Access interface opens to the File menu, which is also called the Backstage view and is designed as a place to handle all of your background processes. From the Backstage view, you can complete a series of tasks that include opening a database, creating a database, changing settings, publishing your database to a SharePoint® server or the Web, repairing your database, and even encrypting your database. You can create a series of databases and they will all be listed in the Backstage view. You can open a database file and simply click *File* to return to the Backstage view at any time.

▲ FIGURE 8.1 Starting the Access application

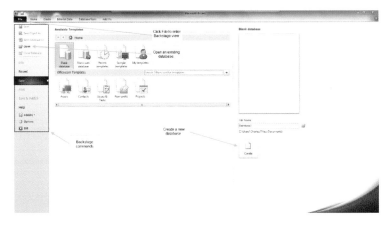

◄ **FIGURE 8.2** Access interface on startup

The ribbon, shown in Figure 8.3, is the easily recognizable toolbar used in all Office applications. This ribbon has different options that you will become familiar with as you continue to work through the Access chapters of this text. There are several ribbon tabs, some of which are visible only at certain times. The four main ribbons you will see when you open your first database are the following:

◄ **FIGURE 8.3** Access ribbon

- *Home*—Provides similar functionality to what you might be used to seeing in other Office applications; used to check spelling and format text.
- *Create*—Creates database objects in your database environment.
- *External Data*—Imports data from other sources, such as an Excel file that has data you want to use in your database.
- *Database Tools*—Provides tools to help migrate your Access database to SQL Server and to analyze your database.

8.2.2 Database Backups

Saving records actually occurs automatically in Access 2010. Anytime you are working with your files and entering or modifying records, the database engine saves all of your work. Most of your data entry will be done directly into pre-designed forms by an Access developer so you will never really have to deal with that portion of the process. In this section you should begin to become familiar with some of the procedures for keeping your database running efficiently and in a healthy state.

Notice in Figure 8.4 that the File menu offers two save options. The Save Object As option is used to save objects with which you are working; you have already used this option. The Save Database As option is used to save a copy of the database. Make sure you save a copy of your database frequently so you do not lose your data. It makes sense to keep a copy of your database at an alternate safe location if you are using the data for an organization and loss of data might cause work stoppages or slowdowns. A backup copy of your database will ensure you can quickly recover and resume database usage. To create a database backup, select *Save Database As*. Keep in mind that Access will close the database and save all objects. Once all objects and the database are closed, a copy is created in the location you chose to store the file.

▼ **FIGURE 8.4** Saving the database

8.2.3 Compressing and Repairing the Database

The Compact and Repair Database feature available in Access helps you improve database performance. At some point after you have created your database and are using it, you may notice that it is slowing down. If the database begins to slow down, naturally your data entry task will also suffer and possibly extend your day into the evening hours in some cases. As the number of records grow in your database performance and maintenance becomes even more critical.

To compress or repair a database, simply select the *File* menu, as shown in Figure 8.5. Select *Info* and then click the *Compact and Repair Database* button. In a new database with few records, the process to compact the database is rather quick. In a larger database, this will take more time; the benefits are well worth the wait, however, as the overall size of the database will decrease.

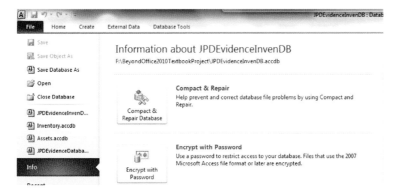

◄ **FIGURE 8.5** Compact and Repair Database option

8.2.4 Using Forms to Add, Delete, and Print Records

An employee or data entry specialist will more than likely be using forms that have been developed for their use. In most cases the person performing data entry task will never see the Design View within Access from which database developers create database tables and other administrative tasks. Most developers lock down the administrative portion of the database so that users cannot modify or change the database objects within the database. Locking down the back end of the database ensures data integrity. Data integrity can be defined as maintaining accurate and correct data within the database. Locking down the back end of the database also ensures a secure environment. You would not want an unauthorized person to damage the objects in your database.

Form view lets you use your new form to modify, add, or delete records. Begin by searching for records using the Form view.

Design view enables the database developer to develop and define the database. It is important to realize that one single instance of Access can manage many databases.

Take a look at the Materials form. Because the form manages items for a store, it is constantly changing. Sold products are removed from the database and new ones are added almost daily. Therefore, much time will be spent updating and searching for records each week.

NOTE   You can use the Materials database included in the student files to follow along with the textbook samples.

There are several ways to search for records. You might have a record that needs to be modified or you might need to acquire information about a specific record in the database. If you have just a few records in the database, you can use the control arrows in the lower-left corner of the form window; these are highlighted in Figure 8.6. If you have many files, you can conduct a search using the Search box at the bottom or, if you know the exact record you need, you can enter the number of the record, such as record 23 of 150.

Another option is to use the filter function to search for records. In Figure 8.7, a filter is being applied to the Product Name text box. Click inside the text box to which you would like to apply the filter and press the *Filter* button in the Home ribbon. Performing this action produces a drop-down box that gives you a list of product options available in the database.

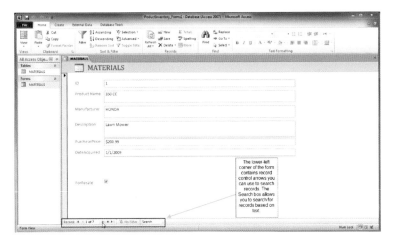

◀ **FIGURE 8.6** Searching for records

Each time you enter a new record into the database with a new product, this list will reflect the changes. For example, if you added "2500cc" for a new product record, the next time you ran the filter you would see "2500cc" in the list of filters.

After locating a record, you can use the form to modify the record. You can delete text and add

▼ **FIGURE 8.7** Entering a new record

To enter a new record, simply press the New (blank) record button.

new data. You might remember from the previous section that you implement business rules into your database by applying constraints to the database tables. Additionally, you might have nulls implemented into your fields. If either of these applies to your table, you will receive errors while updating or modifying your records. If you realize you have made a mistake after updating a record, you can use the Undo button located on the upper-right side of your application window. This will undo your last change; you can click the Undo button as many times as necessary to undo previous changes.

Entering a new record can be done in one of two ways. You can click the *New (blank) record* button on the lower-left side of your form, shown in Figure 8.6, or you can press either of the left arrows to move to the next blank record.

To delete a record, click on the *Home* ribbon and from the *Records* panel select the drop-down menu next to the grayed-out *Delete* button; this will give you the option to delete your record. Another way to delete a record is to click the left margin of your form and press the *Delete* key on your keyboard. In both cases, the Access application will always ask you to confirm the deletion, as shown in Figure 8.8. When you confirm to delete the record, that record will be permanently removed from the database. There is no option that allows you to recover the deleted record once the entire process has been executed.

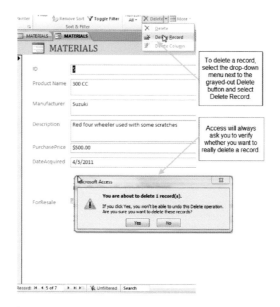

◀ FIGURE 8.8 Deleting a record

You can print the data on a form by clicking *File* and selecting the *Print* option from the menu. If you press Print selection in the Print dialog box that appears, Access will print every record in the database. If you have only a few records, as in the MATERIALS table, this might not be a problem, but if you have several hundred records you could be using up expensive toner on extra records you might not need to print. The best option is to print only the records you need. Choose the *Selected Record(s)* option in the Print dialog box as shown in Figure 8.9 and enter just the records you would like to print.

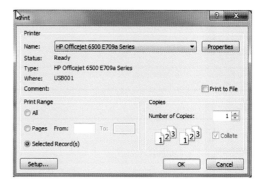

▲ FIGURE 8.9 Printing records

One more important tool at your disposal is the filter and sorting function within the Access database management system. Filtering and sorting can help you retrieve just the records that you need. For example, perhaps you want to select a specific type of product. In the Materials database, you could sort through the records to produce the records for items under a certain price or, because the table mostly contains motorcycles, you could search for one in a specific color.

> A **FILTER BY FORM** *is a search that converts a preselected form into a search tool by adding a drop-down menu and tabs that can be used to add "or" criteria to produce precise search results.*

To begin using the filter options, you should use the Filter By Form feature. This is one of the advantages over sorting in Excel. The Excel application gives you the ability to sort and filter through data that is primarily flat in nature with no relationships between data; with Access, you have the additional power of relationships and the ability to query specific elements within the database. Adding the functionality to filter and sort gives the user the ability to produce precise results based on the data that has been entered into the database. There are three types of filters you can apply in Access:

- *Filter by condition*—Setting a condition produces results based on specific criteria within your data elements. You can produce records based on a filter condition that can include either numbers or text.

- *Filter by selection*—You use this filter when you conduct a query using existing data elements. For example, you might conduct a query that lists all motorcycles with a 350 cc engine.

- *Quick Filter*—This type of filter can be applied to one or more columns using a particular element or multiple elements.

The Filter By Form feature lets you convert one of your forms into a very powerful search tool, as shown in Figure 8.10. You apply a Filter By Form by opening the form where you would like to add search criteria, selecting the *Home* ribbon, clicking the *Advanced* button within the *Sort and Filter* panel, and then selecting *Filter By Form*. A drop-down menu arrow will appear in the form along with three tabs at the lower-left corner of the form. The Look for tab is the original search form and the two Or tabs are used to add additional search criteria.

Once you have created a filter, you might wonder whether you need to recreate your filters each time you want to use one. The answer to this is absolutely not; you can quickly and easily save a filter as a query. By clicking on the *Advanced* button in the *Sort and Filter* panel

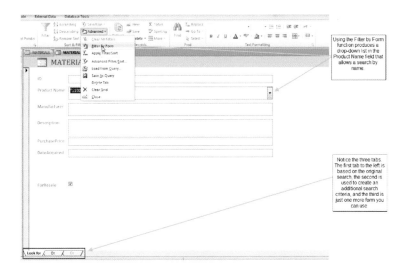

◀ **FIGURE 8.10** Filter By Form

of the *Home* ribbon, you can select the *Save As Query* option shown in Figure 8.11. Once this selection is made, the Save As Query window will appear. Select a name that clearly indicates the type of filter you are using to help you and your users determine what the available redeveloped filter does.

▼ **FIGURE 8.11** Saving a filter as a query

You can add further functionality to the Materials form you have been using, as shown in Figure 8.12. A split form gives the user a multidimensional view of the data by displaying the original form with a one-record-at-a-time view of the data along with a split view containing a list of other records. This lets you compare records listed in the table. You will notice in Figure 8.12 that record 1 is highlighted in the top view and also displayed in the form below.

If you want to scroll through your records in the top portion, you can easily highlight other records to have them appear in the form in the lower portion of the screen.

◀ **FIGURE 8.12** Split forms

NOTE An example Materials database with a split form is available on the resources DVD.

8.2.5   Sharing an Access Database

Access 2010 has enormous Web capability to share your database with others that is beyond the scope of this chapter. However, you can use SharePoint to share your Access database application with others in your organization.

SharePoint is a Microsoft enterprise product used to provide organizations with a Web-based repository where users can collaborate on documents and share all types of information.

SharePoint is also a massive topic and is beyond the scope of what you are learning here. However, you should be familiar with the fact that you can share your Access database by publishing your application to a SharePoint server. In addition to SharePoint, you can place your database in a shared location, such as the shared network drive of your organization's server, where up to 40 people can access the database at any one time. If your user base is much more than that, it is time to upgrade your Access database to Microsoft SQL Server, which is an industrial-strength platform that allows many more users to access your application. Like SharePoint, SQL Server is an advanced topic, and using it can be a difficult task if you lack significant experience; note that there are courses that focus solely on SQL Server.

One of the most common ways for a beginner to share an Access database is when it is hosted from a central location on a network-based asset such as a network drive or using a UNC.

A Universal Naming Convention (UNC) is an industry wide way of identifying resources on the network rather than using drive letters to map resources. Using a UNC is far more efficient because drive letters can appear differently to users in different parts of the organizations. A UNC might look something like\\PersonnelServer\Training\TrainingDB.

It is important to realize that although 40 people can be in the database simultaneously, only 15 can modify records at a time. There are Access gurus who claim to have increased these numbers significantly, but these experts are coding and tuning the database to a point where it operates in an extremely efficient manner. There are some steps you have to take to share your database on your organization's network through the aid of your organization's database administrator.

8.3 KEYBOARDING VIII

In this lesson you should have completed all of your lessons and typing tests. In the following keyboarding lessons you will be completing data entry exercises using the *MEDTEK. accdb* file located within on the companion DVD or found on the companion Web site (*www .keyboardingandbeyond.com*). You can also use the typing application that you have used throughout to practice typing speed for data entry into an application. You are advised to do both so you can see your speed as well as see what it is like to enter this information in a real database application.

Efficient Data Entry

Data entry will be a little different than typing a single document in the Word application. In most data systems you will have to double click on an icon on the desktop to start an application and then use a login screen. The *MEDTEK.accdb* file does not require a password to use, though the administrative portion of the file is locked down to avoid inadvertent damage to the database objects. In most cases, data entry will include a form or window for each function. In the *MEDTEK.accdb* file you will have only one form but have the opportunity to enter single records and multiple records. In most cases you will submit personal data and use the tab key to move from entry point to entry point. You should set your work area free from clutter and have all of the data organized in such a fashion that you can easily view the screen and documents your using to enter data into the system.

Keyboarding Lessons 111–120

Enter the following records into the MEDTEK database. There are about 40–60 words in each record. Several of the exercises have multiple records. Alternatively, you can use the included software to practice for track your time, speed, and errors:

Lesson 8.1 Data Entry Exercise

```
Patient Name: John Smith
Patient Address: 1111 Anywhere Ln
Patient Phone: 228-559-8686
Appointment Date: 10/6/11
Note: Patient contacted clinic on 10-5-2011 with a sore
throat complaint and high fever. Patient reports tonsils are
enlarged and painful to swallow. Patient was scheduled for an
appointment on 10/6/11 at 7:30 am with Dr. Johnson. Patient has
history of chronic sore throat and has been referred previously
to ENT.
```

Lesson 8.2 Data Entry Exercise

```
Patient Name: Paula Smith

Patient Address: 1212 Anywho Ln

Patient Phone: 580-552-8656
Appointment Date: 10/7/2011
```

Note: Patient contacted clinic on 10-5-2011 with back pain complaint due to possible fall. Patient reports she is unable to sit up for long periods of time. Patient was scheduled for an appointment on 10/7/11 at 7:30 am with Dr. Johnson. Patient has history of chronic back pain due to car accident. Patient also consistently complains of pain and has been referred to a pain management specialist.

Patient Name: Jack Smith

Patient Address: 1215 Lowery Ln

Patient Phone: 750-859-8656

Appointment Date: 10/5/2011

Note: Patient contacted clinic on 10-5-2011 due to small deep laceration to finger. Patient reports the bleeding has stopped but insists on an appointment with Dr. Johnson. Patient was scheduled for an appointment on 10/5/11 at 10:30 am with Dr. Johnson. Patient has allergy history to penicillin. Patient was last seen on 9/3/2011 for cold symptoms.

Lesson 8.3 Data Entry Exercise

Patient Name: Chris Jones

Patient Address: 1017 Jackson Ln

Patient Phone: 222-235-8656

Appointment Date: 10/8/2011

Note: Patient contacted clinic on 10-6-2011 with back pain complaint due to car accident. Patient reports he is unable to sit up for long periods of time. Patient was scheduled for an appointment on 10/8/11 at 8:30 am with Dr. Johnson. Patient has already been seen by the emergency room at the local hospital and was referred back to his primary care provider for follow-up. Patient also consistently complains of pain and has been referred to a pain management specialist.

Patient Name: Jessica Garland

Patient Address: 1211 Dolphin Ln

Patient Phone: 850-888-8898

Appointment Date: 10/10/2011

Note: Patient contacted clinic on 10-5-2011 due to annual physical exam. Patient reports she would like a full annual physical exam with Dr. Johnson. Patient was scheduled for an appointment on 10/10/11 at 10:30 am but did not show up. Patient has allergy history to penicillin. Patient was last seen on 9/3/2011 for strep throat symptoms.

Patient Name: Donald Smith
Patient Address: 7777 Any Ln
Patient Phone: 580-552-7885
Appointment Date: 10/7/2011
Note: Patient contacted clinic on 10-5-2011 with back pain complaint due to possible fall. Patient reports she is unable to sit up for long periods of time. Patient was scheduled for an appointment on 10/7/11 at 7:30 am with Dr. Johnson. Patient has history of chronic back pain due to car accident. Patient also consistently complains of pain and has been referred to a pain management specialist.

Patient Name: Bob Smith
Patient Address: 2215 Lowery Ln
Patient Phone: 750-859-2232
Appointment Date: 10/5/2011
Note: Patient contacted clinic on 10-5-2011 due to small deep laceration to finger. Patient reports the bleeding has stopped but insists on an appointment with Dr. Johnson. Patient was scheduled for an appointment on 10/5/11 at 10:30 am with Dr. Johnson. Patient has allergy history to penicillin. Patient was last seen on 9/3/2011 for cold symptoms.

Lesson 8.4 Data Entry Exercise

Patient Name: Michael Smith
Patient Address: 1033 Ocean Ln
Patient Phone: 850-865-8658
Appointment Date: 10/9/2011
Note: Patient contacted clinic on 10-6-2011 with back pain complaint due to car accident. Patient reports he is unable to sit up for long periods of time. Patient was scheduled for an appointment on 10/9/11 at 8:30 am with Dr. Johnson. Patient has already been seen by the emergency room at the local hospital and was referred back to his primary care provider for follow-up. Patient also consistently complains of pain and has been referred to a pain management specialist.

Patient Name: Mary Gore

Patient Address: 1244 Mahi Ln

Patient Phone: 850-777-8899

Appointment Date: 12/3/2011

Note: Patient contacted clinic on 10-5-2011 due to annual physical exam. Patient reports she would like a full annual physical exam with Dr. Johnson. Patient was scheduled for an appointment on 9/15/11 at 10:30 am but did not show up.New appointment set for 12/3/2011 Patient has allergy history to penicillin. Patient was last seen on 9/3/2011 for strep throat symptoms.

Patient Name: Donald Simpson

Patient Address: 333 Eel Ln

Patient Phone: 850-333-8989

Appointment Date: 10/31/2011

Note: Patient contacted clinic on 10-5-2011 with back pain complaint due to possible fall. Patient reports she is unable to sit up for long periods of time. Patient was scheduled for an appointment on 10/31/11 at 7:30 am with Dr. Johnson. Patient has history of chronic back pain due to car accident. Patient also consistently complains of pain and has been referred to a pain management specialist.

Patient Name: Sarah Smith

Patient Address: 2255 Lowery Ln

Patient Phone: 750-800-3004

Appointment Date: 10/25/2011

Note: Patient contacted clinic on 10-5-2011 due to small deep laceration to finger. Patient reports the bleeding has stopped but insists on an appointment with Dr. Johnson. Patient was scheduled for an appointment on 10/25/11 at 10:30 am with Dr. Johnson. Patient has allergy history to penicillin. Patient was last seen on 9/3/2011 for cold symptoms.

Lesson 8.5 Data Entry Exercise

Patient Name: Michael Smith

Patient Address: 1033 Ocean Ln

Patient Phone: 850-865-8658

Appointment Date: 10/9/2011

Note: Patient contacted clinic on 10-6-2011 with back pain complaint due to car accident. Patient reports he is unable to sit up for long periods of time. Patient was scheduled for an appointment on 10/9/11 at 8:30 am with Dr. Johnson. Patient has already been seen by the emergency room at the local hospital and was referred back to his primary care provider for follow-up. Patient also consistently complains of pain and has been referred to a pain management specialist.

Patient Name: Mary Gore
Patient Address: 1244 Mahi Ln
Patient Phone: 850-777-8899
Appointment Date: 12/3/2011
Note: Patient contacted clinic on 10-5-2011 due to annual physical exam. Patient reports she would like a full annual physical exam with Dr. Johnson. Patient was scheduled for an appointment on 9/15/11 at 10:30 am but did not show up. New appointment set for 12/3/2011 Patient has allergy history to penicillin. Patient was last seen on 9/3/2011 for strep throat symptoms.

Patient Name: Chrissy Jones
Patient Address: 1212 Sailfish Ln
Patient Phone: 850-859-8656
Appointment Date: 10/31/2011
Note: Patient contacted clinic on 10-26-2011 due to possible strained muscle on left leg. Patient reports she is unable to run and requested an appointment with Dr. Johnson. Patient was scheduled for an appointment on 10/31/11 at 10:30 am with Dr. Johnson. Patient was last seen on 6/1/2011 for strained back muscle.

Lesson 8.6 Data Entry Exercise

Patient Name: Michael James
Patient Address: 55555 Ocean Ln
Patient Phone: 850-865-8989
Appointment Date: 10/9/2011
Note: Patient contacted clinic on 10-6-2011 with head pain complaint due to fall. Patient was scheduled for an appointment on 10/9/11 at 8:30 am with Dr. Johnson. Patient has already been

seen by the emergency room at the local hospital and was referred back to his primary care provider for follow-up. Patient also consistently complains of pain and has been referred to a pain management specialist.

Patient Name: Jim Jameson
Patient Address: 1244 Snapper Ln
Patient Phone: 850-655-5555
Appointment Date: 12/6/2011
Note: Patient contacted clinic on 10-5-2011 due to annual physical exam. Patient reports she would like a full annual physical exam with Dr. Johnson. Patient was scheduled for an appointment on 9/15/11 at 10:30 am but did not show up. New appointment set for 12/6/2011 Patient has allergy history to penicillin. Patient was last seen on 9/3/2011 for virus symptoms.

Patient Name: Chrissy Jones
Patient Address: 1212 Sailfish Ln
Patient Phone: 850-859-8656
Appointment Date: 12/16/2011
Note: Patient contacted clinic on 11-26-2011 due to possible strained ankle on right leg. Patient reports she is unable to run and requested an appointment with Dr. Johnson. Patient was scheduled for an appointment on 12/16/11 at 10:30 am with Dr. Johnson. Patient was last seen on 6/1/2011 for strained back muscle.

Lesson 8.7 Data Entry Exercise

Patient Name: Jack Johnson
Patient Address: 1215 Blistery Wind Ln
Patient Phone: 750-859-3333
Appointment Date: 12/1/11
Note: Patient contacted clinic on 12/1/11due to small deep laceration to left wrist. Patient reports the bleeding has stopped but insists on an appointment with Dr. Johnson. Patient was scheduled for an appointment on 12/1/11 at 10:30 am with Dr. Johnson and did not show up. Patient has a history of depression. Patient was last seen on 9/3/2011 for cold symptoms.

Lesson 8.8 Data Entry Exercise

Patient Name: Joan Smith

Patient Address: 1111 Manatee Ln

Patient Phone: 850-222-8666

Appointment Date: 11/5/11

Note: Patient contacted clinic on 11-4-2011 with sore lower back complaint and high fever. Patient reports needing assistance to walk. Patient was scheduled for an appointment on 11/5/11 at 2:30pm with Dr. Johnson. Patient has history of back pain due to car accident on 4/1/2004.

Lesson 8.9 Data Entry Exercise

Patient Name: Marcia Smith

Patient Address: 1000 Snowflake Ln

Patient Phone: 222-222-2222

Appointment Date: 12/3/11

Note: Patient contacted clinic on 12/3/11 with dizzy spells and a terrible headache. Patient reports she is unable to sit up for long periods of time. Patient was scheduled for an appointment on 10/8/11 at 8:30 am with Dr. Johnson for a medication refill. Patient has already been seen by the emergency room at the local hospital and was referred back to his primary care provider for follow-up.

Patient Name: Joe Johnson

Patient Address: 1211 Crab Ln

Patient Phone: 850-888-8888

Appointment Date: 12/1/2011

Note: Patient contacted clinic on 11/10/11 due to annual physical exam. Patient reports he would like a full annual physical exam with Dr. Johnson. Patient was scheduled for an appointment on 12/1/2011 at 10:30 am but did not show up. Patient has allergy history to penicillin. Patient was last seen on 9/3/2011 for headaches.

Lesson 8.10 Date Entry Exercise

Patient Name: MJ Smith

Patient Address: 1033 Pacific Ct

Patient Phone: 850-865-8888

Appointment Date: 11/9/2011

Note: Patient contacted clinic on 10-6-2011 with back pain complaint due to car accident. Patient reports he is unable to sit up for long periods of time. Patient was scheduled for an appointment on 11/9/11 at 8:30 am with Dr. Johnson. Patient has already been seen by the emergency room at the local hospital and was referred back to his primary care provider for follow-up. Patient also consistently complains of pain and has been referred to a pain management specialist.

Patient Name: Johhny Tucker

Patient Address: 1244 Rainforest Rd

Patient Phone: 850-777-1111

Appointment Date: 12/3/2011

Note: Patient contacted clinic on 9/3/2011 due to annual physical exam. Patient reports she would like a full annual physical exam with Dr. Johnson. Patient was scheduled for an appointment on 9/15/11 at 10:30 am but did not show up. New appointment set for 12/3/2011. Patient has allergy history to penicillin. Patient was last seen on 6/3/2011 for strep throat symptoms.

Patient Name: Kris Coffer

Patient Address: 333 Stingray Ct

Patient Phone: 850-333-7777

Appointment Date: 10/31/2011

Note: Patient contacted clinic on 10-5-2011 with back pain complaint due to possible fall. Patient reports she is unable to sit up for long periods of time. Patient was scheduled for an appointment on 10/31/11 at 7:30 am with Dr. Johnson. Patient has history of chronic back pain due to car accident. Patient also consistently complains of pain and has been referred to a pain management specialist.

CHAPTER SUMMARY

This chapter covers an introduction to computer information management systems and data entry. The goal of this chapter was to expose you to data systems and learn some of the basic maintenance functions you might become involved with while using the Access application for data entry purposes. The remainder of the chapter focused on data entry exercises to expose you to record entry into a data system. It is important to note that Access is considered a baseline data system and larger companies use larger, more complex data management and data entry systems.

CHAPTER KNOWLEDGE CHECK

1 Most jobs in an organization require at the very least some form of _____ into a computer information management system.

- ○ **A.** Data entry
- ○ **B.** Database administration
- ○ **C.** Database development
- ○ **D.** None of the above

2 Data in its most basic form can be defined as _____.

- ○ **A.** Pure facts
- ○ **B.** Raw facts
- ○ **C.** Inaccurate
- ○ **D.** All of the above

3 An information management system is really only as good as the data that is deleted and then processed into useful information.

- ○ **A.** True
- ○ **B.** False

4 Data entry errors can actually lead to serious consequences and liabilities.

- ○ **A.** True
- ○ **B.** False

5

A flat file database is defined as a system that does not contain _____.

- ○ **A.** Relationships
- ○ **B.** Records
- ○ **C.** Accuracy
- ○ **D.** All of the above

6

A _____ is simply a collection of data structures that are organized to serve the particular needs of an organization or person.

- ○ **A.** Database management system
- ○ **B.** Relational database management system
- ○ **C.** Database
- ○ **D.** None of the above

7

The Access interface opens to the File menu, which is also called the _____ and is designed as a place to handle all of your background processes.

- ○ **A.** File management
- ○ **B.** Backstage view
- ○ **C.** Background window
- ○ **D.** None of the above

8

A record is a collection of data grouped together in an organized fashion contained in a table. For example you might have a table called *customer* which contains many fields such as first and last name, phone number, and address.

- ○ **A.** True
- ○ **B.** False

9

Anytime you are working with your files and entering or modifying records, the database engine _____ all of your work.

- ○ **A.** Deletes
- ○ **B.** Prints
- ○ **C.** Saves
- ○ **D.** All of the above

10

The Compact and Repair Database feature available in Access helps you improve database performance.

- ○ **A.** True
- ○ **B.** False

CHAPTER EXERCISES

1. For this exercise, locate the Materials database from the student files. Once you have located the database, start the application and enter ten new records to the database.

2. Based on the previous exercise you should now have ten records populating the *Materials.accdb* database file. Using the print selection Print Only Selected records, you choose by using the selected records option within the Print dialog box.

3. For this exercise, using the populated Materials database search for files using the filter function. Please explain the results based on the criteria you selected.

4. Using a filter of your choice search through the records in your database. Please list the results and criteria used.

5. Explain the importance of database backups.

6. Please explain the process used to repair an Access database.

7. Explain the theory behind a Relational Database Management System.

8. Define the concept of a database record.

9. How Access databases are commonly shared at the enterprise level.

10. Define and discuss the term Universal Naming Convention.

CHAPTER REVIEW QUESTIONS

1. Locate and identify an example of a data management system you use at work. Write a short paragraph on how the system is used to improve business functionality. If you do not work or are not allowed to release this information, then simply find a database system you interact with in your personal life.

2. Develop a short paragraph describing a fictional business you might like to own. Explain how the business operates and how it generates income. Develop a short essay explaining how a database management system might help improve operations to enhance the chances of success.

3. Using the previous exercise develop six reports your fictional business might develop in order to process monthly and annual data to help business managers make better business decisions.

4. Please explain the difference between a flat file database and a relational database management system.

5. Using the Web, conduct a search for database management system types and list other types of database management systems available and how they operate. Please be sure to list any sources used.

6. Please explain why it might be beneficial to share a database application over the Web.

7. What are the benefits to compressing an Access database and when might it be necessary to perform this task?

8. Using the Web, conduct a search on the term *data integrity*. Please explain how this concept can be achieved and how does the data entry specialist contribute to this concept.

9. Please explain the process used to search for records in a database specific to Access.

10. How are new records saved in an Access database application?

KEYBOARDING DRILLS

1. Enter the following records into the MEDTEK database. There are about 40–60 words in each record below. Several of the exercises have multiple records. Alternatively, you can use the included software to practice for track your time, speed, and errors:

```
Patient Name: Joan Smith
Patient Address: 1111 Manatee Ln
Patient Phone: 850-222-8666
Appointment Date: 11/5/11
```

Note: Patient contacted clinic on 11-4-2011 with sore lower back complaint and high fever. Patient reports needing assistance to walk. Patient was scheduled for an appointment on 11/5/11 at 2:30pm with Dr. Johnson. Patient has history of back pain due to car accident on 4/1/2004.

Patient Name: Paula Garcia
Patient Address: 1212 Wahoo Ln
Patient Phone: 305-444-5555
Appointment Date: 11/10/11
Note: Patient contacted clinic on 11/10/11 with painful sore on left foot. Patient reports she is unable to walk for long periods of time. Patient was scheduled for an appointment on 11/10/11 at 1:30 pm with Dr. Johnson. Patient also consistently complains of pain and has been referred to a pain management specialist.

Patient Name: Jack Johnson
Patient Address: 1215 Blistery Wind Ln
Patient Phone: 750-859-3333
Appointment Date: 12/1/11
Note: Patient contacted clinic on 12/1/11 due to small deep laceration to left wrist. Patient reports the bleeding has stopped but insists on an appointment with Dr. Johnson. Patient was scheduled for an appointment on 10/5/11 at 10:30 am with Dr. Johnson and did not show up. Patient has a history of depression. Patient was last seen on 9/3/2011 for cold symptoms.

Patient Name: Marcia Smith
Patient Address: 1000 Snowflake Ln
Patient Phone: 222-222-2222
Appointment Date: 12/3/11
Note: Patient contacted clinic on 12/3/11 with dizzy spells and a terrible headache. Patient reports she is unable to sit up for long periods of time. Patient was scheduled for an appointment on 10/8/11 at 8:30 am with Dr. Johnson for a medication refill. Patient has already been seen by the emergency room at the local hospital and was referred back to his primary care provider for follow-up.

Patient Name: Joe Johnson

Patient Address: 1211 Crab Ln

Patient Phone: 850-888-8888

Appointment Date: 12/1/2011

Note: Patient contacted clinic on 11/10/11 due to annual physical exam. Patient reports he would like a full annual physical exam with Dr. Johnson. Patient was scheduled for an appointment on 12/1/2011 at 10:30 am but did not show up. Patient has allergy history to penicillin. Patient was last seen on 9/3/2011 for headaches.

Patient Name: Donald Smithton

Patient Address: 7777 Walker Ln

Patient Phone: 888-888-8888

Appointment Date: 12/15/11

Note: Patient contacted clinic on 12/15/11 with left leg pain complaint due to possible fall. Patient reports he is unable to walk for long periods of time. Patient was scheduled for an appointment on 12/15/11 at 7:30 am with Dr. Johnson. Patient has history of chronic back pain due to car accident. Patient also consistently complains of pain and has been referred to a pain management specialist.

Patient Name: Chrissy Johnson

Patient Address: 2121 Marlin Ln

Patient Phone: 750-859-2233

Appointment Date: 12/8/11

Note: Patient contacted clinic on 12/3/11 due to small wart on forehead. Patient was scheduled for an appointment on 12/8/11 at 10:30 am with Dr. Johnson. Patient has allergy history to penicillin. Patient was last seen on 9/3/2011 for cold sores.

Patient Name: MJ Smith

Patient Address: 1033 Pacific Ct

Patient Phone: 850-865-8888

Appointment Date: 11/9/2011

Note: Patient contacted clinic on 10-6-2011 with back pain complaint due to car accident. Patient reports he is unable to sit up for long periods of time. Patient was scheduled for an appointment on 11/9/11 at 8:30 am with Dr. Johnson. Patient has already been seen by the emergency room at the local hospital and was referred back to his primary care provider for follow-up. Patient also consistently complains of pain and has been referred to a pain management specialist.

Patient Name: Johnny Tucker
Patient Address: 1244 Rainforest Rd
Patient Phone: 850-777-1111
Appointment Date: 12/3/2011
Note: Patient contacted clinic on 12/3/2011 due to annual physical exam. Patient reports he would like a full annual physical exam with Dr. Johnson. Patient was scheduled for an appointment on 9/15/11 at 10:30 am but did not show up. New appointment set for 12/3/2011. Patient has allergy history to penicillin. Patient was last seen on 9/3/2011 for strep throat symptoms.

Patient Name: Kris Coffer
Patient Address: 333 Stingray Ct
Patient Phone: 850-333-7777
Appointment Date: 10/31/2011
Note: Patient contacted clinic on 10-5-2011 with back pain complaint due to possible fall. Patient reports she is unable to sit up for long periods of time. Patient was scheduled for an appointment on 10/31/11 at 7:30 am with Dr. Johnson. Patient has history of chronic back pain due to car accident. Patient also consistently complains of pain and has been referred to a pain management specialist.

Patient Name: Sarah Smith
Patient Address: 2255 Lowery Ln
Patient Phone: 750-800-3004
Appointment Date: 1/1/12
Note: Patient contacted clinic on 12/15/11 due to small mole on forehead. Patient was scheduled for an appointment on 1/1/12 at 10:30 am with Dr. Johnson. Patient has allergy history to penicillin. Patient was last seen on 9/3/2011 for cold symptoms.

APPENDIX
A

A. Mobile Typing and Texting

A.1 MOBILE TYPING

In addition to laptops and desktop computers, there are a wide variety of personal and mobile devices which allow for text input. These include traditional cellular phones and the new generation of smart phones including the iPhone® by Apple and Android® phones using the Google® operating system. These devices allow for not only the common form of sending short text messages (called texting) but also the use of full e-mail clients in which you can send and receive traditional e-mail messages. The essential element on these devices is efficient entry of text information. The method of inputting letters is not standard across these devices because they do not have the space to accommodate a full sized keyboard. Therefore, most of these devices support some form of interface which allows you to type with your thumbs. This appendix will introduce you to the common formats for texting as well as the format for e-mail regardless of the device on which it is used or accessed. The appendix concludes with the last five typing lessons in the book which involve texting.

A.2 E-MAIL

Electronic mail, commonly abbreviated as e-mail, is the digital equivalent of a letter or postcard and has become a preferred method for sharing information and resources in businesses and organizations. It is a fast and convenient form of communication that allows for quick transmission of information from one party to another. The benefits of e-mail are its fast transmission speed, the ability to attach electronic files to a message, and the asynchronous nature of the communication.

Asynchronous communication means that both parties do not have to be online at the same time. Instead, the sending party connects at one time and the receiving party can connect at any time after the transmission has been sent to retrieve the message. This is also called the store-and-forward model of information transmission because the message is saved on an email server for the recipient and can be retrieved at a later time.

E-mail Structure

Each e-mail message that is written (such as the one shown in Figure A.1) is housed inside an electronic structure called the *envelope*. This envelope is typically used by the simple mail transfer protocol (SMTP) to direct the delivery of the message to the intended recipient. Like any other transmission over a network connection, it may experience multiple stops in the routing between the sender and the recipient (or recipients); these are handled by an initial mail submission agent (MSA) and passed through mail transfer agents (MTAs) until it reaches the mail delivery agent (MDA) of the recipient. The destination is controlled by the envelope as opposed to the contents, just as it would be with a letter that is sent through the postal service. The various agents in the system can be compared to the postal workers that deliver standard mail.

◀ **FIGURE A.1** Example e-mail message

Within the envelope, an e-mail has two components: the *header* and the *body*. The header contains the subject and addressing information for both the sender and the recipients of the message. Unlike a real letter, a single e-mail can be sent to multiple recipients with ease; this is controlled by the information added to the header. The header commonly contains the following fields:

- *From*—This is the address of the sender. In most e-mail clients, this is not an editable field.

- *Date*—This is the send date of the message. In most e-mail clients, this is not an editable field and may not even be visible.

- *Message-ID*—This is an automatically generated identification value that is used to identify the e-mail message.

- *To*—This field identifies the primary recipient or recipients of the e-mail message; this field is composed of e-mail addresses separated by a comma or semicolon.

- *CC*—This stands for carbon copy; this field is used to send e-mail to someone who is impacted by the circumstances described in the message body but who is not directly involved or does not need to take direct action.

- *BCC*—This stands for blind carbon copy; this will (in most e-mail clients) hide the addresses of the person or persons listed in this field from other recipients. This option should be used for large groups to help protect e-mail addresses and keep the message header size small.

- *Subject*—This is a short description of the contents of the message; it should be a preview of what is contained in the message body.

The header may also optionally contain the following fields: In-Reply-To, Content-Type, Received, References, and Reply-To.

The body of the message is where the relevant content is placed in an e-mail message. In the actual e-mail message format, the body is separated from the header by a blank line. Most e-mail clients separate these two items entirely when viewing the message. The body contains the actual information that you want to send to the recipients. E-mail was once limited to plain text input, but most e-mail clients now allow you to enter HTML tags and formatting into the body of messages, meaning you can perform most of the operations of word processing in an e-mail message.

You can also add attachments to an e-mail message. These are external files that are enclosed in the envelope of the message along with the header and the body. There is no intrinsic size limitation on an e-mail message, but the standard cutoff for most e-mail clients is 25 MB per message including the header, body, and attachments. This is actually a high limit considering the amount of traffic and documents that are passed via e-mail in most organizations. Attachments are governed by the defined multipurpose Internet mail extensions, commonly called MIME types. The *MIME type* is the format of the content that gives the information stored in the message context for interpretation just like file formats in an operating system.

NOTE

You should never open an e-mail message from a source you do not trust. If you have not requested the e-mail and you do not know the sender from prior contact, you should not open the e-mail message, no matter what the subject line states. There are professional scammers and attackers that excel at crafting subject lines to entice you to open harmful or deceitful messages. Any attachment that is contained in an untrustworthy e-mail should be deleted; attachments can contain malicious software that could compromise or destroy your machine. This is particularly true when the attachment is an executable file (one that has the extension .exe on a Windows machine); you should never open an executable file from an e-mail message unless you have verified by outside contact with the sender that the file is legitimate. It is possible to send e-mail falsely from another person's account, so knowing the person from whom you received the e-mail is not a guarantee that it is safe.

E-mail is considered a *push technology*, which means the sender controls the flow of information rather than the recipient. When you are using e-mail, you are therefore subject to any messages that anyone wishes to send you. This is why unwanted messages (termed *spam*) are such an inconvenience; your inbox can be filled with these messages without your permission, and the range of possible e-mail addresses preclude blocking them all. It is therefore up to the spam filter of your e-mail client to try to determine which messages are legitimate and wanted and which messages are unwanted. Texting is also a push technology, so the flow of information is the same as that of e-mail.

A.3 TEXTING

A text message is a short communication with two elements: a recipient (or multiple recipients) and a message body. It operates on the short message service (SMS) protocol and is incorporated into most mobile phone networks in operation. The original limitations of text messages were 140 octets (8-bit sequences) of information, which can equate to 140 text characters depending on the encoding information. Text messages are intended to be short pieces of information that can be typed and transmitted quickly. These can be used when conversation on a vocal phone line is not possible. Texting is one of the most widely used mobile services in existence. It can stand alone in its own application or it can be integrated into a larger network, typically by associating the messages with an email address. Some versions of SMS will allow the inclusion of various media elements such as small images or video, called a media message.

A.3.1 Texting Abbreviations

Because of the typical limitations in space for these messages and the difficulty of typing large volumes of text with the common mobile keypads or miniature keyboards in existence, a number of common abbreviations have been developed to convey phrases or even sentences with a single string of characters the length of a short word. You can see a list of some of the most common texting abbreviations in Figure A.2.

Another type of abbreviation commonly used in texting is the emoticon. This is a combination of symbols that presents a visual picture which can indicate the emotion that should be attached to the reading of the message. This can be essential in texting because there is no emotion or tone in text communication. You can see examples of emoticons and their associated emotions in the list below:

- :) or :-) implies smiling or happiness
- :(or :-(implies frowning or sadness
- :| or :-| implies neutral or expressionless
- >:(or >:-(implies anger
- :O or :-O implies shock
- ;) or ;-) is winking

Characters	Meaning	Characters	Meaning	Characters	Meaning
LOL	Laugh Out Loud	CTRN	Can't Talk Right Now	IK	I Know
BRB	Be Right Back	EOM	End Of Message	IM	Instant Message
K	Okay	EOL	End Of Line	IMO	In My Opinion
THX	Thanks	FTF	Face To Face	JK	Just Kidding
ASAP	As Soon As Possible	GL	Good Luck	NP	No Problem
BTW	By The Way	IDK	I Don't Know	OTP	On The Phone

◀ **FIGURE A.2** Common texting abbreviations

A.4 MOBILE KEYPADS

Because most mobile devices are too small to contain a complete keyboard, several variations have been developed to incorporate the use of the full range of alphabetic characters and symbols into mobile device typing interfaces. The methods of typing also vary, but there are common threads among text entry in these types of devices. This section will explore the various types of keyboard entry that you are likely to encounter in the use of mobile devices. With the exception of the Apple iPad®, the majority of these devices are intended to be used solely with one or both of your thumbs.

A.4.1 The Common Phone Keypad

On typical phones, the alphabet is incorporated into the numeric keypad with three letters per number and the common symbols incorporated with the number 1. The * and # keys serve additional functions, such as operating as a space key or toggling the letter case from upper to lower. You can see an example of this type of keypad in Figure A.3. There are two main types of text input that are supported on these devices, and sometimes it is possible to switch between them. The first type of text input is where you type the number key repeatedly to cycle through the letters and finally reach the number on the key. The other method is where the mobile device will predict the word you are attempting to type based on the sequence of keys; this has the advantage of requiring you to only type the keys once per letter, but it often requires a choice between possible words and the use of the first method for words that are not part of the device's dictionary.

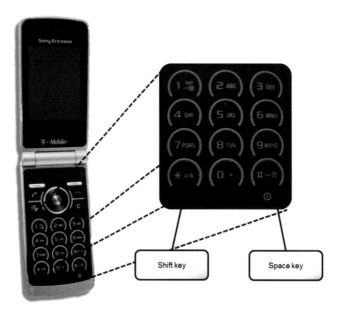

◀ **FIGURE A.3** Common phone keypad example

iOS Keypad

There are two versions of the iOS keyboard; all of them are context-sensitive for the application chosen and will appear whenever an object or element supports text entry. These are all activated by touch on the touchscreen interface of the device and will contract or expand to occupy the bottom portion of the screen based on how the orientation at which device is held. These are found on Apple devices such as the iPhone®, iPod Touch®, and iPad. The iPad (and iPad 2) has almost a full sized keyboard for typing when the device is held horizontally, as shown in Figure A.4. This allows you to type with all of your fingers as you would

◀ **FIGURE A.4** iPad keyboard

for a standard QWERTY keyboard. There are two screens of this keyboard: one contains letters and the other contains numbers and symbols. These are activated by a toggle (.*?123* for the symbol interface when you have the alphabet displayed and *ABC* for the alphabetic interface when you have the number/symbol interface displayed).

The keypad on the iPhone and iPad Touch is smaller to fit the size of the device, so it is intended for you to type on it with your thumbs. You can see an example in Figure A.5. The keypad is similar in layout to the iPad (and this version actually came first). There are two main display screens for the keypad. The first is the alphabet (which contains a toggle *@123* which switches to the second screen) and the second contains the numbers and symbols (which has a toggle *ABC* which switched to the alphabet). On the number and symbol display, there is an additional symbol toggle (*#+=*) which displays alternate symbols. These keypads are all touch type, and they will click when typed to simulate the effect of real keys on a physical keyboard.

▲ **FIGURE A.5** iPod Touch keypad

A.4.3 Android Keypad

The common keypad for the Android mobile operating system has two screens that are activated by touch. The first screen is the alphabetic characters with an alternate number or symbol accessed by holding down the key until the alternate symbol appears. The second screen contains numbers and symbols with the full set of keyboard symbols presented either directly or as an alternate character. You can see an example of these screens in Figure A.6. Both of these screens contain a shift key for switching the letter case, a backspace key (which looks like an arrow to the left with an *X* inside), and an enter key (typically labeled "Go"). There is a version of typing on this keypad that allows you to move quickly from key to key in sequence to construct a word; this is again a predictive method so it will not capture all words and you may have to manually type certain uncommon words or phrases. The typing interface will appear whenever you select an object or element that allows text entry.

A.5 KEYBOARDING IX

This is the final typing section in the text. It is designed to give you practice at texting on the device you will be using to do so. Because there is such a wide array of keypads used on mobile devices, it should be your focus to learn the keypad layout and format for text entry on your own device. The enclosed software is designed to be accessed on mobile devices and has been tested for iOS and Android. This allows you to time your texting speed. The following lessons should be completed as quickly and precisely as possible. These lessons focus on utilizing numbers, letters, and symbols effectively.

◀ FIGURE A.6 Android touch keypad

Keyboarding Lessons 121–125

Texting focuses on the use of your thumbs for quick text input. You should make sure that whenever you are using the auto-fill or prediction feature that the word you select is the one you wish to enter. These lessons will focus on switching between numbers and letters, using symbols, and toggling cases. The software included with the text and available online at *www.keyboardingandbeyond.com* will time the lessons and alert you to any mistakes made while entering the text for these exercises. Because this is practice, you should feel free to redo these lessons and activities as much as you need to improve your performance and form. If your mobile device does not support access to the Internet, you can still practice these tasks using the text message input on your device. Each line is considered one message, so you can use the enter key on your keypad or the Enter button on the software to move to a new line for the next message.

Lesson A.1 Text Entry

In this lesson, you will use your mobile device to enter text. The software will count up the amount of time it takes for you to complete the task, so you can take as long as you need and retry the exercise to improve your speed.

Type the following:

```
i cannot get away at the moment
when did you want to meet
where are you now
how far away are you
```

Lesson A.2 Changing Letter Case

In this lesson, you will use your mobile device to enter text and shift the text case as needed. The software will count up the amount of time it takes for you to complete the task, so you can take as long as you need and retry the exercise to improve your speed.

Type the following:

```
I need to go to Dulles now
Where is the meeting for ASPCA
There is no room in A or B
C train leaves soon and D train left already
```

Lesson A.3 Numbers and Text

In this lesson, you will use your mobile device to enter text and incorporate numeric input with the standard characters. The software will count up the amount of time it takes for you to complete the task, so you can take as long as you need and retry the exercise to improve your speed.

Type the following:

```
The train leaves in 8 minutes
No show for 11 or 15
22 minutes and counting
I have to leave in 30 min
The code is 8 3 4 7
```

Lesson A.4 Adding Symbols

In this lesson, you will use your mobile device to enter text and numbers as well as adding symbols and punctuation. The software will count up the amount of time it takes for you to complete the task, so you can take as long as you need and retry the exercise to improve your speed.

Type the following:

```
How far away are you?
I will be there at 8!
Take #5 left and then take #7.
Where should we meet? 88th and 1st?
```

Lesson A.5 Abbreviations

In this lesson, you will use your mobile device to enter text and practice some of the abbreviations used in texting. The software will count up the amount of time it takes for you to complete the task, so you can take as long as you need and retry the exercise to improve your speed.

Type the following:

```
I have a call - BRB
LOL That is funny!
THX I needed that.
OTP - IM me later.
FTF in 15?
```

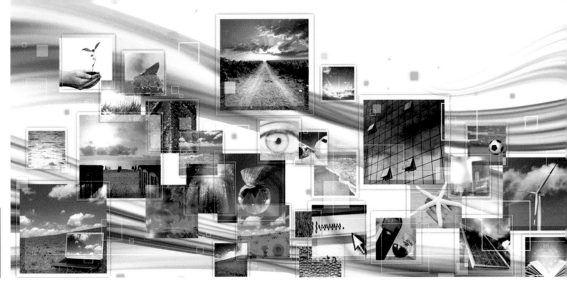

Additional Word Processing Software

B.1 WORD PROCESSING ALTERNATIVES

In addition to Microsoft Word in the Office 2010 and Office 2011 software suites, there are a variety of alternatives to creating word processing documents. This includes options from Microsoft as well as other companies and organizations. One alternative is to use the Windows Live Skydrive® from Microsoft that includes online storage and a Web version of Word (called the Word Web App®); this is a free alternative that requires only account registration. Another online alternative is to use Google Docs® which includes the Web app called Document for use in creating word processing documents. OpenOffice.org™ is another software organization which provides free productivity software for download. There are a variety of other options in addition to these, but these should get you started if you are seeking an alternative to using Word in either a business or personal setting.

B.2 WINDOWS LIVE SKYDRIVE

A Microsoft Windows Live ID is similar to a digital passport which gives you access to document sharing, Web versions of the Office software, and password protected document storage. The document storage for a Live ID account is called the SkyDrive. The SkyDrive gives you 25GB of storage for free with password protection and the ability to share your documents with others. This section covers the creation of a Microsoft Windows Live ID and how to access the Word Web App.

B.2.1 Creating a Microsoft Windows Live ID

If you use Microsoft Windows as your operating system or use Microsoft products on your machine (including Microsoft Office), you may find it very helpful to create a Windows Live ID, which is the equivalent of a digital passport. A Windows Live ID allows you to access services and provide authentication credentials with an e-mail address and a password. Some features of Microsoft Office require you to have a Windows Live ID. To create a new Windows Live ID, you can go to *www.passport.net* in a browser window. The interface for the Windows Live ID site is shown in Figure B.1.

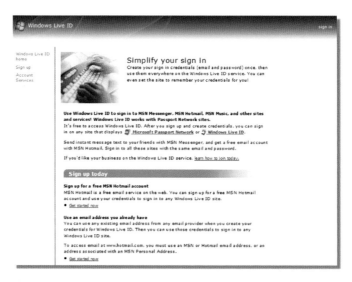

◀ **FIGURE B.1** Microsoft Windows Live ID home page

If you are already using Microsoft Windows Live Hotmail as your e-mail account provider, you can use your account information wherever the Windows Live ID is requested. If you are using another e-mail provider, you can use it to create a new Windows Live ID by clicking the *Get started now* link under the *Use an e-mail address you already have* heading. You will then see the account creation form shown in Figure B.2.

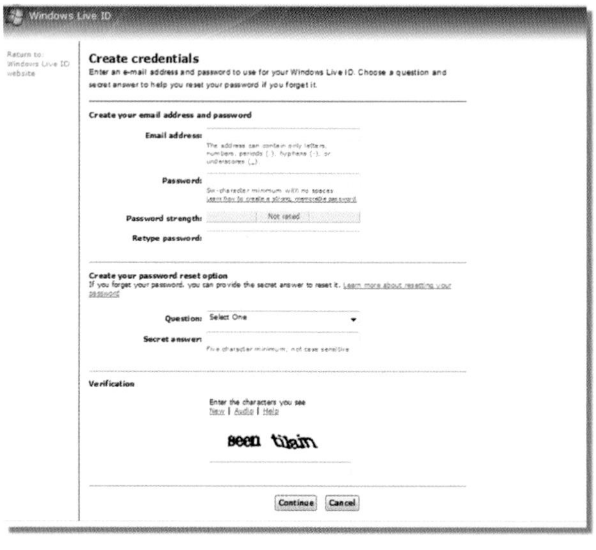

◀ **FIGURE B.2** Microsoft Windows Live ID account creation page

You only need to enter an existing e-mail address, a password for the Windows Live ID (which will be rated by the password strength indicator), a security question, and the answer to the security question. You must enter the characters in the verification *captcha* and then click *Continue*. You will be sent an e-mail to the address that you used to create the Windows Live ID account; you must open this e-mail and click the link contained within it to verify the account and activate the Windows Live ID account. You can access or change your account settings by using the login information at the Windows Live ID home page at any time. Once you have created your account, you can login at *login.live.com* and choose the *Office* or *Skydrive* link at the top of the page. You can see an example of this in Figure B.3.

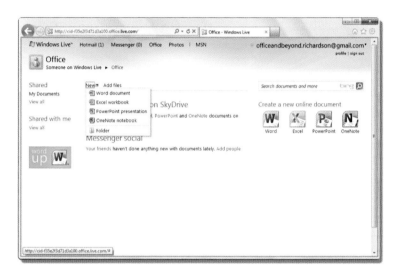

◀ **FIGURE B.3** Microsoft Windows Live SkyDrive access

From your SkyDrive access, you can use the Web App versions of some of the Microsoft Office applications to create new documents online without access to the full version of the software. This includes Word, PowerPoint, Excel, and OneNote. After you have created the documents, you can share them online or download them to your local machine. To create a new document or folder, select *New* and choose the selection you would like to create. The Web App versions of the software have more limited capabilities than the standalone versions available, but they are useful tools for creating quick documents and collaborating with others. When you select a document or folder to create, you will be prompted to give it a name.

B.2.2 Microsoft Word Web App

The Microsoft Word Web App on SkyDrive has three standard ribbons you can use to create your document. The File menu gives you the ability to save your document and to share it with others. You can see an example of the interface for the Word Web App in Figure B.4.

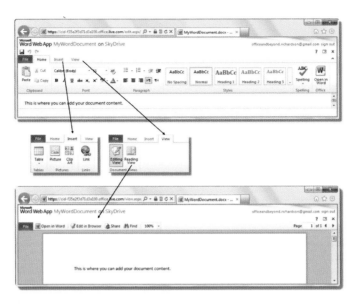

◀ **FIGURE B.4** Microsoft Word Web App interface and ribbons

The Home ribbon contains the standard formatting commands along with copy and paste shortcuts and the *Spelling* icon to check the document spelling. You can utilize styles in this version but you cannot modify the styles themselves. The Insert ribbon allows you to add a subset of media including a table, hyperlink, image, and Clip Art. The Clip Art icon allows you to search all of the available Clip Art from *www.office.com*. The View ribbon allows you to select the default Editing View or an optional Reading View which displays the document without the ability to edit it.

Sharing and Saving Documents

In the Office view of your SkyDrive, you can navigate to the folder where your document is located in order to share or download it. When you have located your document, you can hover over it to get a menu of options as shown in Figure B.5. You can download your document to your local machine by choosing the *More* menu and then selecting *Download*. You will be prompted with instructions for completing the download based on the Web browser you are using.

◀ **FIGURE B.5** Downloading and sharing documents on the SkyDrive

To share a document, you must first edit the permissions of who is allowed to view it. To change the permissions to include additional people (who can all edit the document online for collaboration efforts), hover over the document name and select the *More* menu and then choose *Share* and then *Edit Permissions*. You will be taken to a new page where you can edit the permissions of your document and add e-mail addresses for others who are allowed to access it. Anyone you list must register a Windows Live ID if they do not already have one associated with the e-mail address you enter.

Once you have edited the permissions for your document, you can send a link to the document by hovering over the document, selecting the *More* menu and choosing *Send a Link*. This opens a dialog box where you can select e-mail recipients who will receive a link to the document. Selecting the Get a Link option from the More menu will give you a Web address on which the document can be accessed by those with permission. You can also create a public link to the document which can be accessed by anyone without signing into Windows Live ID; the document can be viewed at the public link but it cannot be edited if it is not made public in the permissions for the file. You can delete your files by selecting the *Delete* menu icon (which looks like an *X*).

B.2.4 Microsoft Office 2011 Document Connection

Microsoft Office 2011 for the Macintosh comes with a special application called Document Connection. This allows you to access your SkyDrive files (or a Microsoft SharePoint site) on your local machine without going through a Web browser. You can read and open documents on your local machine that are saved on your SkyDrive using this application; you can also upload new documents to your SkyDrive directly from your machine. This includes any documents which have been shared via your Windows Live ID account. You must login to your Windows Live ID account to access your documents. You can see the interface for Document Connection in Figure B.6.

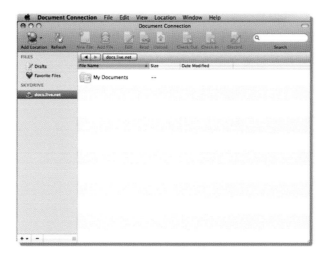

◀ **FIGURE B.6** Microsoft Office 2011 Document Connection interface

GOOGLE DOCS

Google Docs is another online application that provides free file storage and online document creation and collaboration. Google Docs allows simultaneous access to a document by multiple authors (each author must be authorized to edit the document by the original document creator). You can register for a Google Docs account the same way you can register for Gmail by Google. You do not have to have a Gmail address to access Google Docs. You can see the Google Docs interface in Figure B.7. You can access Google Docs by selecting *Documents* on the account interface or by selecting *more* and then *Documents* on the Google home page (*www.google.com*) across the top of the window.

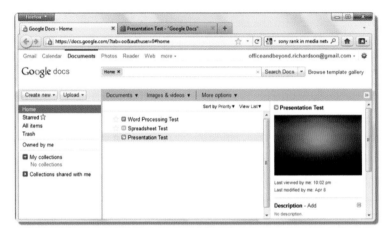

◀ **FIGURE B.7** Google Docs interface

From this interface, you have the ability to upload documents and folders to your Google Docs account, which stores them online. Google Docs provides 1 GB of storage space for any files that are not created in the Google Docs format (or converted to that format). You can view your folders and the documents contained within them. You can open an existing document by selecting the file name in the main interface. You can also create new documents by selecting the document type from the *Create New* menu.

Document

The document application in Google Docs allows you to perform most of the tasks necessary for word processing. The interface, as shown in Figure B.8, is a menu and toolbar interface. The toolbar contains most of the font and paragraph formatting commands. You can use the File menu to save the document, rename it, and close it. You can also use the File menu to download the document (using the *Download As* command) as an ODT, Word, PDF, or HTML document to your local machine.

◀ **FIGURE B.8** Document example in Google Docs

The Edit menu contains the commands for undoing and redoing actions, copying and pasting, selecting all content, and the find and replace functionality. The View menu can be used to toggle the display of the rulers and spelling suggestions. The Insert menu allows you to add hyperlinks, images, headers, footers, page breaks, equations, and symbols to your document. The Format menu has a shortcut to the available formatting effects. The Tools menu contains the command to calculate the word count and the Table menu is used to manage and insert tables into the document.

B.3.2   # Sharing and Saving Documents

To share a document in Google Docs, you can hover your cursor over the document and select the Actions menu; from here, select the Share entry and choose Share settings. This opens the dialog box shown in Figure B.9. You can change the permissions on the document by adding e-mail addresses for people who should be granted access to your document. After you have added the e-mail addresses, you can select the mailing options you want to use. When you click Share, the permissions for the file will be updated and the e-mail notification will be sent according to the specifications you have indicated.

◀ **FIGURE B.9** Google Docs share settings example

You can also select the *Download* option from the *Actions* menu. This allows you to download your online documents to your local machine in the specified format. Microsoft Office, OpenOffice.org, and PDF are all generally supported for document export. You can click and drag the title of the document to move it to a different folder or drag it to the trash to remove it. You can also select *Move to trash* in the *Actions* menu to move it to the trash folder. When you click the *Trash* folder, the option to *Empty Trash* will delete all items in the folder.

B.4   OPENOFFICE.ORG

There is a free alternative to Office that was developed as part of the open source software initiative. OpenOffice.org has counterpart programs for most of the Office suite, including word processing software, presentation software, spreadsheet software, and database software. If you are using OpenOffice.org to complete the exercises in the book, you will still benefit greatly from reading the text outlining the tasks and operations given for the Office program. In most cases, the difference in functionality may be a simple placement issue, and thus the majority of the overview and topic coverage may be found in the sections of the chapter devoted to Office. The OpenOffice.org equivalent to Word is OpenOffice.org Writer.

NOTE   You can download the full version of OpenOffice.org from *www.openoffice.org*. This site services all operating systems for which the software is available. You can also download the source code if you want to compile it yourself, but that is an advanced topic beyond the scope of this text.

B.4.1   Writer

If you are using OpenOffice.org as an alternative productivity software suite, Writer is the program that is used for word processing. Once you have downloaded and installed OpenOffice.org, it will be available in the Start menu on a Windows machine or from the Applications folder on a Macintosh. Unlike the new versions of Word, Writer uses the more traditional menu and toolbar interface. The approach taken in this text is to include the major content and the description of the project in the section detailing the Office product.

When you create a new document in Writer, you should see the blank document interface shown in Figure B.10. There is a list of menus across the top of the interface, along with toolbars that provide a shortcut to some of the more common commands available in the menus. Opening the *File* menu should be a first stop.

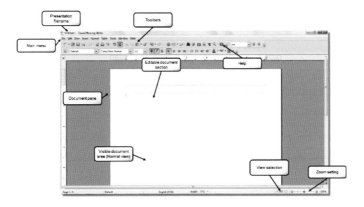

◀ **FIGURE B.10** Anatomy of Writer

The File menu is shown in Figure B.11. As with most File menus for software applications, this is where you can access commands to manage your files, including New, Save, Save As, Open, and Print. You should note that unlike Office, you can open a new file from any of the applications in the OpenOffice.org suite by selecting the *File* menu and *New*. The Help menu gives you access to the OpenOffice.org help interface. On a Windows machine, you can press the *F1* key to access the help interface for OpenOffice.org if it is the currently active application.

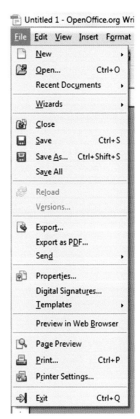

▲ **FIGURE B.11** File menu in Writer

There are a number of toolbars available that will provide shortcuts to common commands. By default, the Standard toolbar, Find toolbar, and Format toolbar are enabled. The Standard toolbar gives you access to file commands (like New, Open, Save, and Print), along with Cut, Copy, Paste, Undo, Redo, and Help. This toolbar also contains several commands that you will use for the projects in this chapter like the Format Paintbrush, the Spelling and Grammar check, and the Navigator.

The Find toolbar allows you to perform a keyword search and move through the results that are found. The Format toolbar is where you will find shortcuts for formatting commands like Bold, Italic, and Underline; this is also where you can change the text size and font selection. The bottom of the interface beneath the document contains the current page number out of the total number of pages, the language in use, the page layout (which can be changed by selecting the icon you want to use), and the current Zoom setting (remember that 100% is the actual size of the document).

The native file type for a word processing document in Writer is ODF text document (.odt). It is possible to save the word processing document in the native Office format but only up to the Word format used in the 1997 to 2003 editions of the software using the *.doc* extension. This document will still open in newer versions of Word without any difficulty. There is an icon in the Standard toolbar labeled *Export Directly to PDF*, which will allow you to save your document in the platform and software independent portable document format (.pdf).

Index